THE DAILY GLOBE

THE DAILY GLOBE
Environmental Change, the Public and the Media

Edited by Joe Smith

Earthscan Publications Ltd, London

First published in the UK in 2000 by
Earthscan Publications Ltd

Copyright © Joe Smith, 2000

Chapter 4 © Robert M Worcester, MORI

A catalogue record for this book is available from the British Library

ISBN: 1 85383 664 8 paperback
       1 85383 669 9 hardback

Typesetting by JS Typesetting, Wellingborough, Northants
Printed and bound by CPD Wales, Ebbw Vale
Cover design by Richard Reid

For a full list of publications please contact:

Earthscan Publications Ltd
120 Pentonville Road
London, N1 9JN, UK
Tel: +44 (0)20 7278 0433
Fax: +44 (0)20 7278 1142
Email: earthinfo@earthscan.co.uk
http://www.earthscan.co.uk

Earthscan is an editorially independent subsidiary of Kogan Page Ltd
and publishes in association with WWF-UK and the International Institute
for Environment and Development

This book is printed on elemental chlorine-free paper

CONTENTS

List of Acronyms and Abbreviations

ACBE	Advisory Committee on Business and the Environment (UK)
AIDS	acquired immune deficiency syndrome
AIR	All India Radio
BP	British Petroleum
BPEO	best practicable environmental option (UK)
BSE	bovine spongiform encephalopathy
CAP	Common Agricultural Policy (EU)
CEO	chief executive officer
CFC	chlorofluorocarbon
CIES	Cambridge Committee for Interdisciplinary Environmental Studies (UK)
CJD	Creutzfeld-Jacob Disease
CO_2	carbon dioxide
CSEC	Centre for the Study of Environmental Change
CSERGE	Centre for Social and Economic Research on the Global Environment (UK)
CSR	corporate social responsibility
DDT	dichlorodiphenyltrichloroethane
DETR	Department of the Environment, Transport and the Regions (UK)
DNA	deoxyribose nucleic acid
DTI	Department of Trade and Industry (UK)
EA	environmental activist
EEA	European Environment Agency (EU)
ENDS	Environmental Data Services (UK)
EPA	Environmental Protection Agency (US)
EPE	European Partners for the Environment (EU)
ESRC	Economic and Social Research Council (UK)
ESRU	Environment and Society Research Group
EU	European Union
FDA	Food and Drug Administration
G8	Group of Eight (leading industrial nations)

GC	green consumer
GCC	Global Climate Coalition
GDP	gross domestic product
GHG	greenhouse gas
GM	genetically modified / genetic modification
GMOs	genetically modified organisms
GNP	gross national product
HFC	hydrofluorocarbon
IAS	Indian Administrative Service
IEA	Institute of Economic Affairs (UK)
IPCC	Intergovernmental Panel on Climate Change (UN)
ITN	Independent Television News
LA21	Local Agenda 21
MORI	Market and Opinion Research International
NATO	North Atlantic Treaty Organization
NERC	Natural Environmental Research Council (UK)
NIMBY	not in my backyard
NGO	non-governmental organization
OECD	Organisation for Economic Co-operation and Development
OPEC	Organization of Petroleum Exporting Countries
OST	Office of Science and Technology (UK)
PCB	polychlorinated biphenyl
ppmv	parts per million by volume
PR	public relations
rBGH	recombinant bovine growth hormone
RCEP	Royal Commission on Environmental Pollution (UK)
RSPB	Royal Society for the Protection of Birds
TTT	Turning the Tide (UK)
UK	United Kingdom
UN	United Nations
UNCED	UN Conference on Environment and Development
UNED	UN Environment and Development Committee
US	United States
USDA	US Department of Agriculture
USFWS	US Fish and Wildlife Service
VNR	video news release
VSO	Voluntary Service Overseas
WCED	World Commission on Environment and Development
WWF	World Wide Fund For Nature
WBCSD	World Business Council for Sustainable Development

LIST OF FIGURES AND TABLES

FIGURES

TABLES

PREFACE

The need for this book was suggested by the experience of organizing, jointly with Roger Harrabin, the Cambridge Media and Environment Programme of seminars. These seminars have brought together senior media decision makers and the environmental policy and academic community in an attempt to overcome the obstacles to effective reporting of environment and sustainability issues. Our work is ongoing, but it was clear at an early stage that there is a wider audience in the media, policy and academic communities looking for a published account of these issues.

The sponsors of the first phase of the programme of seminars, comprising Allied Domecq, Bowrings Insurance, Economic and Social Research Council Global Environmental Change Programme, Générale des Eaux (now Vivendi) and the Reuters Foundation are gratefully acknowledged. This work is based on what has, for me, been an enormously rewarding partnership with Roger Harrabin which developed during his tenure as a Wolfson Press Fellow at the University of Cambridge in 1996.

A seminar and evening lecture held in May 1998, organized by the University of Cambridge Committee for Interdisciplinary Environmental Studies (CIES), and sponsored by Allied Domecq, was the starting point for several of the contributions to this volume. Therefore, thanks are due to all the participants in the seminar and Allied Domecq for their support. Thanks also to my former colleagues at the CIES (the institutional home of the media seminars) including Anne Lonsdale, Keith Richards, Siobhan Carew and Bhaskar Vira, who have all been very supportive of this work.

Thanks are also due to the contributors to the volume, who have kept (in a broad sense) to challenging deadlines despite a range of more immediate professional pressures. The willingness of all parties to take part in 'border crossing' and self-reflection has made for a rich and appropriate mix of insights. For most, the volume has made unusual demands: for journalists to reflect deeply on their own practice; for academics to write for a wider audience; for policy makers to stand back from their established role to consider the part they must play in enabling better communication and debate. The contributions suggest a sophisticated understanding of the challenges among some of the key players, and there are numerous signs within the book of creative approaches that promise dividends in terms of a better quality of understanding and debate.

Thanks to Jonathan Sinclair Wilson and the staff at Earthscan, particularly Akan Leander, and those individuals who assisted with the preparation of individual texts and figures, including Ian Agnew, Chris Beacock, Andrea DeGirolamo, Boyce Miller, Richard Pitts, and Robert Williams.

Finally, thanks to my wife and sons, Renata, Tomasz, Lukasz and Stanislaw, for their acceptance of my need to work late and take calls in the attic office during the summer holidays, when I should have been outside playing.

Cambridge, August 1999

Biographical Information on the Authors

Paul Brown is environment correspondent for *The Guardian*, the paper widely credited with the most consistent specialist coverage of environmental issues in the UK. He is author of *Global Warming: Can Civilization Survive?* (Blandford, 1996).

Graham Chapman is Professor and Head of Department at the Department of Geography at the University of Lancaster. He is co-author of *Environmentalism and the Mass Media: the North–South Divide* (London, 1997).

Chris Church is consultant to the Community Development Foundation and the UN Environment and Development Committee for the UK (UNED-UK). He was Local and Regional Development Manager for Friends of the Earth from 1984–1990. He has worked and written extensively on Local Agenda 21 issues and managed the Local Sustainable Development programme for ANPED, the Europe-wide 'Northern Alliance for Sustainability'.

Julian Darley undertook a Master's degree looking at the communication of environmental issues after ten years working in the US film industry. His chapter is based on a year of research into the shaping of environmental issues on the BBC Radio 4 *Today* programme.

Cherry Farrow is Campaigns and Media Officer for the Royal Society for the Protection of Birds (RSPB), and formerly Communications Officer at the World Wide Fund For Nature (WWF). She started her career as a journalist at the Press Association and worked as a TV producer and director at Channel Four, CBS and the BBC. She was a Field Director for the Voluntary Service Overseas (VSO) in Papua New Guinea and undertook postgraduate work in nutrition and community development at London University.

Ivor Gaber is Professor of Broadcast Journalism at Goldsmiths College, University of London and a radio and television producer specializing in UK politics. He is the co-author of *Environmentalism and the Mass Media: the North–South Divide* (London, 1997).

David Gee works on Information Needs Analysis and Scientific Liaison at the European Environment Agency (EEA). He was formerly Director of Friends of the Earth (England and Wales) and spent much of his early career working on health, safety and environmental issues in the British trades union movement. He recently contributed to chapters in *Environment in the European Union at the Turn of the Century* (European Environment Agency, 1999).

The Rt Hon John Gummer is Conservative MP for Suffolk Coastal and former Secretary of State for the Environment (1993–1997). He was a Cabinet Minister under both Margaret Thatcher and John Major and has played a prominent role in international negotiations on climate change, biodiversity and human settlements. In addition to political and business interests, he is active in a range of environmental projects, including his appointment in 1998 as Chairman of the Marine Stewardship Council, a partnership between NGOs and business that aims to establish sustainable fisheries.

Roger Harrabin is an environment specialist on the BBC Radio 4 *Today* programme and Associate Press Fellow, Wolfson College, Cambridge. He has worked in local and national print media and in both BBC TV and radio news and current affairs; he was also the first presenter of Radio 4's *Costing the Earth* documentary series. He is a Co-director of the Cambridge Media and Environment Programme.

Sir Robert M May is currently Chief Scientific Adviser to the UK government and Head of the UK Office of Science and Technology. He is also Professor of Zoology at Oxford University and at Imperial College, London. Trained as a theoretical physicist and applied mathematician, for the past 20 years he has studied various aspects of the way populations and communities are structured, and how they respond to change, both natural and human-created.

Frank McDonald, environment correspondent for *The Irish Times* since 1986, is Ireland's longest serving environment journalist. He is credited with initiating the media exposure of planning and political corruption in Ireland and has been prominent in describing and questioning the nature of Dublin's rapid development. His books include *The Destruction of Dublin* (1985), *Saving the City* (1989) and *Ireland's Earthen Houses* (1997).

Greg Myers is Senior Lecturer at the Department of Linguistics, Lancaster University. His books include *Words in Ads* (Arnold, 1994), and *Ad Worlds: Brands, Media, Audiences* (Oxford University Press, 1998).

Richard Pitts is a policy manager in the UK Office of Science and Technology's Science in Government Directorate, where he has been responsible for cross-departmental food, health and environment related issues. He is currently on secondment in the secretariat of the Human Genetics Commission at the Department of Health. He has a background in analytical chemistry and has pursued a science and technology career within the Department of Trade and Industry.

Devinder Sharma is a journalist and author with a genetics background. A former development editor of *Indian Express*, he is also coordinator of the New Delhi-based Forum for Biotechnology & Food Security. His books include: *GATT to WTO: Seeds of Despair* (Delhi, 1995) and *In the Famine Trap* (Delhi, 1997).

Joe Smith is Lecturer in the Faculty of Social Sciences, Geography Discipline at the Open University and was formerly Director of Programmes at the University of Cambridge Committee for Interdisciplinary Environmental Studies (CIES). His research explores aspects of governance and environmental sustainability in Europe. He is a Co-director of the Cambridge Media and Environment Programme.

Vikki Spruill has been Executive Director of SeaWeb since 1995. SeaWeb is an innovative project which has developed a communications strategy designed to make oceans a national environment priority in the US. Previously, she was a Senior Vice President in the Washington DC office of Ruder Finn, one of the largest independent public relations firms in the world.

Bronislaw Szerszynski is Lecturer in Environment and Culture at the Centre for the Study of Environmental Change, Lancaster University. His research interests include risk and modernity, religious and philosophical aspects of environmentalism, the mass media, voluntary associations and social movements. He edited *Risk, Environment and Modernity* (Sage, 1996) with Scott Lash and Brian Wynne.

John Urry is Professor in Sociology at the Department of Sociology, Lancaster University. His recent books include *Consuming Places* (Routledge, 1995), *Contested Natures* with Phil Macnaghten (Sage, 1998) and *Sociology Beyond Societies* (Routledge, 1999).

Heather Voisey is undertaking research into community development in Glasgow. She was formerly Senior Research Fellow at the Centre for Social and Economic Research on the Global Environment (CSERGE) at the University of East Anglia. She has worked on two major European funded projects looking at the implementation of sustainable development, and co-edited a special issue of the journal *Environmental Politics* and two books in this area.

Bob Worcester is Chairman of MORI (Market and Opinion Research International) and Visiting Professor at the London School of Economics and Political Science, City and Strathclyde universities. He has acted as adviser to two UK prime ministers and a range of NGOs. His books include *British Public Opinion* (Basil Blackwell, 1991) and *Explaining Labour's Landslide* (Politico's Publishing, forthcoming).

PART I

Global Environmental Change, the Public and the Media

1 INTRODUCTION

Joe Smith

Pick up a newspaper; turn on the news. These are great cultural products, drawing on vast experience of producing stories that bring together conflict, drama, personality and events. Journalists and editors know what we want from 'news'. Yet they struggle to tell some of the most important stories about the ways in which human activity is proving a hazard to the global environment. This book brings together policy makers, communications professionals, academics and journalists to try to explain and respond to this major challenge.

Global environmental change issues present enormous challenges to politicians and policy makers on a national and international level. They require a radically improved level of cooperation between governments on issues such as trade, technology and pricing of raw materials. Environmental change, and policies intended to mitigate or adapt to these changes, will reach far into the economic, social and political life of all human societies.

The necessary changes require an informed and supportive public. Yet these challenges to humanity mean little to the person in the street. The concept of sustainable development, which underpins our response to global environmental change, is still a mystery to most people.

The public's understanding of global environmental change and sustainability issues has been badly served by the media. As the science of climate change and biodiversity has matured, media coverage of these issues has, perversely, reduced. The need to report dramatic news has proved an obstacle to discussion of the slow unravelling of the science and policy debates surrounding global environmental change issues. While the media has proven willing to cover one-off events such as major conferences, the dramatic implications of such political and scientific statements have not fed through to day-to-day reporting of 'mainstream' transport, energy, economics and business stories.

However, the bland assertion by politicians, the public and the pressure groups that 'the media are to blame' reflects a poor understanding of the context of, and constraints upon, media reporting. It is difficult for the media to report long-term systemic processes, threaded through with scientific uncertainty and contentious debate. Neither are the stories presented with the energy required: government press officers are employed as gate keepers, and their first instincts are defensive. Furthermore, science is, quite properly, the most conservative profession in the world and is reluctant to see complex, sometimes ambiguous, results edited down to a punchily written 'story'.

Major challenges exist both for the media and the policy community: how to tell stories about highly complex science and policy debates which unfold slowly in meetings and journals? How to give recognition to popular narratives about environmental values that don't fit 'official' framing of problems? How to ensure that coverage of the deep underlying issues of environment and sustainability don't get bounced out of the way by late-breaking news items? How to represent issues that are important and new, but not 'news'?

The chapters in this book are directed at these questions. The remainder of the Introduction outlines key themes and points of the chapters.

In his role as Chief Scientific Adviser, Robert May is charged with advising the UK prime minister and the Cabinet on science and technology matters. In Chapter 2 he and Richard Pitts observe that:

> *'Global environmental change is undoubtedly one of the really big issues, and scientific challenges, of our time. . . At first sight the issues seem dramatic enough to ensure good coverage and plenty of interest.'*

This book is driven by an awareness that this has proven not to be the case. May and Pitts' chapter surveys some of the obstacles to effective action and understanding. They do not argue purely for the communication of facts, or the elevation of science per se, but rather point to the need for a wider appreciation of science as a process of inquiry. They note that, in addition to the need for greater public understanding of science, there is a need for greater understanding – among scientists – of the public. This is particularly true of the range of global environmental change issues where the scientific debate is about narrowing bands of uncertainty rather than working towards certain knowledge. The chapter closes with an astute comparison of one way in which the media's sense of a story resembles the working of human eyesight:

> *'[O]ur own eyesight is much more keyed in to seeing movement than stasis. Out of the corner of our eye, we often notice a fly in the corner of the ceiling when we have not consciously taken in*

*the entire foreground. It is an evolutionary adaptation, particular
to organisms with eyes that look forward. Newspapers are like
this.'*

Hence the media may not give regular space to a major global
environmental change issue – where there has been complex and
lengthy debate over levels of risk and uncertainty – at a time when
there is sudden movement in what may be a far less significant story
about an event, a personality or a mainstream political conflict.

John Gummer builds on this last point and offers a sharp-eyed
insight into the difficult and narrow path available to politicians who
want to take climate change policies forward. His long experience of
domestic politics as a senior figure in the Conservative governments
of the 1980s and 1990s, and of international environmental politics, is
deployed in an account of the reality of making good policies in the
face of competing interests. He recounts the difficulty of managing
both long and short-term interests in the face of media obsession with
'today's' conflict stories. The transformation of scientific debate into
headlines has also stood in the way of sound long-term decision
making. Bi-partisan policies on domestic or international political
stages can help, but the realities of winning elections can intrude:
'Anybody who thinks that we do not have a common view in Europe
should recognize that one of the commonalities is that we all react
exactly the same as an election approaches, wherever it may be!'
However, the global reach of environmental problems has seen
questions of equity between rich and poor countries move from being
philosophical to being a necessity; nevertheless:

> *'[e]xplaining to people that we must help to enable India to grow
> in a way which costs us money but reduces the impact on our
> climate is a piece of oratory which will test even a Margaret
> Thatcher.'*

The level of public environmental understanding and commitment is
the core theme of Chapter 4. Robert Worcester draws on his peerless
experience of advising senior decision makers on public attitudes to
the environment to offer a concise summary of the state of public and
'expert' opinion. The chapter draws on Market and Opinion Research
International's (MORI's) extensive UK and international polling data.
But it offers more than an opinion poll snapshot: the commentary on
the figures draws a fuller picture of ambiguous signals and underlying
forces. People have low levels of trust in the messages of established
institutions about the environment, and are skeptical about business

performance in this area. They are contradictory in wanting greater environmental protection, but wanting the freedom to continue what they know to be environmentally damaging lifestyles. Even though 'environment, conservation, sustainability, pollution is not on the top of many people's agenda . . . it lies there, sleeping perhaps, until something, a Torrey Canyon, an *Exxon Valdez*, a Chernobyl, a *Brent Spar*, awakens it.' Worcester notes that it is companies, above all, who should take note of this, and suggests that 'the time to dig the well is before you need to draw the water'.

Part II sees four experienced environmental journalists take stock of their experience of trying to make the environment news.

Roger Harrabin has worked for over a decade to make environment and sustainable development stories fit the demands of existing news and current affairs formats. His chapter reflects on this experience to try to account for the persistent failure of otherwise excellent news media to give full weight to these important themes. He includes discussion of numerous cases from his own experience that illustrate:

> *'the demand for drama, conflict and novelty in the mass audience media... These trends have made the reporting of the abstract notion of sustainable development more difficult. Sustainable development is not a story – it is an idea, and what is more, an idea which has already been expressed.'*

Harrabin expands on this to show how newsroom culture, concern with audience figures, and space and time constraints stand in the way of effective coverage of long-term, complex issues. His account of a series of seminars that have sought to bring together senior media decision makers and the environmental policy and research community offers a rich insight into these obstacles. More positively, it also indicates a willingness on the part of all the key players to reconsider their responsibilities.

In Chapter 6, two of the print media's most experienced environment journalists debate their experience of trying to present environment and sustainable development stories within mainstream newspaper pages. There are strong continuities in Paul Brown and Frank McDonald's experience: of obstruction by news editors; of the difficulty of making news out of important but abstract policy debates or slow-drip science stories, and of resource and time constraints. Yet they have also succeeded in working with the grain of existing news values to get global environmental change issues covered by presenting them as human interest, mainstream economic or political conflict stories.

This is the direct voice of working journalists, committed not just to the environment but to the idea that environment *is* news. They illustrate how they have overcome obstacles presented by disinterested colleagues, uncommunicative science and policy experts and slow, complex processes. The chapter sheds light on the (creative) tension that arises out of the need to toe a line between committed advocacy and professional standards. The tension has been overcome in these and other cases by working hard at telling a story, and working within the system to ensure it gets into the paper on the basis of existing newsroom values. The rest is up to the reader.

It is still rare to find a journalist with a science background. Devinder Sharma draws on his experience as both journalist and geneticist to address the particular responsibility of the media in enabling good debate and decision making about some of the fastest moving questions in science and technology. The storms raging around genetic modification, particularly its applications in agriculture, are of truly global significance. Sharma outlines the issues and concentrates on the role of the media, in its probing investigative role, as a key line of defence against the over hasty introduction of unproven and hazardous technologies. The 'journalist as advocate' question is again raised. The issue has greater urgency in this field than perhaps any other. The chapter's robust critique of the current plans for the promotion of genetically modified (GM) technologies in the developing world reflects the decision of this journalist to give up the insistence in his training to present a strenuously balanced picture. Rather, Sharma proposes that the GM issue is so serious that the media must continue to vigorously interrogate every corner of the story, even at the risk of being charged with being partisan or anti-progress. Ultimately, he argues, the GM issue may have the unexpected benefit of reviving the media's role as an independent defender of societies' widest interests.

Part III draws together academic researchers who have addressed different aspects of media, environment and society relationships.

Action by citizens is viewed by environmental decision makers as a keystone of adequate responses to global environmental problems. Decision makers have viewed the media as a prime route for communicating appeals to people to get them to act locally in some way on behalf of the environment. Szerszynski, Urry and Myers have sought to explore the degree to which people think of themselves as 'global citizens'. Chapter 8 provides a summary of a ground-breaking research project into the ways in which novel experiences of travel and communications have brought about a 'broadening of moral boundaries, so that problems of global distance or global scale are seen as "our" business'. Through interviews with media professionals, analysis of outputs and focus group discussions they explore the making and take-up of global imagery, narratives and appeals, and the degree to which this results in a sense of global rights and responsibilities.

In looking at the links between the environment, citizenship and what they term the 'banal globalism' of the media, they have questioned the line drawn between genres that are seen as 'civic' – news, current affairs, documentaries – and others linked to consumption and popular taste – advertisements, music videos and soap operas. As a result, there is an emerging, if fragmented, sense of global citizenship, and this 'has been profoundly shaped by this mediated nature of the contemporary public sphere'. In the face of pessimistic accounts of how economic globalization is limiting the capacity of citizens to 'act for the good', this chapter hints at ways in which the global media may be opening up new ways of thinking about, and acting on, environmental issues.

Drawing upon extensive experience as a producer with the UK's biggest news organizations, Ivor Gaber is in a strong position to analyse the apparently cyclic nature of news reporting of environmental issues. Chapter 9 blends this experience with empirical research, including content analysis, survey data and indepth interviews, to explore how, in contrast with economic or political reporting, environment reporting does not tend to be linked to the passage of environmental 'events'. The degree of coverage of environmental stories appears to be linked to the state of economic and political fortunes, and media reading of public tastes and political fashion. This presents all of those concerned with the effective communication and debate of pressing environmental issues with a challenge: how to work with these prevailing forces to ensure that the proper significance of climate change and biodiversity loss is fully represented in broadcast and print journalism?

The response to this challenge will differ significantly depending upon the culture. Different societies perceive, debate and report on the environment in different ways. This important, albeit simple, observation is often lost in the context of the seemingly all pervasive influence of Western media. Graham Chapman draws on cross-cultural empirical research on the mass media and environmentalism in India and Britain to examine these issues. Taking the empirical research as his starting point, Chapter 10 also explores some of the philosophical issues raised. The conclusions point to why, at the international level, different civilizations around the world do not treat the global environment as an equally significant 'problem'. The chapter notes how the West has assumed, because its media is a dominant global influence, that its assumptions are universally held. By extension, the West 'assumes a single global consciousness, whereas in fact there are many'. Chapman argues that single, centralized definitions of environmental issues, and centralized communication of these (in the manner of the dominant Western media), are not just an ineffective means of approaching solutions: such approaches are themselves part of the problem. In a conclusion that is of significance for negotiating the whole range of global environmental change issues, he suggests that if the West is sincere about wanting to resolve environmental problems:

> *'its first job is to find out how to listen to the silent majorities of the South. Their senses of "crisis", of "before" and "after", are not the same as the North's. At the deepest cultural levels, the trajectories of "becoming" may not be the same.'*

The BBC Radio 4 *Today* programme is one of the flagship news and current affairs programmes in British broadcasting. It is also the source of some of the best quality coverage of environment and sustainable development stories. Hence it represents an important and revealing case for research. In Chapter 11 Julian Darley splices empirical evidence drawn from interviews, observation and analysis of programme output, together with material from media studies and cultural theory, to explore the strengths and weaknesses of broadcast media news formats for exploring global environmental change issues.

These strengths and weaknesses were clearly displayed in the coverage of one of the defining moments of modern environmentalism: the fate of the *Brent Spar* oil storage facility. Joe Smith describes how news reporting made the *Brent Spar* one of the most recognized industrial structures in the world. The conflict between Shell, owners of this redundant North Sea oil installation, and Greenpeace is one of a small number of incidents and issues credited with transforming business thinking about sustainable development, about decision making and about the way large corporations relate to their publics. For most people, the conflict was mediated through television and print journalism. The story offered the media three ingredients they find difficult to resist: conflict, event and personality.

Yet, in the wake of Shell's capitulation to Greenpeace's demands, all players, including senior media decision makers, were critical of the media's performance. Perhaps the most serious, yet under-discussed, aspect of the media's failure was that – despite the fact that the opposition to dumping the installation was driven by deeply and widely held environmental values – most media coverage insisted on portraying it as a story of conflicting scientific truth claims. Chapter 12 summarizes the events, emphasizing media treatment of the issue and the impact of the *Brent Spar* on business thinking. One of the main protagonists wrote that '[t]he *Brent Spar* was, as one journalist has written, just an "incident". It has changed attitudes to the environment and to industrial responsibility, but not that much. Out there, somewhere, is another, similar incident waiting to happen' (Rose, 1998, p7). The media will need to look to new areas and forms of reporting if, through future reporting of '*Brent Spars*', the business community and public are to be drawn into giving the concept of sustainable development practical meaning.

Part IV demonstrates some important new ideas for, and institutional approaches to, tackling the challenges outlined in the first sections of the book.

Even their most strident critics would recognize that environmental non-governmental organizations (NGOs) have been prime movers of current awareness of global environmental change issues. Communications professionals have been central figures in this process. Cherry Farrow draws upon her experience as a journalist and TV producer and director, and more recently in senior NGO media posts at two of the UK's most influential NGOs, to outline the challenges of communicating the science and policy issues behind climate change and biodiversity. Previous campaign icons – usually photogenic habitats and species – offered straightforward messages and clear campaign goals. The route to the public and decision makers was clearly mapped out. The uncertainties inherent in climate change science, and the difficulty of locating responsibility, be it with governments, business or householders, make for a complex communications task.

But the NGOs, with their high levels of public trust and mix of science, policy and communications staff, are increasingly playing an important role in this field. They offer a bridge between expert knowledge and hard-pressed media professionals. By reference to both their sound science and mass memberships they can claim a legitimate role in taking this complex debate forward. Recent years have seen the NGOs move on from communicating the urgency of the issues through specialist journalists. Farrow describes how they have become increasingly involved in promoting solutions, and have started to address their messages directly to mainstream foreign affairs, economics, transport and business correspondents.

The United Nations Conference on Environment and Development (UNCED) or the Earth Summit, held in Rio de Janeiro in 1992, gathered world leaders to map out a common framework for acting on key environmental problems. It was widely agreed that action would have to build on broad public participation at a local level. However, the term coined to describe this – Local Agenda 21 (LA21) – has made little impact on the public imagination, perhaps in part because the media has not reported the process itself. Heather Voisey and Chris Church combine academic and local government experience in their approach to researching the links between public and media attitudes to LA21. They explore some of the reasons for the media's reluctance to cover or 'brand' LA21 stories. The chapter suggests that 'effort is being wasted trying to embed LA21 in the public memory and imagination'.

Local government officers and activists should give up hoping for a public spirited interest in the slow document and process-based work of LA21: 'Journalists don't want to "write for the spike"; they have to compete with simpler, more topical stories'. Yet, those journalists who have looked inside LA21 feel that behind the slogan there is plenty of good material for local and regional media. Chapter 14 suggests that a more strategic approach to LA21 communications at national level, investment in media training at local level, and less anxiety about branding good stories with local government jargon could see dramatic improvements in the coverage of the underlying issues.

Chapter 15 reminds us that the media already serves as one of the main sources of environmental information for the public. The media also provides the stage for the battle between competing claims about environmental risks. Yet, preceding chapters have shown how there is a widespread feeling among societies around the world, among the science and policy communities, among pressure groups and business, and increasingly among media decision makers that the media is failing to play its full part.

As other chapters in this book have shown, uncertainty, complexity and risk are not easy to represent within the existing formats of broadcast and print news. Nevertheless, there are signs of positive change. David Gee shows how European institutions, above all the European Environment Agency (EEA), have recognized the need to work directly with journalists. They need to be given access to well-researched, fully referenced and professionally edited materials that allow them to communicate the state of scientific and public debate. The media can also offer a means whereby some synthesis is achieved. Remembering issues raised in Chapters 8, 10 and 14, the range of transnational, national and local media can also respond to people's needs to have environmental debates set within contexts to which they can relate.

Of course, there are tensions in this model. The media and a body such as the EEA each serve to shape perceptions through the information they publish. However, the EEA's aim is to reduce controversy by helping people to agree on what is happening to the environment, whereas the media thrives on creating controversy. Much depends upon the quality of material that the media receives.

The book concludes with an account of an impressive project that directly addresses this last issue in relation to one specific, underreported, environment. It looks at how the world's oceans face a range of devastating pressures; yet decision makers and the public have failed to recognize this state of affairs. Ocean scientists and environmentalists have long felt poor media coverage, even relative to terrestrial environmental issues, to be a source of this problem. These simple facts were the driver behind an important innovation in information management. SeaWeb is a novel US programme aimed at bridging the gap between environmental knowledge and the media.

Vikki Spruill's summary of the experience of setting up this new venture, and her account of its successes, are of significance for environmental, academic, policy and media communities around the world. Chapter 16 points to the need for a strategic response to poor media handling of global environmental change issues. It also discusses how this project has sought to manage the challenge of communicating uncertain science. The success of SeaWeb has been based upon creating and nurturing a live network of links between the knowledge base and the media. Crucially, the staff and wider network at SeaWeb combine first-class scientific and policy expertise with professional media, editing and management experience.

CONCLUSION

'Action today is hugely disproportionately important; yet our institutions are forged by evolutionary forces that select for self-interest on a short time scale. To propose action in the long-term global, collective interest against short-term individual interests is to ask a great deal. That is something of much greater significance than the obstacles created by the way the media works, or the uncertainties of the science.'

Of course, Robert May and Richard Pitts are right; but there will be no progress in addressing this dilemma until the media take up the professional challenge of communicating what stakes are involved. For this to happen, other players have to take up their own challenges.

This book refers to a range of recent projects and institutional developments that may serve to support new approaches in the media:

- social and environmental reporting by major corporations;
- sustainable development indicators, and new 'sustainable' measures of economic growth produced by national and local governments;
- increasingly professional editing and presentation of complex scientific and policy debates;
- media training for experts, and indepth explanation of the context of global environmental change stories for journalists;
- increasingly creative (and unpredictable) 'surveillance' of government and business performance by NGOs, and the development of new media strands and technology;
- recognition by institutions that 'expert' definitions of issues must be balanced by recognition of diverse public values.

Global environmental change issues need to be presented to the media with fluency and confidence, by means of well-resourced communications strategies. Science and policy figures need to be willing to speak plainly about the implications of their findings, and to explain how uncertainties and debates are a normal part of their ways of working. This will make it easier for the mass media to move away from presenting climate change, for example, as 'for and against', and instead allow reporting of the 'narrowing bands of distribution of opinion'. Greater investment in specialist science reporting can in turn ensure that controversial and potentially important outliers gain appropriate coverage.

Journalists, not institutions, set the media agenda. Journalists are fulfilling some of the most basic tenets of their professional training when they insist on balance and editorial independence. Many in the media accept that they have an important part to play in communicating the breadth and significance of global environmental change issues. When they take up this challenge they need not lose a shred of their impartiality and balance. They are just applying old skills to new problems. NGOs, academics and policy makers all have a responsibility to ensure that these new problems are presented to the media more effectively.

A number of contributors to the book argue that mainstream politics has the largest responsibility. Too much of this debate has been undertaken in relatively closed expert arenas. Presidents and prime ministers have been willing to rubber-stamp the outcomes of international conferences, but have been careful not to become too closely associated with debate on the detail (or reasons) behind politically contentious decisions on, for example, climate change mitigation policies. However, the media can only start to report the politics and economics of action on climate change or biodiversity when sustainable transport, energy or agriculture policies are thrashed out in the public realm. Bi-partisan support for action exists, in theory, in many parts of the world, but has tended to collapse as the opposition parties sense the opportunity for near-term gains at election time. Politics needs to go beyond debates about the need for action; it needs to show leadership and imagination in debating the best course.

REFERENCES

Rose, C (1998) *The Turning of the Spar*, Greenpeace, London

2 COMMUNICATING THE SCIENCE BEHIND GLOBAL ENVIRONMENTAL CHANGE ISSUES

Sir Robert M May and Richard Pitts

Global environmental change is unquestionably one of the really big issues, and scientific challenges, of our time. This chapter will outline some of the science and look at some of the obstacles to communicating it to key decision makers and – via the media and other means – to the wider public. At first sight, the issues seem dramatic enough to ensure good coverage and plenty of urgent interest. The Earth's biodiversity is diminishing at an alarming rate and the great majority of scientists agree that the climate is warming – in both cases as a result of human activity. In responding to these issues, the international scientific community addresses four interconnected questions:

- Detection: what is the evidence for global environmental change?
- Understanding: how are the natural processes changing?
- Impacts: what effects do these changes and human activity have on one another?
- Solutions: what can be done to mitigate these effects?

Climate change presents the best, and perhaps most pressing, example of scientific activity on global environmental change. If we ask questions about climate change, there are some certain facts, some things that seem probable and some that remain as open questions. The facts include the following.

The amount of carbon dioxide (CO_2) going into the atmosphere – the amount *in* the atmosphere now as a result of our inputs – is 25 to 30 per cent more than it was about 100 years ago. Methane levels have doubled over the last century.

These and a basket of other things constitute what are called 'greenhouse gases', simply because they contribute in a complicated way to the phenomenon whereby energy coming in from the sun at short wavelengths is reradiated from the Earth's surface at longer wavelengths; and in a manner much akin to a greenhouse, these gases can capture the heat in ways which have many refinements, non-linearities and complications.

Given these alterations to the input of these gases – and, indeed, to many other natural processes – by our activities on a scale that rivals natural processes, a good starting point is to assume that they are more likely than not to cause changes in climate and other matters. The question is whether changes in climate can be detected.

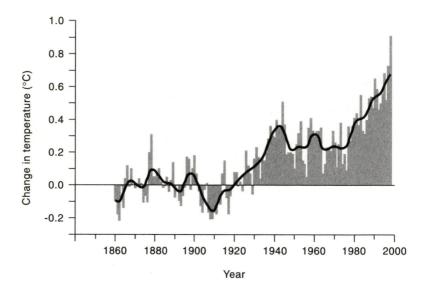

Figure 2.1 *Observations of global mean surface temperature 1860–1998*

A sort of running average of the Earth's surface temperature since decent records started to be kept slightly less than 150 years ago (and illustrated in Figure 2.1) shows that the top of the league table is 1998, while the silver medal goes to 1997 and the bronze to 1995. The natural, but not necessarily the correct, interpretation is that this is no coincidence: that is, as we have been putting CO_2 and other gases into the atmosphere, they have been having an effect on global average surface temperatures. Equally, there have been fluctuations of about 1° Celsius in global average temperature at the surface of the Earth over the last 1000 years. Arguably, therefore, this temperature change is just another fluctuation.

The Intergovernmental Panel on Climate Change (IPCC), which points the way towards the future in many more ways than just climate change, is an organization that draws together scientists from some 150 countries. Britain has had an input into the deliberations out of all proportion to its size or spending on the science budget. The IPCC exists because it is seen that climate change happens on a global scale, and that to try to discuss it or to take action country by country is a nonsense.

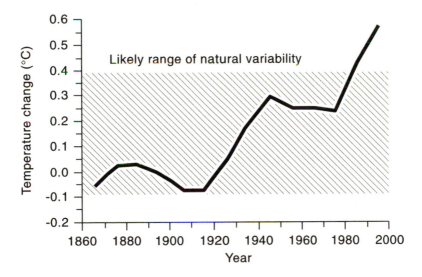

Figure 2.2 *Observed global temperatures have risen well above natural variability*

The temperature trend is shown in Figure 2.2 against a shaded background which represents a consensus of what the likely excursions in temperature might ordinarily have been over that period. The consensus summary finding of the IPCC in 1997 was that the balance of evidence suggests a discernible human influence on the global atmosphere.

The IPCC is an interesting organization, and worth dwelling on briefly. It embraces dissent; there is no unanimity among the approximately 3000 people involved. All opinions are embraced before arriving at a consensus – as is the case in almost any scientific issue of interest for policy formation. The notion conveyed to us, so unfortunately but so understandably, by the natural processes of forming undergraduate, primary or secondary school curricula is misleadingly that science is a set of nice hard answers. That never was true in most of science, and is certainly not true in the areas that are often of most interest: in highly non-linear systems where our activities are changing things. Whether we are talking about biological diversity or climate change or any one of a wealth of things, the notion that science gives precise answers comes only from an ignorant lack of acquaintance with what science is about. Science should be understood as a way of sharpening questions and defining the areas of uncertainty.

This is what the IPCC tries to do. It produces narrowing bands of distribution of opinion – not two sides, but more often a distribution of opinion with a sort of consensus round the middle, and sometimes outlying spikes. It does this on a global scale. For many of the problems of the future in biology, it makes no sense for one country to regulate them because the error made in any one country will have global consequences. This is true of the ethical questions of cloning, the more practical questions of the safety involved in putting into ourselves organs from all sorts of other animals (hearts from pigs, livers from baboons etc), and of possible new plagues created by the unprecedented viral concatenations that we create. The IPCC's process of international consensus forming is a model for much future activity as the next century unravels the opportunities and the threats of our increasing fluency in the Book of Life itself.

The way the IPCC has gone about its business, embracing dissent, putting out the facts and letting opinion contend in the market place, is a sound example of how science can inform policy making: that is, embrace widely, bring in non-experts, make the data available, and deal with the resulting messy discourse in the market place. This is how science happens; this is the way confidence is engendered. On a similar note, in 1997 the Office of Science and Technology (OST) published a note on 'The Use of Scientific Advice in Policy Making', offering guidance to departments when dealing with these kind of issues. It promoted:

- early identification of the issues: based on information from a variety of sources;
- access to the best available scientific advice: drawing on a sufficient range of independent and expert sources, and releasing data as early as possible for the research community to build upon;
- openness: in both the formulation of scientific advice and the presentation of policy.

Scientific information and expert advice are increasingly important to the government when making policy and regulatory decisions – particularly on sensitive environmental issues and those involving people's health and safety, and animal and plant protection. These are often characterized by significant scientific uncertainty and diverse scientific opinion, which has too often led to incomplete media reporting and poor public understanding of the scientific debate. Global environmental change is a good example. There is widespread public awareness of global change issues because of media interest; but how much of the science is communicated is more uncertain. Public uncertainty about global change science has in part been created by scientists disagreeing on the interpretation of available data. This arises because few individuals outside science understand how it operates. Leading edge science does not deal in certainty. Scientific advance thrives on openness, honesty about what is known, uncertain or unknown, and competition of ideas.

Current research into climate change is largely aimed at reducing the uncertainties that abound at almost all the stages of climate prediction. A very few experts still doubt that global warming is happening and others query the extent to which the observed warming is unusual or attributable to human activities. It is very important to reduce these uncertainties so that the scientific evidence can carry greater weight. However, we have to recognize that significant reduction in some of the key uncertainties will still take a decade or more.

We live in a society where most people feel uncomfortable about dealing with uncertainty. They are happier with absolute answers and science is still expected to provide these. In government, the role of the scientist in public presentation is not to provide comfort but to provide information and explain scientific advice. Ministers or officials are there to explain how policy has been framed in the light of this and other advice.

The language used by scientists must be relevant to the audience. They must have some understanding of what drives the media – for example, the tendency to want to reduce the number of shades of grey in the full scientific argument or to focus on just one newsworthy aspect of an issue.

To take an example, there have been claims for some time that global temperature changes over the past 100 years are largely due to variations in solar activity, although variations in solar radiation over the last 20 years have been less than 1 per cent. Recent research by two Danish meteorologists led them to contend that much of the warming of the last century can be explained by changes in solar output linked to sunspot frequency. This is an interesting theory but it is only speculative at present and requires further exploration and review. It is still more likely that human-induced increases in greenhouse gases are, and will be, largely responsible for climate warming. However, the report in *The Observer* (12 April 1998) entitled 'Solar wind blows away theories' would have us believe that there is a good chance that greenhouse gases are no longer a problem.

As a result, public understanding of science is not necessarily just about improving the public's knowledge of scientific facts or elevating the importance of science as an activity. Improving the public's knowledge of the process of scientific inquiry is at least as important. Indeed, as well as 'the public understanding of science', we should also be considering 'science's understanding of the public,' seeking an understanding of how people develop their attitudes to science and scientists. In one survey members of the public were asked which scientists they would have most confidence in to tell the truth about bovine spongiform encephalopathy (BSE) (Durant and Bauer, 1997). Scientists in universities were regarded as the most reliable, followed in order by those in industry, consumer groups and government, with scientists writing in newspapers and journalists at the bottom. Conversely, if asked which scientists they would have least confidence in, those in government were less trusted than anyone except journalists. The conclusions were that, overall, scientists in industry come out as well as anyone, and that today scientists are regarded by the public just as critically as any other authority (which perhaps in some ways is a good thing).

It is encouraging that the government is keen to improve the level of understanding between scientists and the public, and the OST's Public Understanding Unit has an important role to play. Economic and Social Research Council (ESRC)-funded research shows that where a political culture of social contract exists, then individuals are more likely to accept shared responsibility for environmental action (Burgess and Harrison, 1997). We need to continue a steady process of making scientific findings available and accessible through a wide range of outlets and the research councils have an important role to play. For example, with regard to climate change, the Natural Environment Research Council (NERC):

- has briefed bankers on the uncertainties and economic implications;
- ran a conference, jointly with the British Association, for sixth formers on climate change in 1998; and
- is involved in a project (the TSUNAMI Initiative, British Antarctic Survey, Cambridge) aimed at improving the insurance industry's

understanding of natural hazards, including predicting extreme climatic events.

It is probably true that large segments of the business community in some industrialized countries are not yet convinced of the scientific evidence of global climate change. In the UK the Foresight programme has a role to play here. The programme, managed by the OST, aims to promote wealth creation and better quality of life by developing visions of the future and looking at future needs, opportunities and threats, as well as examining how developments in science could help the UK to meet those challenges. Sustainable development is an underlying theme of the programme. All outputs from Foresight point to environmental change as being a key driver for the future. Two main aims are to increase business awareness of the risks and opportunities and to encourage the formation of partnerships to tackle specific issues.

Either way, the policy debate is moving on. Despite the uncertainties, and occasionally clumsy treatment of them in the media, the significance of the likely impacts of climate change have brought the UK government and the international community to the point of seriously considering the difficult practical steps that will have to be taken to reduce greenhouse gas emissions and to meet future legally binding targets (8 per cent for the European Union – EU). The UK has additionally set its own ambitious domestic aim of a 20 per cent reduction in CO_2 emissions by 2010. Achieving this will have an impact on virtually everyone's lifestyle or business.

Therefore, in the coming months and years, as measures are introduced, it will be more important than ever that the scientific evidence for climate change and the scientific basis for action are effectively communicated to business, the media and the public – and between government bodies and scientists. Unless the general public is persuaded of the need for action, potentially unpopular measures such as curbing private car use and energy waste stand more of a chance of floundering. Ministers have a collective responsibility to lead the British people to better appreciating the need for firm and early action.

The scope of required action, nationally and internationally, falls broadly. For example, when focusing on CO_2, the major greenhouse gas, if we ask who and what is putting it into the atmosphere in the UK, the answer is as follows:

- Road transport: about 22 per cent;
- Domestic activities, broadly defined (heating): about 27 per cent;
- Industry: about 28 per cent; and

- A miscellaneous set of other things, such as air transport, marketplace activities, shopping centres, etc: about 23 per cent.

Acting to reduce CO_2 emissions across these sectors should not only be portrayed as bad news. The situation represents major opportunities to take the lead in creating the key global technologies of tomorrow, and to develop greater industrial efficiency and competitiveness. Those opportunities are present every bit as much as the inconveniences and threats.

A US study using a different categorization looked at extreme things that could be done within the bounds of feasibility (Romm et al, 1998). It suggested that the input of CO_2 could be reduced by changes of practices as follows:

- The utilities: 10 to 22 per cent;
- Industry: 10 to 17 per cent;
- Better buildings : 7 to 10 per cent;
- Transport: 15 per cent.

Looking ahead to 2010, and assessing the economic impacts in terms of billions of dollars, the costs roughly balance the benefits. There are benefits to some and costs to others. The tricky thing is that, although the costs and benefits across the US may average out, there are winners and losers – which makes for policy difficulties.

There is an interplay between climate change and biological diversity which deserves more emphasis than it usually gets. The driver of anthropogenic climate change is increasing numbers of people, differentially amplified in different places by varying patterns of resource consumption. So, the current acceleration in rates of extinction of species ultimately derives from growth in numbers of humans and their activities.

The total number of distinct species of plants, animals and fungi that have been named and recorded is roughly around 1.5 million, but even this simple number is uncertain to around 10 per cent (mainly because we lack a synoptic database; consequently, obtaining an accurate total is complicated by synonyms – the same species being independently 'discovered' under different names in different collections). Estimates of the true total number of species living on Earth today are uncertain to within a factor ten. My guess would be around seven million, with a reasonable range of five to 15 million, although much higher guesses can be defended.

Given these uncertainties, it is impossible to accurately gauge the number of species becoming extinct each year. But we can make comparisons between documented extinctions in better known groups (birds, mammals) against the average rate at which species have gone extinct over the 600-million year sweep of the fossil record. Such estimates suggest that, over the 20th century, extinction rates increased by a factor of roughly 1000, compared to the average background rate. And a variety of guestimates, each of them uncertain in different ways, points to a further tenfold acceleration in extinction rates over the next 100 years or so. This elevation of extinction is on the same scale as the Big Five events of mass extinction in the fossil record, such as the one that saw off the dinosaurs.

Discussions of biological diversity in the context of climate change tend to focus on more particular considerations, such as the ability of species to 'move with the climate' across a landscape whose fragmentation will often prevent any such movement. I think that much of this discussion misses the real point: the same processes (human activities which by many measures rival the sweep and scale of the natural processes that maintain the biosphere) which make for anthropogenic changes in climate will also cause great impoverishment of the Earth's biota. Although the meeting of the Earth Summit in Rio, and the Biodiversity Convention which came out of it, made a start on international recognition of these problems, they do not seem, since then, to have received as much attention as has climate change. They should.

Politicians increasingly recognize that if the public is to be drawn into an understanding of policy actions based upon uncertain science, it must have a stake in the development of those policies. For example, in the UK, the Department of the Environment, Transport and the Regions (DETR) has developed an excellent climate change consultation paper. This document recognizes that it will not be possible to do anything about global environmental change in the UK unless we bring everyone with us, precisely because the burden of doing something about it falls broadly.

If we are uncertain about the science, this is nothing beside our continuing uncertainty and lack of understanding about our own nature and institutions. As an example, consider the difference between the dialogue on this subject in the UK and in the US. Here, industry and government are more or less on the same wavelength. Just before John Prescott left for the key climate change conference in Kyoto in late 1997, the prime minister held a meeting at number 10 with the core cabinet (the foreign secretary, the chancellor and the transport and environment ministers), the leaders of industry (the head of British Petroleum (BP), Shell and the automobile industry), and leading figures of the science advisory establishment. I came to that meeting feeling in private that much more reservation and hesitation would be expressed by people from, for example, BP and Shell. In fact, this did not happen and, in order that such feelings be aired, I found myself voicing the notes of dissent.

Contrast that with the US where the oil industry has been (one can almost only use the word) virulent in opposition to any change. There are some signs of shifts in the US towards the UK situation, but a deep problem remains. A key factor in ensuring that government and business have a more unified position in the UK arises from the fact that the previous Conservative government (one member of which also contributes to this volume) played a remarkable role of leadership – a leadership role to which the present Labour government pays tribute. The baton was handed on to a government equally committed to taking a lead in this.

The way in which the media enter this is interesting. In what may seem a wild digression, I observe that our own eyesight is much more keyed to seeing *movement* than *stasis*. Out of the corner of our eye, we often notice a fly on the ceiling when we have not consciously taken in the entire foreground. It is an evolutionary adaptation, particularly to organisms with eyes that look forward.

Newspapers are like this. The media respond to breaking news, to new things, to change. When did you last read something about AIDS in the newspaper? Do you think that pandemic is not still growing, that it is still not a problem in Europe? It is like a sloth that has adapted to predation by moving slowly: it is yesterday's news. It is not the fault of the media; it is inherent in the way we react – it is our fault, not the media's. The tendency to report a dissident, often crackpot, view of climate change – to look for the two sides as if we were reporting a sporting event, rather than to describe this more complicated distribution of opinion with occasional odd spikes – is inherent in the way our society works and is not to be blamed on the media.

The Kyoto climate change talks represented a surprisingly good beginning – though no more than a beginning. It was a train moving out of the station. It was also surprising because we are asking for action for the future: the real problems lie decades ahead. The serious problems are for our children and grandchildren, but action today is hugely multiplied into the future. There are time constants on the scale of centuries in this system, in the ocean and the atmosphere. Action today is hugely disproportionately important; yet our institutions are forged by evolutionary forces that select for self-interest on a short time scale. To propose action in the long-term global, collective interest against short-term individual interests is to ask a great deal. That is something of much greater significance than the obstacles created by the way the media works, or the uncertainties of the science.

REFERENCES

Burgess, J and Harrison, C (1997) *After Kyoto: Making Climate Policy Work*, Climate Change and Changing Lifestyles, Special Briefing No 1, ESRC Global Environmental Change Programme, University of Sussex

Durant, J and Bauer, M (1997) 'Public Understanding of Science in Britain: 1996 National Survey', The Science Museum, London (unpublished)

Office of Science and Technology (1997) *The Use of Scientific Advice in Policy Making: A Note by the Chief Scientific Adviser*, Sir Robert May, DTi Publications, London

Romm, J, Levine, M, Brown, M and Petersen, E (1998) 'A Road Map for US Carbon Reductions', *Science*, vol 279, pp669–670

3 POLITICS, THE PUBLIC AND THE ENVIRONMENT

The Rt Hon John Gummer MP

It has always seemed to me that, in dealing with global warming, a sensible place to start is with two simple points about the world as we know it. Firstly, from all our experimentation and all the work done, and money spent, on astronomy, it is clearly rather an unusual world. It appears that there are no others quite like it. When people get enthusiastic about life on other planets, it is usually rather boring life like lichen. By that we do not mean 'life' but something rather different. Therefore, it might be reasonable, though not necessarily true, to suggest that what is unusual and rare might actually be fragile, and therefore we ought to be rather careful about it. It is important for us that life is sustained; so being careful about it is not an unreasonable basis upon which politicians should approach these issues.

Secondly, there is the question of sheer volume. The difference between a few people living in clearings in the woods burning the odd stick, and millions upon millions of people producing huge quantities of what are called 'greenhouse gases' before throwing them into the atmosphere, ought to be sufficient at least to *suggest* that we should be that much more careful. So, even before we reach the science, those two simple points should be enough for politicians to take the issue seriously. Then, as we look at the science, even a non-believer reaches the stage of recognizing that not to take it seriously would be an irrational stance. But, of course, it is hard when dealing with science. Scientists never say something is *certain*, and there is always a scientist to be found who will suggest something else. Even more importantly, the reporting of science is often understood in terms of the headlines, rather than the contents, of the article. The sunspot arguments or the global cooling arguments, if read carefully, can be fitted into a proper appreciation of the issues, but when seen – as most people see them – only in terms of the headlines, a proper appreciation is never reached.

Politicians are constantly under pressure to make decisions in circumstances where people have formed opinions largely from headlines. The context in which we have been working is one in which politicians – particularly in this country – have increasingly accepted that science makes it more sensible to act cautiously. For example, the results of looking at increases in population and the effects on the Earth's atmosphere suggest that precautionary measures should probably be taken.

This is the context in which we operate, but the trouble is that when that generality meets reality we start to say how *difficult* it all is. Robert May points out that domestic activity is one of the two largest producers of greenhouse gases. However, as soon as we consider domestic activity, we have to think about encouraging people to live rather differently, restricting the way they live and perhaps taxing some of the things they do. Once the generality meets *that* reality, it is surprising how quickly people run away from it.

The bi-partisan policy on these issues that we now have in the UK goes some way towards overcoming the problems arising out of this; but the debate on changing domestic fuel taxation points to the ways in which near-term political goals can erode cross-party support for a longer-term principal. In this case, there was wide support for a certain amount of taxation on domestic heating; yet people who had been in favour of that – publicly and universally in favour of it, and indeed wanted to go further because of the pressure for carbon taxes and the like – changed to the other side in the space of a single by-election. The most remarkably refined arguments can be produced. There are instances where the party which had gone in for the taxation is now likely to be very much on the side of the motorist if the present government presses ahead with current proposals for changes in the taxation of private car use.

This is not the singular activity of one side or the other. However even at a time of bi-partisan political view, it is a hard view to hold once it moves from *generality* to *reality*. At that point, of course, all the doubts are recalled. The moment we get into a position in which it would be easier not to take the difficult decision, people want it to go away. The way politicians help it to go away is to say, of course we do not really quite know; there is not sufficient evidence at the moment for us to take so large a step. Perhaps we ought to have some more research, ask some more questions, wait for a while or wait for the moment that is suitable, wait for the media to encourage the people to take this more seriously. Let us give ourselves a bit of elbow room.

In fact, the key issue for the politician is that, having got to the generality, the difficulties are only just beginning. It is the particularities that cause the problems, and the easiest way out of those problems is to wait. This is why one must underline the arguments of Robert May, that the longer we wait the more difficult it will be. These are the most important years of all. If we get it right now, changes can be made that will make global warming possible to live with at a price which is bearable. We cannot change it; we cannot set it back. Much of what is already happening cannot, in any sense, be reversed. What *can* be done is to make the degree of global warming tolerable and containable *if* it is right that we are causing it.

This can be done only if measures are taken now; and, in general, the European scene is in favour of doing this. The problem for us politically is that this is not true in the US. Robert May is right to make that contrast clear. The Global Climate Coalition believes that global warming will not happen, that what we say is happening is not happening. In any case, even if it were, it is so expensive to stop that it is better to leave it to someone else later on. That is their view, and it is the view in a country which is peculiarly vulnerable to the pressures of industry. I think that in no other nation in the world is there a government that so often speaks with the voice of industry. For example, it would be difficult to put a single piece of paper between the American government policy on genetically modified organisms with that, until very recently, of Monsanto.

I am afraid that this has been a problem for the US for a long time. What happens is that, in general, President Clinton says 'measures must be taken'; Al Gore writes books to show why this is a decision which quite clearly has to be taken, and that to ignore it would be like ignoring *Kristallnacht* (the quotation he used) – but, in the end, very little is done.

The contrast can be made by comparing two companies: Shell, which honourably, and I think with great courage, resigned from the Global Climate Coalition, and Esso, which almost single handedly is determined to press the argument that nothing need be done because, in fact, nothing is actually happening.

Of course, this is crucially important in a world where Americans are responsible for 25 per cent of the emissions. To put this into perspective, every American child born will expect to benefit from the work of 120 people to provide it with the energy it needs. For every European child, it is 60, every Chinese child eight, and every Bangladeshi child will have to make do with only one (probably his own energy). The comparison, therefore, is clear. Unless the Americans can be persuaded to take action, unless US politics make it possible, action that is sufficiently great to make a real difference will not be taken.

There is a real issue about the influence of politics globally to achieve any kind of result. This is the key to the problem. It is a *global* issue which needs a global solution. We are uncertain in politics about how to deal with a global issue. When I went to the European Union (EU) with the toughest policy that Britain had ever produced on global warming, colleagues who had given me the best degree of elbow room that any minister could be given mentioned, in passing, that it would be a good idea if India and China also did their bit. It is, quite rightly, much more difficult to get people in Britain to take measures if it can easily be pointed out that other people are not doing so. Even if those other people are way behind us in the emissions they are producing, and even if their standard of living is much lower than ours, it is still politically hard to say that we must act even if others do not.

We are seeing this in the EU at this moment, despite the brave words and fine signatures for which we worked so hard. There is now the excuse of a rather different figure on a rather different basis after the 1997 climate change conference in Kyoto, so people are busy moving backwards – and some of the biggest mouths are shut remarkably quickly. Holland, a country which has been ruder about the UK in relation to the environment than almost any other, is now busy explaining why – although it signed up to a 2025 per cent reduction – it unfortunately does not think it can do anything at all. It is amazing how the proximity of elections has that effect upon individuals universally. Anybody who thinks that we do not have a common view in Europe should recognize that one of the commonalities is that we all react exactly the same as an election approaches, wherever it may be!

This is an issue which can be solved only on a global basis, and only over time. The point must be pressed that the quicker we move the easier it is to do, and the longer it is left the more impossible it becomes; but I still have to say that the problem of time is extremely difficult. We see this when people decide on which issues they wish to concentrate. Global warming is accepted in principle by politicians of all parties in this country. There is now a bi-partisan programme, so at Kyoto it was possible for the negotiating Labour minister to point to the previous Conservative minister, myself, as being more extreme than he was. Therefore, the Americans had better settle because it would be worse if it was left to anyone else. This kind of bi-partisanship has given us a great strength in the world.

However, even though this is true, just look at how the choices are made. In general, it is of course easy to attack trends in road transport. I believe recent research has shown clearly that the almost universal view held by people about the motor car is simple: a great deal more should be spent on public transport in order that *other* people may use public transport, giving more space on the road for *me*. When we talk about doing something about transport in general, it all sounds good – before we have the *White Paper*. It is when we get the *White Paper*, and begin to talk in particularities about what we will do about transport, that we are in trouble, even though road transport has been picked as the key element. The phrase 'integrated transport policy' is telling in its ambiguity: it is the sort of phrase you use when you do not know what your transport policy is going to be.

Politicians are now coming to the tough times. We will have to be prepared to pass up immediate political advantage and make decisions which will otherwise be impossible. Of course, there are some areas where it will be easier to make decisions if only we are prepared to take on particular vested interests. We have to face the degree to which vested interests can make a huge difference, and a distorting difference, to the way that politicians operate.

Let me give one example. Hydrofluorocarbons (HFCs), the chemicals widely suggested as the alternative to chlorofluorocarbons (CFCs) to protect the ozone layer, are in fact more than 2000 times as powerful a global warming agent than carbon dioxide (CO_2). By the year 2010, they will account for 4 per cent of the emissions of greenhouse gases in the UK, even taking the most conservative and most favourable scenario. With a less favourable scenario, it might be twice as much. HFCs are not widely used yet because they are coming into operation as an alternative. If measures were taken to see that they were not used, but that hydrocarbons, ammonia or some of the other possible mechanisms were used instead, *before* there is a problem of a vested interest, we could contribute significantly towards our total package. Consider the importance of that 4 per cent when we are only talking about an 8 per cent overall reduction. If we talk about that as a greenhouse gas, we are talking about quite a serious contribution to the UK target. But, of course, the manufacturers of HFCs are already out there fighting the battle, saying it is impossible, there is no alternative, there is something wrong with everything else. The chemical companies are all there because they have done a deal in their minds – in the US again – that they will support the giving up of CFCs as long as the alternative is a chemically run refrigeration system, so that there can be a chemical alternative in order that they can make an alternative profit.

We need to recognize that it is better to take on a vested interest *before* it has a vast number of supporters who have bought the product, rather than leave it until the product has been sold – by which time the battle has almost been lost. I hope very much that we can take measures of that kind. Politicians have to take what are the easier means to solve this problem because all the means are difficult.

I want to finish with two key points for politicians, but also for the rest of us. Firstly, I think that one of our biggest problems is that we never bring these issues down to earth. We are so busy talking about global warming – these *huge* concerns – that we forget such issues strike the public only when they are brought down to earth. Later chapters describe what happened when Mrs Thatcher started talking about global warming: it created a means of bringing the issue to people's attention – bringing it into their compass. The argument goes something like this: if she thinks that, even though it is clearly difficult for her, there must be something in it. It brings the issue close to people's hearts and minds.

This is true of global warming in another way. We have not yet been prepared to face the fact that one of the issues about which the public care most is air pollution; the quality of air is right at the top of any list of the public's concern everywhere in the world. Hence, one of the ways we have to deal with global warming is to deal with air pollution. It is much easier to get people to be concerned, for example, about road traffic if it is clearly linked with particulates, cancer and triggering asthma. This does not stand in the way of taking measures which contribute, at least in part, to dealing with global warming; rather, it reinforces the need for action in people's minds.

In other words, politicians have to be increasingly willing to seek out the issues about which the public instinctively feel strongly – which tend to be those closest to the public – and use them to bring the public to an understanding of the bigger issues. In reality, these are the more terrifying because they could signal the end of the way in which we live on this planet.

The second point is the sheer revolution which the issue of global warming demands. This is illustrated by a case, in 1997, when the Danes made a great fuss about the closure of their last coal-fired power station. Indeed, there was a good deal of media coverage. Within six months, the same Danish government thrilled the world by announcing that, as part of its aid programme, it was giving to India one of its old power stations – the same coal-fired power station that it had just closed down. The link between the two took some time to be established: it does not matter where in the world the rubbish is put, it has the same effect as far as global warming is concerned.

This is a devastating fact that politicians have not even begun to come to terms with. For the first time, what has been up to now merely (I use the word 'merely' carefully) a moral consideration – that we in the rich North should be helping the poor in the South – becomes a practical necessity. In the past, people have had to explain to others that it is because of the brotherhood of man or the fatherhood of God;

there has had to be a philosophical or theological reason to explain why we must help other people. Sometimes we have used a pathetic explanation about how it helps the markets as a by-product and that these other people might be able to buy our products. These arguments, deep down, play on people's guilt.

Today, politicians have to come to terms with the fact that our climate will change in a way with which we cannot cope, if a method is not found to allow the Indians and Chinese to grow, develop and provide for their populations without destroying the atmosphere. We know this can be done only if *we* take a smaller proportion of what will become the allowed level of emissions. In turn, through our technology and investment, we enable developing world countries to make more for their people with the emissions that they will be allowed.

Suddenly, we are facing a world in which justice becomes not the prerogative of the moralist but the necessity of the practical politician. I do not believe that any politicians fully understand what this will mean over the next 20 years. Explaining to people that we must enable India to grow in a way which costs us money but reduces the impact on our climate is a piece of oratory which will test even a Margaret Thatcher.

4 PUBLIC AND 'EXPERT' OPINION ON ENVIRONMENTAL ISSUES

Robert M Worcester

INTRODUCTION

The pace of change – corporate, product, political and consumer – is accelerating at an increasing rate. Great Britain is at the end of a long mutation; society has basically transformed itself. The Thatcher revolution has run its course. Privatization has reached its limits. We are on the 'Third Way'.

But there is a growing sense that daily life has become too stressful, and that security is undermined. In the application of Maslow's 'Hierarchy of Human Needs', sustenance is assured, but security is threatened. Esteem is under attack, and self-actualization comes hard (Maslow, 1954).

Crude hedonism is on the rise: more drugs, and more anti-social behaviour, growing faster with young women than young men. Too many are what we call the *'underwolves'*, which we define as the *underdog who bites back*.

Resentments are building up which threaten the fabric of our society. For the longest period in this century, the economies of the developed nations have been on the rise; but when the downturn does come, there are stresses that may cause the fabric to rip. The fault lines include the employed younger against older retired citizens, which will inevitably be exacerbated by the declining proportion of those in work to those who demand that pension promises be met. They also involve the poor against rich, as bands between the well paid and the poorly paid widen; rural dwellers against those living in urban areas, as housing demands encroach rural landscapes and greenbelts, and urban public transport continues to soak up scarce resources while petrol taxes penalize the rural motorist. Further stresses on society will be initiated by scientists against the people, as trust in science and scientists to solve intractable problems wavers; producers against consumers, as consumer society is encouraged by governments everywhere; trade unions lose power and people no longer believe in their institutions to do what is best for the people against the interests of pressure groups.

People against institutions will become increasingly the order of the day, faith in institutions declining. In this country, and likely in others, central government will also be pitted against local government – here the heritage of the Thatcher consolidation of central power. Everybody will be against big business, as mergers and downsizing, short product cycles and fat-cat salaries are outed by an envious press and people become cynical about business commitment to sustainable development and corporate social responsibility.

Another strain already apparent is that engineers want high tech, but people want high touch, and, most importantly, people are realizing here, and survey evidence makes clear elsewhere, that the media are seen to be part of the problem, not part of the solution (see Table 4.1) (Worcester, 1998).

As can be seen in Table 4.1, journalists have the trust of fewer than one person in five, and rank even below politicians. Half of those individuals who trust business leaders trust journalists, while only a third of those who trust civil servants and pollsters, a quarter of those who trust the police and scientists, and a fifth of those who trust professors trust journalists.

In the results from last year's Latinobarometre, carried out annually throughout Latin America by Marta Lagos of MORI Chile, in countries where institutions are trusted least, the media are trusted most; but in the majority of countries from Argentina to Mexico, the media, both broadcast and print, have the trust of few of their listeners and readers.

In light of these changing needs and wants, what does the following signify?

- Eight in ten individuals have over the past 11 years, year after year, agreed that: 'I would find it very difficult to adjust my lifestyle to being without a car'?
- Crime is the top worry for most people (48 per cent), followed by illness/health care (42 per cent), and fear of unemployment (29 per cent), and anything environmental struggles to make tenth place.

Meanwhile, people are moving from concern about ecology to daily environmental awareness.

- Nearly half of the British public agrees that: 'the motor car is ruining the British countryside', and only a third disagrees.

Table 4.1 *Trust in professions*

Q *Now I will read out a list of different types of people. For each, would you tell me whether you generally trust them to tell the truth or not?*

	April 1997			January 1999		
	Trust %	Not %	Net %	Trust %	Not %	Net %
Doctors	86	10	+76	91	7	+84
Teachers	83	11	+72	89	7	+82
Clergymen/priests	71	20	+51	80	14	+66
Professors	70	12	+58	79	10	+69
Judges	72	19	+53	77	16	+61
Television newsreaders	74	14	+60	74	17	+57
Scientists	63	22	+41	63	27	+36
Police	61	30	+31	61	31	+30
Ordinary individual in the street	56	28	+28	60	28	+32
Pollsters	55	28	+27	49	35	+14
Civil servants	36	50	−14	47	41	+ 6
Trade union officials	27	56	−29	39	47	− 8
Business leaders	29	60	−31	28	60	−32
Government ministers	12	80	−68	23	70	−47
Politicians	15	78	−63	23	72	−49
Journalists	15	76	−61	15	79	−64

Base: circa 1000, 1997; circa 2000, 1999; British adults
Source: MORI/The Times, 1997; MORI/British Medical Association, 1999*

- More than twice as many people trust pressure groups, such as Greenpeace or Friends of the Earth, than trust government scientists to advise them on the risks of pollution.
- One in four say that they would trust government scientists least out of ten spokesmen, and nearly half say that it is government ministers they would trust least.
- Seven in ten of the public believe that 'industry and commerce do not pay enough attention to their social responsibilities', as do two-thirds of the nation's editors and 83 per cent of Labour MPs.
- One person in six (17 per cent) says that he or she has boycotted a company's product on ethical grounds, and one in five (19 per cent) has chosen a product or service because of a company's ethical

reputation. That is the purchasing decisions of some five million households!

• There has been a sharp and sustained drop in individuals who say they believe that 'the profits of large companies help to make things better for everyone who buys their products and services' over the past two decades. In the late 1970s, some 55 per cent said that they thought this to be true. By last year, the percentage of those agreeing had been cut in half to 26 per cent.

And what are the implications of the following? Nine people in ten – 91 per cent – say that they think the problem of air pollution in Britain is serious. Nine in ten – 92 per cent – say that they think disposal of society's waste products is serious. Nineteen people in 20 – 95 per cent – say that they think pollution of our rivers and beaches is serious. Seriously.

About two-thirds of the public recycle – that's good; but that percentage has not increased in the past decade – and that's bad. But six people in ten say that they have selected an environmentally friendly product over another because of its environmentally friendly packaging, and three in ten say they do so regularly. That's some 12 million British adults! And that's good – but not good enough.

Environmental Consumerism

There was a sharp rise in the proportion of the British public who participated in various green activities: to a lesser extent in such sedentary activities as walking in the countryside or watching environmental programmes on TV; to a greater extent in the case of green purchasing, doubling from 1988–1991. During that period, the proportion of environmental activists (EAs; defined as those who have engaged in five or more of the listed activities) increased from 14 per cent of the adult population in 1988 to 31 per cent in 1991, before falling back to 23 per cent by 1992 as the state of the economy, or rather the state of economic optimism, declined. Since then, environmental activism, green consumerism and other green activities have levelled off in Britain, with about one British person in four identifiable as an environmental activist, and four in ten as a green consumer. In August 1998, 27 per cent were classified as EAs and 33 per cent as green consumers (GCs).

MORI conducts a study on business and the environment annually, and has done for over a decade. Alongside this national survey of the

British public, we also interview the nation's environmental journalists on national daily and Sunday newspapers, magazines and on the broadcast media. In addition, two years ago we conducted the UK Department of Environment's triennial survey of public attitudes towards the environment. In it we found that the British public 'talk green', even if sometimes they do not 'act green'. In fact, while the UK Treasury holds most of the cards – those not held by the Bank of England anyway – and few in power pay much attention to the environment minister – by a massive 86 per cent to 12 per cent – the British public thinks that the environment should get at least equal billing to managing the economy.

But the environment is 'off-message'. Politicians think that there are no votes in it (they are wrong); and in New Labour at least, if it is not health, education, law and order or jobs, it is not for this parliament, and greenies have not made the connections with prime issues to get their concerns back on the agenda.

Public priorities, furthermore, have shifted since the heady days (for environmentalists anyway) when pollution, conservation and the environment were seen to be the most mentioned and important issues facing the country, and the prime minister (Thatcher, of all people) was making speeches at the Royal Society and in the United Nations (UN) about it. Many manufacturers have bought into being green, as have the political parties to some extent – so what might have been exceptional then is commonplace now.

So what are the public's concerns to do with the environment, and how are they changing?

As can be seen, the big jump in 1998 was in toxic waste – it hit the headlines and was the subject of much controversy. Genetically modified organisms (GMOs) will continue to be a big hit when we go to the public in this year's survey; up 17 per cent in 1998 over the previous year, and a big jump again in 1999.

So, three people in four are of the view that 'industry and commerce do not pay enough attention to their treatment of the environment'. And while that is some improvement over a decade ago, there is still some way to go before a sceptical public is convinced that business can be trusted with the environment.

And it is not just the ordinary citizens of this country, either, it is environment journalists, it is MPs and especially Labour MPs – and it is captains of industry also; and if they do not know whether or not British companies pay enough attention to their treatment of the environment, who does?

For over a decade, I have been pointing out to anyone who will listen that public mistrust of scientists is a problem that needs attention;

Here are some statements about the balance between economic and environmental considerations. With which one of these do you agree most?

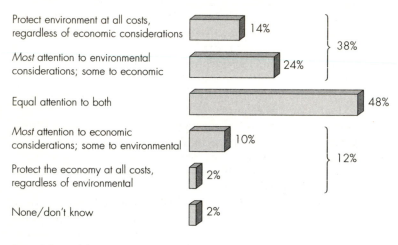

Protect environment at all costs, regardless of economic considerations — 14%

Most attention to environmental considerations; some to economic — 24%

} 38%

Equal attention to both — 48%

Most attention to economic considerations; some to environmental — 10%

Protect the economy at all costs, regardless of environmental — 2%

} 12%

None/don't know — 2%

Base: 1782 adults 18+ in England and Wales, 1996–97
Source: MORI/DETR, 1996–97*

Figure 4.1 *Balancing environment and economy*

I am glad to say that it seems, finally – and following the panic over BSE and CJD, beef on the bone, and the like – that people in positions of power are beginning to be concerned about the decline in confidence in institutions and scepticism about what science can deliver. But when nearly twice as many people who trust green NGO scientists as trust government and industry scientists, and when Greenpeace makes GMOs 1999's big thing, you do not need to be reminded of the *Brent Spar* to know that when they talk, people listen. It's not much better when you ask people who they can trust generally to tell the truth either: while scientists get a 63 per cent veracity score, business leaders get a lowly 28 per cent. But that's better than government ministers, who are trusted by only 23 per cent!

The proof of the pudding is in the eating. When we asked people their purchasing criteria, putting quality and price equal, 57 per cent of the public said that they put a company's environmental responsibility as 'very important'. And some 12 million people tell us that they have 'bought green', not just talked it.

Which, if any, of these environmental and conservation issues most concern you these days?

97–98

Exhaust fumes from cars/lorries	52%	+3
Toxic/chemical waste/toxic dumping	50%	+11
Sea pollution/waste disposal at sea	48%	+4
Pollution of rivers/streams/water	48%	+2
Air pollution	48%	−1
Crop spraying/insecticides	33%	+7
Industrial pollution	32%	+7
Genetically modified foods	30%	+17
Food safety	30%	+8
Loss of natural resources	29%	+10

Source: MORI/Business and the Environment (4–11 September 1998, 1823 respondents)*

Figure 4.2 *Public environmental concerns*

Do you agree or disagree that:

*British companies do **not** pay enough attention to their treatment of the environment?*

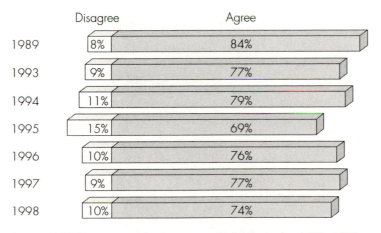

	Disagree	Agree
1989	8%	84%
1993	9%	77%
1994	11%	79%
1995	15%	69%
1996	10%	76%
1997	9%	77%
1998	10%	74%

Source: MORI/Business and the Environment (4–11 September 1998, 1823 respondents)*

Figure 4.3 *Companies' green performance – 1*

British companies do not pay enough attention to their treatment of the environment

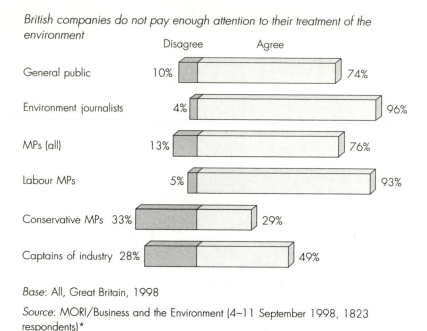

Base: All, Great Britain, 1998

Source: MORI/Business and the Environment (4–11 September 1998, 1823 respondents)*

Figure 4.4 *Companies' green performance – 2*

How much confidence would you have in what each of the following have to say about environmental issues?

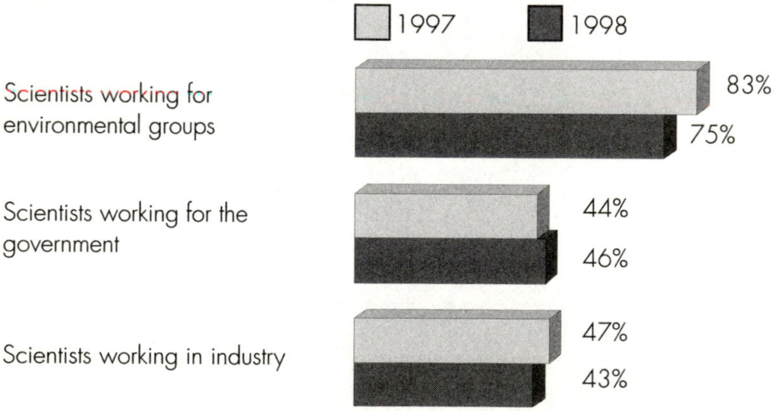

Source: MORI/Business and the Environment (4–11 September 1998, 1823 respondents)*

Figure 4.5 *Trust in scientists*

How important are the following to you when choosing between products and services, where quality and price are equal?

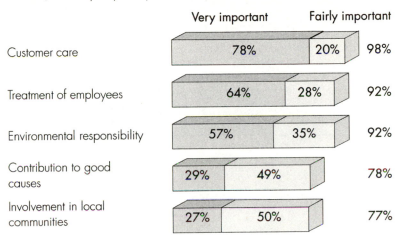

Base: circa 1000 British adults aged 15+, 1998
Source: MORI/Corporate Social Responsibility, 1998*

Figure 4.6 *Purchasing criteria*

Different opinions exist as to whether companies' social and community contributions should benefit only those they are trying to help, or whether it is acceptable for companies to derive some benefit too. Which comes closest to your own?

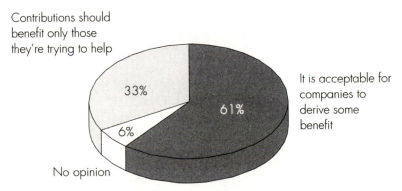

Base: 996/939 British adults aged 15+, July–August 1998
Source: MORI/Corporate Social Responsibility, 1998*

Figure 4.7 *Who should benefit?*

When forming an opinion about a particular company or organization, how important is it to you to know about their activities in society and the community?

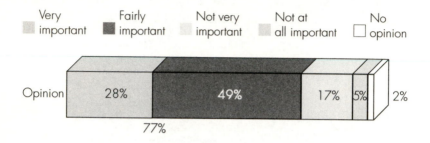

When forming a decision about a product or service from a particular company or organization, how important is it to you that it shows a high degree of social responsibility?

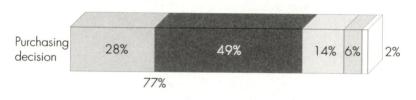

Source: MORI/Corporate Social Responsibility, 1998*

Figure 4.8 *The Importance of corporate social responsibility*

CORPORATE ETHICS

To be fair to the public, it does not see corporate social responsibility as a one-way street. Most folks think it is okay for a company to do good, out of doing good. Nearly twice as many people in this country find it acceptable for companies to derive some benefit out of their community and social involvement.

And when forming an opinion of a company or product or service, the public tells us that it is important to know what that company is doing to meet what it sees as the company's social responsibility.

Can you tell me which of the things on this card, if any, you have done in the last 12 months?

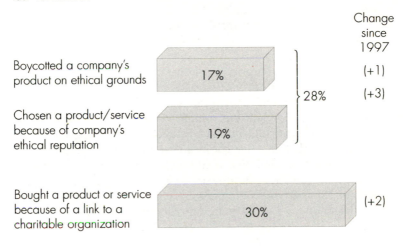

Base: 1935 British adults aged 15+, July–August 1998
Source: MORI/Corporate Social Responsibility, 1998*

Figure 4.9 *Corporate social responsibility and purchasing behaviour*

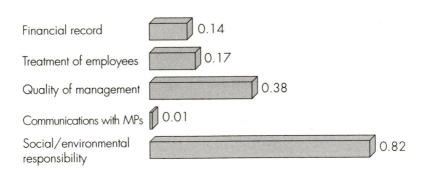

Note: 1 = Perfect correlation
Base: 100 MPs, November 1997
Source: MORI/Survey of MPs, Winter 1997*

Figure 4.10 *Drivers of favourability – MPs*

Earlier I said that the proof of the pudding is in the eating. The set of findings in Figure 4.9 makes the point, when you consider that every percentage point represents the behaviour of approximately 420,000 consumers. In other words, a quarter of the public is over ten million consumers; three in ten approaches 13.5 million. That's a lot of people.

And finally, let us stop for a minute and reflect on who has the power of life and death over businesses and NGOs? MPs do. When we looked at the 'drivers' of favourability in 1997, we expected to find that those companies who were thought to be good at communicating with MPs would score high on the key favourability score. We found, to the contrary, that effective communications per se had almost nil correlation with favourability, as did their financial record and even their treatment of their employees. What really paid off was the impression MPs had of a company's reputation for meeting what they saw as the company's social and environmental responsibilities.

CONCLUSIONS

All in all, then, the environment is alive and well and living in the hearts of your fellow countrymen. At an Anglo-North American conference on the topic of business and the environment held at Lake Louise several years ago, the opening British speaker – amongst governmental, business and NGO leaders – said that the environmental issue would take care of itself in another few years as concerned youngsters grew into adulthood. They would then express their concern to government, industry and commerce and force them to take care of the environment – and he was the chairman of a water company!

The fact is that most of us are green when we are 15; but then we leave school, some of us unprepared for work, either because of illiteracy or innumeracy or both. And when we find we cannot get a job, the environment as an issue falls away from first or second, in the order of concerns, to eighth, ninth or right off the agenda. I call it the 'Alligator Principle' – when you're up to your neck in alligators, you don't worry a lot about global warming. But global warming is a greater threat to most of us than alligators.

The environment, conservation, sustainability and pollution are not on the top on many people's immediate agenda, but it lies there, sleeping perhaps, until something – a Torrey Canyon, an *Exxon Valdez*, a Chernobyl, a *Brent Spar* – awakens it, and then it becomes a monster, wrecking anything in its path. Tomorrow's company takes care to ensure its future by worrying about its social responsibilities before called upon to do so by consumers, the media or government. The time to dig the well is before you need to draw the water. Monsanto failed to do this; it will be many a year before it recovers what was once its good name.

REFERENCES

DETR (1998) 'Public attitudes to the environment', *Digest of Environmental Statistics*, no 20, HMSO, London

Maslow, A (1954) *Motivation and Personality*, Harper, New York

Worcester, R (1998) 'What does the World Values Survey say about trust in government?', paper read at AAPOR/WAPOR, 15 May 1998, Panel on Media, Polls and Trust in Democratic Institutions

NOTE

* Full details of published polls are available from MORI, 32 Old Queen Street, London SW1 9HP, Tel: +44 (0)20 7222 0232, Fax: +44 (0)20 7222 1653.

PART II

Reporting Global Environmental Change

5 REPORTING SUSTAINABLE DEVELOPMENT: A BROADCAST JOURNALIST'S VIEW

Roger Harrabin

A straw poll of the public would probably elicit the view that people keep up with the news to 'find out what is happening in the world'. There is a gap, though, between expectation and delivery as the news media does not quite report what is happening in the world, but rather concentrates its energies on whatever topics happen to be at the top of a narrow and subjective list of events that appear to be new to the editors of the day.

One illustration is the reporting of genetically modified (GM) crops in the UK, the US and Germany. The steady move towards GM crops, for instance, was progressing in Britain for several years almost totally unremarked by the news media, until in late 1998 it suddenly gained acceptance as a story with editors and accordingly went on to dominate media debate for more than six months. Meanwhile, in Germany the GM debate had been raging in the media for several years before it became an issue in the UK: whilst at its peak in the UK media, GM had not been recognized as a news issue in the US. In all three countries the scientific, ethical and environmental issues were very similar, although the issues were treated very differently by the media in different news cultures under varying degrees of influence from agribusiness, scientific research and green pressure groups.

It could be argued that sustainable development is still at the 'undiscovered story' stage. The very phrase is enough to send a news editor to sleep before the end of the seventh syllable. And there are many barriers to improving the media's reporting of so broad, diverse and difficult a topic.

NEWSROOM CULTURE: CHALLENGES OF TIME, SPACE AND COMPLEXITY

News culture is a major barrier. The newsmachine has always been driven by events, which literally constitute 'news'. But in recent years the trend has intensified, with a stronger demand for drama, conflict and novelty in the mass audience media. Many observers have also chronicled the increasing tendency to narrate events and explain ideas by personalizing the news. Harry Evans, the legendary former editor of *The Sunday Times* who wrote the textbooks which still influence each new generation of young journalists, offered the definition 'News is People'. This dictum is exemplified by the media's treatment of stories focusing on topics as diverse as personal crises for soap opera stars, the battle for the US presidency, or the NATO punishment bombings of the Serbian bad guy Milosevic.

Even the upmarket news outlets in the competitive information market increasingly appeal to people's hearts as well as (sometimes instead of) their minds. These trends have made the reporting of the abstract notion of sustainable development more difficult. Sustainable development is not a story – it is an idea, and what is more, an idea which has already been expressed. Any attempt by a journalist to do a story on sustainable development per se is almost doomed to failure. Even the surreptitious deployment of the phrase buried deep within the body of a journalist's text can raise editorial eyebrows.

Time scales are another problem. News explains the events of the day selected by the professional and personal preferences of editors, and examines their potential short-term consequences. It is extremely difficult to engage the newsmachine with discussion of consequences that may or may not result in 50 years' time. So, the idea that the world may warm with potentially catastrophic consequences over the next century is an old story – it may be massively important, but unlike the latest cricket score, we have heard it before. Therefore, taking the key example of climate change, the story tends to be explored in the media through individual events in the natural world which appear to confirm or deny the global warming theory now, such as bird habitats shifting northwards in the UK, or frogs mating earlier, or the world's coral reefs being badly bleached by a sudden surge in sea temperatures during 1998. These narrowly focused reports sometimes attempt to place the issue within the broader debate over whether global warming is induced by man; but often they tend to be presented as bald statements of natural fact, with the global warming phrase tossed in.

Environment journalists often go to considerable lengths to overcome these obstacles by disguising reports of long-term environmental change as news events. In attempting to raise the news significance of the massive coral bleaching episode that affected reefs round the world in late 1988, I invited the UK's Deputy Prime Minister John Prescott to join me on a scuba dive off a damaged reef. The venue was fixed as the Maldives, because Mr Prescott was already on an official visit to India. The addition of a heavyweight politician provoked infinitely more interest than would have normally have been manifested in a report on coral death, and the story ran prominently to millions of listeners and viewers on the BBC. But in the print media the initiative backfired badly as leader writers condemned Mr Prescott for enjoying himself at the taxpayers' expense. The story was written by political correspondents whose focus was on the political row raised by opposition politicians over the expense of the trip, rather than by environment correspondents wishing to highlight the environmental implications of the coral damage.

Once the 'news line' of a story is established ('MP in Freebie' – rather than 'Global Coral Death'), it can be hard for individual reporters to take an independent line. News editors are voracious consumers of other media, and despite an ambition of editorial independence, many have a natural human inclination against being found to be on the wrong track. This can lead to a narrowing of the potential news agenda. It was hoped that new TV channels would allow a broadening of the agenda, but many observers have commented that the reverse has happened as hard-pressed producers concentrate their efforts on maximizing their coverage of the few chosen topics of the day.

The problems of established news cultures and the long time scales involved in many global environmental change stories are compounded by the difficulties of reporting complexity. Whatever the aspirations of editors towards the intellectual higher ground of dispassionate analytical journalism, it is still the case that stories make a more powerful impact if they have a clear moral message. Like the old Western movies, it engages the passions of the viewer if it is clear who is the goodie and who is the baddie. I once presented an *Assignment* documentary for BBC2 on the impact of big dams in the Indian subcontinent. The story was complex, and the conclusions ambivalent. Many people in some areas had lost their homes to big dams, and the dams and irrigation systems were often poorly maintained. But in other areas fewer people had been moved out, and dams had successfully increased agriculture by irrigation and provided cheap, non-polluting electricity which fuelled an industrial export boom to help the country's balance of payments crisis. The documentary was warmly received by some viewers, but two television critics complained that the message of the film was insufficiently clear. 'Are we supposed to be for or against big dams?' one newspaper critic asked in irritation. Even inside the BBC there were mixed feelings about the programme. The documentaries which attract the largest audiences and win most awards are often the most partisan, and BBC editors would not be human if they did not have at least half an eye on audience figures.

Available space is also a fact which limits the ability of journalists to embrace complexity. Space is at a premium in many news and current affairs media. In morning broadcast news bulletins on BBC Radio 4, the reporter is often allowed no more than 50 seconds to tell the story. At an average of three spoken words a second, that means a story has to be told in 150 words, relating all the pertinent facts whilst being written in an accessible fashion that will engage the listener when he or she is at the bathroom mirror or sorting out the children's breakfast cereal. No wonder complexity is hard to convey. The business of news and current affairs journalism often involves painful compromise in which the journalist is well aware that he or she is oversimplifying the picture, but cannot find another way to tell the story. These problems are exacerbated by the inevitably tight limits on journalistic research time. The more angles a journalist explores in any given story, the more time it takes. When journalists are under pressure to publish or broadcast, and many news media are cutting costs by reducing their staff, this is a problem.

The nightly TV news bulletins allow around two minutes per filmed report. This is not much more helpful, especially as the reporter has to fit the script to the available pictures while also trying to tell a story of broader import. TV is a uniquely difficult medium in which to explore sustainable development issues because the concrete nature of film images does not easily lend itself to the discussion of discursive or abstract ideas. Even in broadsheet newspapers, space is sometimes uncomfortably tight, as papers increasingly tend to offer acres of space to whatever big running story happens to be in the news at the time, thereby robbing space from other important issues.

Specialist journalists who want to make connections between the sustainable development agenda and other areas of specialist interest are also hampered by the aforementioned lack of space. Let us suppose that an energy correspondent, for instance, wanted to insert at the bottom of a ten-paragraph story a couple of paragraphs touching on potential environmental implications of a given news event. Let us then suppose that because of shortage of space, the last two paragraphs were cut either by the journalist or by the subeditors. If this happened five times, there would have been enough green news copy on the notional newsroom spike to make an environment story all of its own.

Time is also a major factor at the point of commissioning a story. Commissioning editors are often bombarded with story ideas from a plethora of sources. If a journalist cannot sell his story to a commissioning editor within the first sentence, the story is sometimes discarded without further investigation. Many specialist journalists wanting to sell a complex story exploring sustainable development devise a shorthand tabloid-headline version of the story in advance. For example, I reported for the *Today* programme and for BBC TV on a complex sustainable development story in Cameroon, which called into question the use of European Union (EU) grants. One EU grant had been given to employ forest rangers to protect a rainforest reserve, while another grant had been given to upgrade a road so that farmers could get produce to market. The trouble was that the road ran next to the protected rainforest reserve, inadvertently enabling poachers to drive from the capital Yaounde to kill gorillas, chimps and other animals, then load them on to lorries for sale in the bush meat markets in town. As a result of the widespread poaching there was less bush meat available for a tribe of pygmies who lived in the reserve. When we visited them they were eating barbecued caterpillars. The sexy headline 'EU fat cats make pygmies eat worms' was coined to give the reports a helping hand onto the airwaves when we returned home. The story was broadcast but the flippant headline, of course, was not.

Cross-sectoral issues are difficult for news organizations which are structured into separate specialisms reporting on different areas of interest. News organizations will often have separate specialist correspondents in business, economics, environment, transport, health, energy, politics, social affairs and development. The sustainable development agenda as defined by the Rio Earth Summit of 1992 encompasses all of these issues and more. The desire to expand the economy while protecting the environment and the social fabric has led the government to create a number of cross-sectoral initiatives to coordinate policy throughout government departments. The government initiative has so far met with some success, but this has arguably not been reflected in news coverage. Stories which concern more than one area of interest have often fallen between the gaps in journalistic specialisms. Environmental economics, for instance, was not taken seriously by most mainstream economics correspondents until the point when it was about to be launched on the unsuspecting public through fiscal weapons in the UK budget.

Similarly, the environmental aspects of transport were long ignored by transport correspondents who relied for their information on sources within the transport sector, who had not themselves grasped the implications of rising emissions of pollutants. The environmental impacts of transport are now mainstream since the New Labour government launched its *White Paper* on integrated transport. But the social equity implications of supporting a car-dominated society in which 30 per cent of car-less people are, in effect, second class citizens are still not discussed as fully as they might be. There are many potentially fruitful areas of contentious media debate: do rich cars drivers from the suburbs have the absolute right to drive to work through poor areas where most people do not own cars, imposing upon those areas noise, pollution and accident risk, for instance?

Global issues also tend to fall between journalistic specialisms. It is often unclear where responsibility lies for reporting on the debate on developing world debt – it tends to fall between religious correspondents and economics correspondents. Population policy is a badly undercovered area, which is perhaps cross-sectoral more than any other. It is staggering that as the world population hits six billion, there is to date almost no debate on the issue.

New but not News

Environment is a new issue for editors who have usually received their journalistic training from old hands well versed in making decisions on the value of stories in the fields of crime, politics, foreign affairs, etc. Decision making on environmental issues appears more erratic, and too often dominated by the agenda of the big pressure groups. Many of the stories on the sustainable development agenda are completely new issues on which there is little journalistic precedent. Many news editors fear the scorn of their colleagues and are reluctant to give space to a new issue unless it has been verified as a valid news story by another (or preferably more than one other) news outlet. News editors desire scoops – but generally only in story areas where there have been scoops before. The saga of genetically modified organisms (GMOs) is a perfect example. A small number of campaigners were warning for years of the potential risks from GMOs, and of the domination of government thinking by GMO businesses, but few news editors had the confidence to highlight such an unusual story. Then, stories on GMOs eventually began to break in the news, until the critical mass of news editor knowledge was reached and GMOs were certified as a 'good story'. Since then a degree of knowledge about GM has become mandatory for news decision makers, and the media has more than made up for lost time by running acres of material on GMOs – some of it of distinctly dubious value. At these junctures, though, the news editors will often prefer to chase hot stories that appear in other media than to follow the more cautious advice of their own specialists in the field.

Even informed editors are faced with the fact that the costs of reporting sustainable development can be high. The sharpest focus of the sustainable development debate is arguably not in Europe, but in developing countries where disparities in individual wealth and health are extreme, and where fragile environments are being destroyed through pressure from business, poverty, ignorance or population growth – or a combination of them all. Around half the world's people live in rural areas. But travelling to far-flung locations in developing countries costs large sums of money, including the air fare, the internal travel (often by expensive four-wheel drive vehicle), and the salary costs of the journalist's travelling time. The 1998 G8 Summit in Birmingham attracted up to 100,000 protesters on to the streets demanding the cancellation of developing world debt; yet the BBC did not manage to offer a TV news film from a debt-ridden country. The issue suffered similar neglect at the time of the large 1999 protest in London, as news budgets had been exhausted by the expensive coverage of the Kosovo war. Both cases were extensively covered from the UK perspective.

Editors keen to report on sustainable development issues often blanche when faced with a bill for two reports from, say, Madagascar at the same cost as five reports from America. There has been substantial discussion of the ubiquity of cheap American drama and entertainment programming on TV stations round the world; but there is relatively little analysis of the pervasiveness of American images in the news, which far outstrip their real news value as missives from the world's only superpower.

It is a simple though regrettable fact of journalistic economics that the farther from major international centres that events take place, the less likely they will be reported. This leads to difficult choices for organizations such as the BBC. If Greenpeace is offering us film footage of a news event which we would never be able to film out of our own resources, should we accept that footage? The same question would be raised over, say, NGO film of oil company activities in the jungles of South America.

CONFLICT

Stories tend to be reported in terms of bi-polar conflict. This means reporting in black and white when sustainable development stories often come out in shades of grey. The debate on water pricing is an example: the media usually reports the battles between water companies and poor consumers, or water companies and birds and bugs, whereas the real balancing act is between the companies, the consumers and the birds.

In the broadcast media we actively seek conflict in the form of debate. Most TV and radio news and current affairs journalists will characterize the most extreme positions in the national debate on any given subject. This is not just unhelpful because it discourages progress by consensus – it also has an inevitable distorting effect on the portrayal of the debate itself. Many debates, for instance have the majority of people grouped slightly to one side of a central position. What is the effect on perception if we journalists choose two spokesmen from the far wings of the debate?

There was a classic case on a radio programme discussing the merits of a suggestion that British summer time should be extended all year round. This was a measure which attracted overwhelming public support in England, and the UK Parliamentary Bill was popular among around half of Scots. The total percentage of the UK population supporting the measure was approximately 80 per cent. The radio programme, though, wanted to inject life into a broadcast debate by choosing spokespeople from either side, and a producer was dispatched to find 'the person who would suffer most' from the change. The sponsor of the bill was duly confronted on air by a farmer in Orkney; but the point was rather lost when the farmer was asked about the impact on his life of the sun not rising until late morning. He replied: 'To be honest, we get so little daylight up here in the winter that it doesn't matter when we get it.'

SCALE AND COMPLEXITY

Some issues are too big for the media to handle. Some of the biggest stories in the world – such as global species loss, resource depletion, fisheries, food security, population growth or developing world debt – are among the hardest for us to cover. We like to focus (particularly in broadcast media) on the personal story with a national connection. This leads to significant distortions. Sometimes, strong pressure from

UK NGOs can succeed in forcing an international sustainable development issue onto the agenda. Domestic campaigners on developing world debt, for instance, have been extremely successful in promoting international debt as a legitimate issue to be discussed in the media. It is partly as a result of the pressure that has been brought to bear by large public demonstrations and the accompanying media coverage that the UK government has become something of an international leader in debt relief policy.

An issue such as world population growth has no such well-organized champions to propel it into the media. Unlike the debt story, it does not offer such a clear moral tale of victims and oppressors. And it is mired in controversy generated in the US by anti-abortion groups who oppose the funding of any international family planning groups who do not condemn abortion. The tension over that tiny element of the population issue appears to dazzle the media whenever population is discussed, and it is very rare for the media to examine broad issues linked to population growth. The population story often manifests itself in the guise of another 'debate' over whether the 19th century cleric Thomas Malthus was right or wrong when he said world population would become unsustainable and millions would die of hunger. The general conclusion was that because Malthus was not proven right by his predicted date, his fundamental premise was wrong.

Some population thinkers such as Dr Norman Myers of Green College Oxford protest that millions have died anyway – but that the deaths have not been related by the media to population growth because they have happened in different parts of the world over different periods of time. There is almost no examination of the fundamental premise to see whether it might prove right over a longer time scale. Likewise, there is very little projection of the world's carrying capacity, or environmental limits. This concept is fundamental to the idea of sustainable development, but the research is highly theoretical, contentious and underdebated, making it near impossible to find space for it in the news pages.

Environmental limits are only one of the new ways of thinking that have been generated by the sustainable development agenda and that have been underreported by the media. Other related issues that suffer the same fate include the 'perverse' economics of subsidy, ethical trading, new forms of protest and social organization, free trade and the environment, and sustainable development indicators. Many environmentalists argue, for instance, that the environment will never be properly protected until it is properly valued by society. That means changing the indicators by which society measures its progress, so that instead of relying solely on gross national product (GNP) as a measure of success, we also look to broader environmental and social indices. Ideas like this are of fundamental long-term importance, but are difficult and complex to tackle in the context of short news bulletins. Climate change offers perhaps the most pressing example of this problem. Much of the media is still preoccupied with the 'is global warming happening?' debate, while the policy makers have moved on to frame the issue as a matter of global risk assessment – how much can we afford not to do?

These new ideas have come from outside the mainstream political process, so it has been more difficult for the news system to debate them as we tend to turn to politicians to validate ideas. Yet, the media would also find good stories within mainstream politics if it were to look: different departments are grappling with the principles of sustainable development from different and sometimes opposing perspectives. News coverage of the report from the UK Department of Trade and Industry Select Committee in July 1999 on business reaction to the government's proposed climate change levy (an energy tax on business) almost universally failed to explore the ramifications of the report on plans by the Department of the Environment, Transport and the Regions (DETR) to cut carbon emissions by 20 per cent.

Most news executives and decision makers are immersed in the business of daily or weekly journalism. It is imperative that they have a good grasp of all the main issues of the day (issues defined as newsworthy by their inclusion in other areas of the mainstream media). They are often involved in the day-to-day minutiae of output and production to a degree which would amaze captains of industry who are content to delegate to trusted personnel. It helps to remember that they are producing a new product every day or every week. They drive the process so closely that it is often difficult for them to find space to step back and take a broader view.

DEBATING THE CHALLENGE TO THE MEDIA

The Cambridge Media and Environment Programme has held two one-and-a-half-day seminars bringing together BBC News executives and senior editors with academics and policy makers in the field of sustainable development. The seminars were strongly supported by the chief executive of BBC News, Tony Hall – a key factor in securing the involvement of extremely busy journalistic decision makers. The seminars have generated enormously positive responses from all sides, and the participants believe that the BBC has improved and expanded its coverage of these issues as a result. To my knowledge, no other media organization in this country has attempted such a process involving its senior management.

Feedback from the second Cambridge seminar acknowledged, though, that:

- the BBC still needs to improve its coverage of issues which cut across traditional specialist boundaries;
- its reporting of politics and business needs a broader perspective;
- its traditional foreign reporting is strong, but its reporting of supranational issues and long-term processes remains under-strength if it is to achieve its objectives defined in its own strategy review;
- senior editors are beginning to take a much broader view of news, but many output editors are still wedded to older news values. Many younger editors are fearful of exposing themselves to ridicule by suggesting stories off the defined news agenda.

At one of the seminars we devised a news values quiz to determine how the journalists and the outside experts might assess the newsworthiness of certain issues. The results made fascinating and instructive reading, and illustrated the enormous difficulty of explaining long-term changes in the news media. We prepared a list of news headlines and asked the participants to give each headline marks out of ten for newsworthiness. The headlines were designed to explore ten topics, with two headlines devoted to each topic – but exploring the issue from a different perspectives. We wanted the participants to make gut decisions on the headlines, and not to engage their intellects in devising the 'right' answers; so we conducted the quiz at a very fast pace (three seconds to mark each headline) and we did not advise them in advance that there were pairs of headlines scattered through the list.

One of the most instructive pairs of headlines concerned the fires that raged in two of the world's three great rainforests in 1997. We offered two headlines: 'Smoke haze envelops South-East Asia' and 'Brazilian Amazon Burns Again'. Journalists and academics alike scored the Indonesian fires seven out of ten. But the journalists awarded the Brazilian fires only four out of ten, while the experts scored them eight out of ten. This should come as no surprise – we journalists pride ourselves on defining our news values independently. Yet such a wide disparity between the journalists' and experts' perceived importance of major issues which may affect the world's climate and biological diversity might make us pause for a little analysis.

The BBC's preferences reflected the values of the broader media. A search of newspaper cuttings on the Indonesian fire will gather enough material to paper a bedroom wall. It was indeed a cataclysmic environment story. Palls of choking smoke drifted across six neighbouring countries, bringing normal life to a halt and creating serious diplomatic tension as more than a million people fell ill with respiratory diseases.

The inferno devastated wildlife, too. The Indonesian islands have some of the most diverse plant and animal species in the world. They suffered terribly as 17,000 square kilometres of forest were burned to the ground. After ignoring the story at first, the British media compensated with a full repertoire of news reports, glossy features and dramatic broadcast news dispatches. You would have had to be in strict media purdah to have avoided the news. Contrast the public's awareness of the latest statistics on the devastation caused by the fires in Brazil. The burning has laid waste to 20,000 square kilometres of the Amazon rainforest – that is, 3000 more than the Indonesian fires. Yet the UK media offered only a handful of reports on the fires in Brazil – even though they arguably pose a greater twofold threat to the global environment (pollution from the fires adds to the gases that may be altering the climate, and the forest loss also reduces the capacity of the world's trees to soak up carbon dioxide). In terms of potential climate change, the year-on-year forest burning in Brazil should arguably worry us far more than the sudden outbreak of fires in Indonesia, where the soil is better and trees are more likely to grow back.

From the journalistic perspective, some of the elements in the Indonesian story are clearly much stronger than those in the Brazilian story. The Indonesian fires may have received relatively little attention if they had been confined within the nation's borders; but they gathered news value as the smoke began to drift into the Malaysian capital of Kuala Lumpur. The 'haze' offered dramatic pictures of the effects on human and economic health – people with masks on their faces, children suffering from lung disorders.

Other factors were accessibility and cost. Most news media were able to fly their Far East correspondents quickly and cheaply into Kuala Lumpur. TV crews could transmit pictures on the same day, offering clear value for money to news editors. It would have cost substantial time and money to cover the Brazilian fires in the same way. The Indonesian fires also offered an important second wave of stories as diplomatic tension began to grow – and later a third wave as the fires became a metaphor for the economic and social ills of a region which had previously seemed to be leading the world into the next century.

These were all reasons why the newsmachines were cranked into fire-fighting in the Far East rather than South America. But there was another major factor. There is nothing new about fires in Brazil. We have been hearing about the burning Amazon rainforest for 20 years, and news editors are bored by it. It is old news. Everybody knows that the Amazon burns. In the literal sense of the word, it is not news.

The uncomfortable paradox is that the longer some problems persist, the less they hold the attention of the media. Unless a strong political campaign or a subjective editorial prejudice forces them continually onto the agenda (like crime rates), they slip quietly from the bulletins to be replaced by real news. Sometimes the story substitution is particularly perverse. This is important because the way issues are framed by journalists has an impact on public opinion and political decision making. Sometimes our politicians may be swayed in their decision making because we journalists have focused on apparently news-making events rather than long-term systemic change. The media treatment of transport danger may offer an illustration. At the end of the last century, railway accidents were commonplace; but the frequent episodes of personal tragedy attracted very little attention in the newspapers. They happened so regularly that they were inherently unnewsworthy. Over the decades the ratchet of legislation has been tightened so that railway safety manuals have swelled into heavy tomes.

The more safety on the railways has improved, the more unusual and dramatic rail accidents have appeared, and the more inherently newsworthy they have become. Reporting of a train crash nowadays follows a fairly predictable pattern. Step one: report the scene of the crash, the numbers injured and the preliminary estimates as to the cause. Step two: continue the dissection of what went wrong. Step three: nominate a culprit, then demand that steps are taken by the relevant authorities to ensure that such an accident will never happen again. One year later: revisit the story to see if train safety procedures have been improved.

THE PUBLIC INTEREST

Our fascination with the train crash story is understandable. A jack-knifed train offers spectacular pictures for TV and newspapers. Trains hit each other so infrequently that a crash has genuine news value. Large numbers of people are usually involved, and the potential exists for large numbers to be injured or shocked if not killed. We perceive that the event of the crash reveals an element of risk which we are duty bound to transmit to the public. And even normally neutral media organs are not embarrassed to adopt a campaigning tone in the interests of reducing further risk to travellers.

The scale, depth and urgency of the reporting have a direct influence on the official response to the crash. Rail unions and safety campaigners join forces with concerned politicians anxious to impress viewers and listeners of the need to improve safety measures whatever the cost. A leader writer will almost inevitably raise the question: 'After all, what is the value of the life of a loved one?' Yet, it might be argued that media treatment of rail accidents could perversely be increasing the risk to the public. Much of the cost of improved safety has been paid over recent years by the rail traveller through the cost of the ticket. Rail fares have soared above the cost of car travel, and this has contributed to the greater use of cars – where the risk of passenger injury is 15 times greater than on the train. There is a double irony: the high risk of road transport is consistently underplayed in the media. An average of ten people die every day on the roads, but because car crashes happen so often they are inherently unnewsworthy and we rarely feel compelled to report them.

The news values survey at the BBC sustainable development seminar produced an enlightening contrast of opinions on this issue. Journalists and experts were offered a headline: road accident – three dead. Both parties scored the story a lowly two out of ten. They were then offered a second headline: train crash – three dead. The experts gave the story the same score of two out of ten. But the journalists scored the story six out of ten – three times higher than a road crash in which the same number died.

The news values quiz revealed many more disparities between journalists' and experts' judgements of significance. This is understandable. But an examination of just the two examples discussed here should raise questions about whether we have the balance right. If our journalism leads people to believe that fires in Indonesia are a problem, but that fires in Brazil have stopped happening, we will create a seriously distorted picture of environmental problems facing the world. We may also impact on policy by influencing public opinion. If our journalism leads to extravagant improvements to an already safe means of transport (rail), and prompts some people to take a riskier form of transport (cars), then we fail if our goal is to promote the public interest. This even holds true in the instance of the appalling German high-speed rail crash which killed 98 people. This was the first crash anywhere in the world after 34 years of high-speed trains running on dedicated track. German rail has a magnificent safety record compared with German roads.

A greater readiness by journalists to set events in context and debate the nature of our journalistic prejudices and preferences might produce healthier reporting, deeper public understanding and possibly even lead to better public policy.

6 HAVE WE 'HAD ENOUGH OF ALL THAT ECO-BOLLOX'?[1]

Paul Brown and Frank McDonald

From:	Frank McDonald
To:	Paul Brown
Date:	June 1999
Subject:	'eco-bollox'

Paul, remember that conference we attended in Cardiff in May 1996? It was organized in the aftermath of the *Brent Spar* by the Centre for Journalism Studies at the University of Wales, with 'Capitalism Goes Green' as its rather optimistic working title. The idea, as you recall, was to bring together environmental activists, journalists such as us and top people from industry, throw them into the same lecture theatre for a couple of days, and see whether this might generate any consensus on such crucial issues as sustainable development and global environmental change. It was based at least to some extent on the notion that few movements had marshalled the media to their cause more effectively than environmental activists. 'The determination and single-minded dedication of the green lobby over more than three decades has pushed the environment to the top of the news agenda', the conference brochure said. 'That, in turn, has made it a political priority. And much of the resulting flood of legislation and regulations that has followed now impacts forcefully on business and industry.'

Sir Crispin Tickell, Thatcher's one-time ambassador to the United Nations and later chief environmental adviser to the British government, was the keynote speaker. But it was not his urbane and wide-ranging address that sticks in my mind from the Cardiff conference, nor the very frank and witty contribution by Sir John Banham, chairman of Tarmac plc, nor even the after-dinner speech by Dr Chris Fay, chairman and chief executive of Shell UK, in which he promised to do better in the wake of the *Brent Spar* and the controversy over Shell's treatment of the Ogoni people in Nigeria. What I remember most is that conversation we had over lunch with Geoffrey Lean, doyen of newspaper environment correspondents.

I hadn't seen Geoffrey since he left *The Observer* for *The Independent on Sunday* and I was keenly interested to find out why. He told us he had approached someone on the newsdesk at *The Observer* one day to let him know that he was working on some environmental story, so that he could put it on the news schedule. To his utter astonishment, the response was: 'We've had enough of all that eco-bollox.' Practically speechless, he returned to his desk and immediately wrote out his letter of resignation, which was then accepted. It was a shocking end to Geoffrey's long years of service at *The Observer*, during the course of which he had done more than most to highlight serious threats to the environment. Had it been *The Sun* or *The Mirror*, one might have understood; after all, the environment is not something that sits easily with the 'infotainment' pap they serve up to their readers. But this had happened in a quality broadsheet newspaper with a very distinguished record, not least in its environmental coverage. It sent a shiver down my spine. If Geoffrey Lean could come a cropper, what hope was there for the rest of us, I thought. Was it a case of 'for whom the bell tolls'?

Of course, as we all know, the environment has declined markedly in terms of media priorities since the heady days of the Earth Summit in Rio de Janeiro back in 1992. We were all there for what was billed as the largest gathering of world leaders to discuss any issue ever. The United Nations Conference on Environment and Development (UNCED), to give the summit its official title, was certainly an extraordinary event – and a nightmare to cover. Almost day after day, it made front-page news in the broadsheets, with oceans of analysis and supplementary reports on inside pages, and there was no dearth of television and radio coverage either. With the world coming to grips with the threats posed by global climate change and the rapidly growing pace of biodiversity losses, there was a real sense of urgency about what was going on in Rio. It reminded me of that great line of Flash Gordon's, in the final stage of his battle with Ming the Merciless: 'Dale, I love you, but we only have ten seconds to save the Earth!'

Six years later, a follow-up UN conference in Bratislava, bringing together the countries which had solemnly signed the Biodiversity Convention in Rio, received almost no media coverage. And when it came to the Fourth Conference of the Parties to the UN Climate Change Convention in Buenos Aires in November 1998, *The Irish Times* – as you know – decided not to cover it, even though I had soldiered with you and some of our fellow hacks at the previous gatherings in Berlin (1995), Geneva (1996) and, of course, Kyoto in December 1997. Apparently, the editor's reasoning, which was communicated to me by one of the deputy news editors, was that since Buenos Aires was merely a follow-up to the crucial conference in Kyoto and seemed unlikely to produce anything in the way of concrete results, it didn't make much sense to be sending me 'half-way around the world' to cover it. I could have argued, I suppose, that we needed to stay in touch with the climate negotiations and keep abreast of what was happening in relation to developing Kyoto Protocol mechanisms for carbon trading, either in 'hot' or 'superheated' air. But any mention of this sort of stuff, as you know, induces yawns and glazed eyes among hard-bitten newsdesk personnel; it might just about make the science page, don't you think?

From:	Paul Brown
To:	Frank McDonald
Date:	June 1999
Subject:	'eco-spin'?

I missed you in Buenos Aires, Frank. I was hoping we might catch John Prescott or Michael Meacher in a tango joint tasting the forbidden delights of eating beef on the bone. As it happens, neither of them did; they were too busy preventing the climate talks from collapsing. But it would have been the sort of story that our newsdesks might consider worth sending us for, rather than the boring old business of saving the planet. There were only about 10 per cent of the number of journalists in Kyoto the year before and, if anything, the talks went backwards rather than forwards. We got some stories out of it, but mostly they were about related issues such as the rise of wind power, the widespread bleaching and death of large parts of the world's coral reefs because of excess sea temperatures, and the battle for control of the international carbon trading market. I am not at all sure that the foreign editor will consider sending me next time, either.

Going back to Cardiff, and that conference. The glazing over of the eyes of *The Guardian's* news editor of the day, and news editors are all the same, can be guaranteed on use of key words. Certain words have been banned from my vocabulary for years. Sustainability was the first to go, along with biodiversity. The word 'environment' also has a high boredom value; in fact, if I do not want to do a story, the useful key phrase is 'of course, this is an important environment story'; this is almost certain to get it wiped off the news schedule. On the other hand, if I do want to do a story, it is important not to mention the environment at all, and make it sound as little to do with our specialism as possible. For example, a big hit was the introduction of termites into Devon. They came in a packing case from eastern Europe and ate someone's conservatory virtually overnight. The story was that although everyone thought they had been exterminated, they had survived the winter and eaten the porch of a nearby house the following spring. It was unheard of for the winters in England to be warm enough for termites to survive, but now this dread pest from southern Europe was out there surviving in the countryside and presumably here to stay. The story came to me as a global warming story but I managed not to mention this until well into the copy. I also organized a big picture of a very ugly termite – so global warming got on the front page, but the word environment did not appear in the text. Stories of new creepy crawlies, exotic weed species, extinctions of plants and animals because it is getting too warm, or because they have been eaten by runaway mink, all come into the same category. The key is they are of so-called 'general interest' and do not mention the environment or biodiversity. The same goes for health stories – the old chestnuts of malaria in southern England or air pollution from traffic only mention global warming way down the story.

On sustainability, one of the 'buzz' words at Cardiff, and slung about in a meaningless fashion, there has been no progress in the news sense. The *Brent Spar*, which changed the attitude of executives across the world, was a story because of the classic Greenpeace David and Goliath act. The huge size of the *Brent Spar* made wonderful pictures as the ant-like protesters scaled its sides in the towering seas. Never mind the arguments – it made great pictures. Then there was the very unpopular Tory government urging Shell, a very unpopular multinational, to dump a very large, dirty and ugly object. (By the way, Frank, don't you think 'dump' is a lovely word, as in nuclear waste dump, toxic dump, and using the world's seas as a convenient 'dumping' ground? So much more exciting than the idea of recycling, reuse or sustainability.) The other great thing about the *Brent Spar* was the politics. We had German and other continental countries without oil rigs telling the UK that sea dumping was not on. As a matter of principle, those who made the mess – the polluter – should pay. In other words, those who created the *Brent Spar* and gained the profit from it should shoulder the cost of disposing it, and not dump it in the Earth's most important commons, the sea. This was the most powerful argument. From the news point of view, it became an adventure saga on the high seas which went on for days, getting more and more tense as the moment to dump got closer. All this against a background of Shell being under heavy pressure from consumer boycotts, and finally falling out with the British government and calling the whole thing off.

A similar epic tale was fought out about French testing in the Pacific two years later. Again, the same principles. A state using the common heritage to test nuclear weapons, bringing the additional element of misuse of colonial power and the riots of the locals in protest at the tests. Greenpeace was onto a winner, governments in the region joined in, it was politics mixed with people in rubber boats taking on the French navy. Everyone remembered the *Rainbow Warrior*. Interestingly, in both stories Greenpeace also caught a cold. Now a multinational organization in their own right, they got the science wrong at the *Brent Spar* and got pasted for it by both the government and the press. At Muroroa, they got their tactics wrong and their two big ships were arrested and impounded by the French. The story that made the lead in *The Guardian* about the campaigners in Tahiti criticizing the campaigners at sea for losing the Greenpeace flagship went round the world. The subsequent sackings in Greenpeace showed how like a corporation the organization had become. In a sense, those campaigns were the last hangover from the great boom in environment reporting in the 1980s. Issues were simpler then. It was a story to discover a hole in the ozone layer, and report the struggles to ban chlorofluorocarbons (CFCs). The same with global warming – first the science, then the politics and now the effects. But the simple big stories have all been told; now it is all in the details. It is harder and harder to get these issues on news pages, as I'm sure you will agree.

From:	Frank McDonald
To:	Paul Brown
Date:	June 1999
Subject:	'jam yesterday, jam today and jam tomorrow'

You're absolutely right, of course. But my biggest problem at the moment is that in Ireland there's too much else going on. The Republic is in the grip of its so-called Celtic Tiger economy, with unprecedented GDP growth rates of between 7 and 9 per cent per annum, and we're all run ragged trying to keep up with it. Not surprisingly, this boom is taking a toll on the environment because of the inevitable tendency, as it enters a phosphorescent phase, for 'sustainable development' to become the major casualty. Irish people with loads of money tend to spend it on private chariots, as a first priority. Sales of new cars in the Republic have rocketed in recent years. The number of cars on the road in Dublin has doubled in less than a decade and the city is now virtually strangled by its own traffic. Gridlock and soaring house prices have become the principal preoccupations of the chattering classes, even among those who are wedded to their top-of-the-range company cars. Funding for public transport is even worse than it is in Britain – and that's saying something. Yet, it has taken a long time for the penny to drop in government circles that public transport offers the only viable solution; so now, finally, a lot of money is going to be spent on buses, trains and other much-needed hardware.

I remember advocating this case way back in the mid 1980s, at a time when Dublin Corporation was pulling down whole streets lined with old buildings to turn them into dual-carriageways to cater for all the traffic coming in from the suburbs. A transport researcher at University College London, Dr Martin Mogridge, had just produced a paper on urban traffic in London, wittily entitled 'Jam Yesterday, Jam Today and Jam Tomorrow'. In it, he put forward 'Mogridge's Conjecture' that traffic in urban areas would always expand to fill the road space provided for it and the only thing that made sense was to invest in rail-based public transport. Our road engineers regarded this as the height of heresy and it didn't help when we all discovered that Dr Mogridge looked like a 'Green groupie', with his long hair, long wispy beard, jeans, sandals, check shirt and corduroy jacket. Nonetheless, he was proved right, as even your roads-mad ministry of transport more or less conceded when Prescott forced it to abandon its traditional policy of 'predict and provide' for traffic growth. However, our National Roads Authority is still infected by the disease and wants to spend IR£6.2 billion on further improvements to the country's main roads over the next 20 years.

Everyone who reads *The Irish Times* knows where I stand on the major environmental issues. As you know from our conversations over the years, I see nothing wrong with being an advocate as well as a reporter. In general, the paper gives me space to express my opinions and analyse public policy from my particular standpoint – though it might sometimes invite a spokesman for the roads lobby, for example, to write a response. As the longest-serving environment correspondent in Ireland (since 1986), I am also plagued by invitations to address this or that conference or to do interviews on radio and television. Last year alone, I did more than 75 of these 'gigs', and concluded that this was clearly unsustainable. In 1997, I found myself in the thick of a ding-dong battle with one of our columnists – former Taoiseach (Prime Minister) Garret FitzGerald, no less – over the issue of whether Dublin should, as planned since 1994, have street-running trams in the city centre. I strongly favoured this precisely because it would take road space away from cars and dedicate it to public transport. Dr FitzGerald contended that the proposed light rail system should run underground in the city centre, to avoid disrupting other traffic. But although independent consultants – the British firm of W S Atkins – recommended proceeding with the original plan, the government caved in to pressure from business interests and decided that part of the system should, indeed, be forced underground.

There is every reason to be concerned about transport, not only because too many people using cars cause congestion and pollution at a local level, but also because road traffic, in particular, is now the fastest-growing contributor to the greenhouse gas emissions that are causing climate change. In June 1998, Irish Environment Minister Noel Dempsey signed up to a legally binding EU 'burden-sharing' deal under which the union, as a whole, is meant to achieve the Kyoto target of reducing total greenhouse gas emissions by 8 per cent on 1990 levels by 2010. Under this deal, Ireland as a relatively small, underdeveloped EU member state is permitted to increase its emissions. Current predictions as I write this are that, because of burgeoning economic growth and the consequential increase in energy and transport demand, emissions would rise by between 40 per cent and 60 per cent under a 'business as usual' scenario. And though this would be unlikely to burst the EU 'bubble', it would reflect very badly indeed on our ability to manage our affairs – quite apart from incurring hefty EU fines for non-compliance with the legally binding Kyoto targets.

Noel Dempsey is not a fool; he realizes that firm measures must be taken domestically to curtail the growth in Ireland's greenhouse gas emissions, even if he does plan to avail himself of the carbon trading loophole. His real problem is that there is no consensus among the 'social partners' – industry, trades unions and the country's farmers – on the need to take action. This is reflected in a level of public apathy and even ignorance about global climate change, despite intermittent efforts over the years by *The Irish Times* and other organs of the media to make it clear that the most serious environmental threat facing the planet really does exist and must be addressed. Maybe we have simply failed to get the message across. As many others have pointed out, the current level of public apathy, in Ireland and elsewhere, is almost certainly due to a realization that tackling the problem of climate change is bound to be a very complex challenge which will take decades to produce results – and, quite possibly, there isn't an awful lot we can do about it anyway. Meanwhile, most people just want to get on with living their own lives.

Inevitably, more immediate problems – environmental or otherwise – take precedence. To all but the best-informed activists, the macro level of global environmental change seems quite diffuse and ill defined compared to, say, the micro level of a sand-and-gravel company seeking planning permission to diversify into cement production on a site just down the road from where you live. And yet, the two issues are related because the cement plant will emit a tonne of carbon dioxide (CO_2), liberated from its limestone raw material, for every tonne of cement it produces. Similarly, the eutrophication of lakes on the River Shannon is caused by phosphate runoff from farms in the catchment due to an overuse of fertilizers. This, in turn, is reflected in higher methane emissions from cattle and other farm animals, which account for a significant proportion of Ireland's total output of greenhouse gases. But every time, it is the local issue that wins out over the global in the way stories are covered and the space which is allocated to them.

There would, for example, be no problem in getting a page to outline and assess the environmental impact of the latest mega-development planned for the Docklands area of Dublin. Or to write an illustrated exposé of the dramatically damaging effects of a tax incentive scheme that was meant to boost the failing fortunes of 13 traditional seaside resorts, but has instead resulted in the endless proliferation of suburban-style clusters of holiday homes. These, too, are examples of unsustainable development, but at a merely local level. Linking what happens locally to the wider problems of global environmental change is the real challenge – and in this, I must confess, the media has too often failed. Only when it comes to such dangerous examples of unsustainable development as the Sellafield nuclear reprocessing plant do Irish people really sit up and take notice. Rightly, we believe that Ireland should not have to put up with the risks inherent in the Sellafield project, just 60 miles across the Irish Sea, when it receives absolutely none of the economic benefit – and this view has been reflected in media coverage of its failings over the years. For that reason alone, the nuclear lobby would have a tough task persuading Irish people that it can offer a viable alternative to burning fossil fuels.

We have also been raking over old coals. Staff resources are consumed covering judicial tribunals inquiring into where our disgraced former Taoiseach Charles J Haughey got his money from and what he might have done in return for all the largesse, or what bribes were paid to politicians and officials to secure land rezonings or planning permissions in County Dublin over the past 20 years. Sensationally, the former Dublin county manager was arrested by the Criminal Assets Bureau after stepping off a flight from the Isle of Man with IR£300,000 in cash and cheques, virtually in a bag marked 'Swag'. And two of our most senior judges were just recently forced to resign when it was revealed that they had both intervened to secure the early release of a Dublin architect who had been sentenced to four years in prison for a drunk driving incident in which a working-class mother of three was killed, after he had spent just 12 months in one of those middle-class open prisons. Against this hectic background, it is hardly surprising that day-to-day news stories dealing with environmental issues may slip off the schedule. There is only one guaranteed exception to this rule – anything to do with genetically modified (GM) foods. Mercifully, the titanic struggle between Monsanto and the green activists who oppose its ambitions is ably covered by our food science correspondent Kevin O'Sullivan, whose appointment reflects how seriously this area is taken by *The Irish Times*. The paper also has a part-time development correspondent, Paul Cullen, who has often brought home the grim realities facing much of sub-Saharan Africa; the fact that his job embraces coverage of Ireland's less-than-honourable treatment of immigrants from Africa and elsewhere gives it an added piquancy.

From:	Paul Brown
To:	Frank McDonald
Date:	June 1999
Subject:	Is planetary survival 'news'?

All I say to you Frank is that you have the luck of the Irish. The GM foods story has fallen firmly in the lap of environment correspondents in the UK. We do have a science correspondent who dabbles, a consumer affairs and food man who helps out, but one of the big political issues has been the effect on the wider countryside. The supermarkets gradually banning GM foods has been a story; but the reason that GM crops have hit the headlines is the potential effect on wildlife and the rest of the farming community. Can organic farming survive large-scale introduction of genetically modified crops which threaten to cross pollinate? Will insects and birds survive massive doses of herbicides on GM crops designed to withstand them? The government, particularly the prime minister, was caught on the back foot by the public reaction. Only Michael Meacher, waving the 'precautionary principle' flag, has saved the government from looking like Monsanto's poodle. There will be much more of this.

But again, like your situation in Ireland, there are other immediate short-term issues blocking out the more complex and longer-term dangers of a deteriorating environment. As I write, we have Kosovo, nail bombs in London, the murder of TV presenter Jill Dando – all compelling human stories that must be told. But in general, even when life is quieter, one of the problems of getting the environment in the paper is that it has fallen off the political agenda. We still retain our environment section on a Wednesday where serious issues are discussed and it remains very popular with readers. The battle remains to get the environment on the mainstream pages. This is easier on the business or foreign news pages where the environmental disasters, forest fires, famines and the like are still news. On the home news pages it is far more difficult. Tony Blair's promise after the election that environment would be at the heart of government has proved to be hot air. John Prescott and his transport reforms have been sidelined, action on global warming is slight, big issues such as energy conservation in homes are not tackled on the scale required. Even promised wildlife legislation and the right to roam have been postponed more than once. It is difficult to write about issues that are not even being discussed by politicians – even the opposition parties. So we fall back on being devious. We talk about discharges at Sellafield and the lack of somewhere to put Britain's nuclear waste in terms of loss of jobs, planning blight and public protests. We try to get the Irish and Nordic governments to put pressure on the UK to stop discharges. We fall back on weather stories, like the 1998 Easter floods, and the fact that 1998 was another world record hot year to keep the issue of global warming alive. We too have the local planning issues which are environment stories and are part of the big picture. It is always the protesters who bring these matters up and the developers that dismiss them as mere NIMBYs.

The bright spot in all of this is that industry, at least part of it, has understood that despite the fickle nature of politics, the environment is here to stay. BP, Shell, ICI and other companies have been stung with large fines for causing spills, and in their boardrooms they have taken hard decisions about at least attempting to address global warming. There is now a clear division between Exxon, the giant US multinational, and Shell and BP – which at least gives another line of stories for the city pages. But again, while the environment is in the background, the story is about personalities, market share, oil exploration in developing countries and pristine environment areas, the costs of fossil fuels versus wind and solar power, and jobs. The strange thing about this hard sell we have to use on bored news editors – omitting mention of the environment but emphasizing the entertainment value of battlegrounds and personalities – is that it works. If you look at the cuttings, we get a lot in the paper. We are becoming adept at confidence tricks. Developing world debt, Indian farmers revolting over Monsanto banning them from planting their own seeds, growing crops for British supermarkets in Africa while the locals go hungry are all environment stories. The key is to keep the human interest in order to write about issues. Serious stories about medium-term, or worse, long-term threats to health and wealth, and even survival of the human race, are harder and harder to get in the newspaper. Do you agree Frank?

From:	Frank McDonald
To:	Paul Brown
Date:	June 1999
Subject:	don't let the bastards grind you down

Funny that you should mention Tony Blair betraying his pre-election promise that the environment would be at the heart of New Labour's policies in government; our Taoiseach, Bertie Ahern, has done exactly the same. The trouble is that only senior officials of the Department of the Environment are really up to speed on the issues and they have the nearly impossible task of convincing other departments with narrower agendas – energy, for example – that climate change is a very serious matter that has to be addressed. The most sceptical of all, at least in Ireland, is the Department of Finance – and I rarely lose an opportunity to castigate its Mandarins for their obstruction of 'green' taxes. I once heckled the deputy head of the department at an economic conference on this issue! We must also accept that we are up against dark forces, such as the Global Climate Coalition and the likes of Donald Pearlman, the Washington lawyer who was dubbed by *Der Spiegel* in 1995 as 'King of the Carbon Club'. I still treasure the photograph I snapped of him talking to an OPEC delegate in the coffee bar of Kyoto's conference centre. He was outraged, told me I was rude and refused to shake my hand. I told him: 'You are ruder, if I may say so.' After all, if this particular Don manages to get his way, the world is pretty well on its way to hell in a handcart. I later used the photograph as my only slide in a lecture on Kyoto to the director and staff of the Irish Energy Centre, so I can't say that it hasn't come in handy. Whatever happens, the only motto that makes sense to me is: 'Don't let the bastards grind you down.' See you at the next climate change gig – assuming I get to go. All the best, Frank.

From:	Paul Brown
To:	Frank McDonald
Date:	June 1999
Subject:	Beyond 'eco-bollox'

More than 50 days into the Kosovo crisis I finally got nearly a whole page on the possible environmental consequences of the war. This mainly concerned the damage to the Danube, wildlife and the spread of dioxins but included the use of depleted uranium weapons by NATO. My only previous piece about the war was also about depleted uranium ammunition being in use, and it took a week to get into the paper. It is a classic example of how the long-term consequences of using radioactive material are ignored because it happens to provide cheap and effective weapons against tanks. Never mind the effects on the health of the next generation of Kosovans. Not that I am despondent. The interest in the wider environment from city and foreign departments outweighs the yawns coming from the home newsdesk. The analysis pages have expanded in our recent redesign and are hungry for 1000-word pieces at the moment that are not about the war or the future of Sellafield, for example.

We have discussed over a tincture or two whether the world as it currently operates could be described as civilized and I think we agreed it could not. But even civilization as the World Trade Organization understands it is in a parlous state (and already doomed in my view). The optimists believe we can find techno-fixes to the environment and that we will be able to carry on much as usual. My view is that we are doing too much damage too quickly to the environment to stop 'civilization' from collapsing as natural resources run out and climate change takes hold. This does not mean we are all going to die; far from it, merely that the kind of anarchy that occurred after the fall of the Roman Empire will ensue. That was incorrectly called the

Dark Ages but there were lots of pockets of civilization amid the ruins. If I remember rightly, Ireland was one of them. That is what I think will happen all over again. Meanwhile we will have to keep bashing away at the philistines on the newsdesk and elsewhere in the hope that we can at least mitigate the worst of the disaster to come. How's that for a cheerful thought.

See you soon, Paul.

NOTE

1 This chapter was drafted as an e-mail dialogue undertaken in June 1999.

7 Genetic Modification, Food and Sustainable Development: Telling the Story

Devinder Sharma

On a flight from London to New Delhi cruising at 35,000 feet above the highlands of the Hindu Kush Himalayas in Afghanistan, the personal video screen receives a news flash fed to the aircraft via satellite. The TV anchor breaks news: researchers at the Roslin Institute in Edinburgh have succeeded in cloning an animal – a sheep.

For the next seven days, Dolly the sheep hogs the limelight. From the Vatican to the White House, and to the crowded streets of New Delhi, the talk is the same. Television and newspapers have already numbed the brain. Some are excited and others dismayed. The more people watch television, the more they get confused. The Vatican calls it playing God, and the US president imposes a ban on human cloning. Scientists are divided. And the public remains baffled.

Welcome to the world of modern electronic media. In an age of information technology where news and entertainment have merged to keep you glued to the television screen for most of the day (and night), it is becoming increasingly difficult to tell the difference between a soap opera and the dramatic happenings in the field of biotechnology and genetic engineering. For most viewers, genetic engineering is a flip side of science fiction. For others, it is a brave new world in the offing. And for journalists and media people, genetic engineering provides good copy – often front page.

The birth of Dolly, followed closely by her cousin Polly, only signals the beginning. New evolution, as many microbiologists propose, will be a matter of science and technology, tempered by ethics and political choice. Cambridge physicist Stephen Hawking told an august gathering – at a millennium lecture at the White House – that humans are likely to redesign themselves completely in the next 1000 years: 'I am not advocating human genetic engineering as a good thing. I am just saying that it is likely to happen in the next millenium whether we like it or not.'

Writing in *The Guardian*, Tim Radford analysed the decommissioning of the evolutionary process of natural selection. Replying to
Princeton University's Lee Silver's argument in his book *Remaking
Eden*, Tim Radford quoted Lord Winston, one of the giants in the field
of reproductive biology, who speculates, astounded, on the sheer speed
with which genetics might be harnessed to robotics and computing:

> *'All of a sudden, they invent the DNA chip. It is a little chip,
> just like a computer chip, but you can put a million different
> little drops of DNA detectors on it. What these little drops do is
> to detect the presence of a gene. We only have 100,000 genes, or
> fewer, perhaps 70,000. On this little chip you put down the ten
> most common forms of each of our genes. And you put them all
> down on this little chip and then you take blood or cells and put
> them on this chip, and the chip will tell you exactly what form
> of every gene you have got.'*

While the redesigning of *homo sapiens* may not be plausible in the next
few years, the release of genetically engineered organisms into the
environment, in the wake of the use of genetically engineered crops
for precision farming and genetically altered products for medical
diagnosis and therapy, has already raised a storm. Biotechnology and
genetic engineering are gearing up to transform the very concept of
agriculture by turning 'farming' into 'pharming' – manipulating farm
animals to produce pharmaceutical products. There are hardly any
more controversial and emotive issues in science today than genetic
engineering. The media in every part of the world has a role to play
in presenting the debate on managing risk and the future of agriculture.
This chapter will explore whether the media is in a position to play
this part to the full. It will note how the media has, in general, failed
to maintain its independence from commercial interests in the last 20
years, but that the media has performed surprisingly well in the face
of this important test. It has, perhaps against the odds, served as the
public's scrutineer of these complex and risky new technologies.

MEDIA AND PROFITS

At a time when the corporatization of the media all over the world
has turned news into a marketable commodity, multinational
corporations have tied with the media conglomerates to blacken out
alternative viewpoints. Even though these conglomerates may have
different names and external appearances, they share the same values

for earning more profits. The resulting paradigm shift in news presentation has brought about a simultaneous change in the public perception of journalists and media personnel. The media is seen as having abdicated its civic role and become another vehicle for making money.

Certainly the media gave heavy coverage to industrial pollution and images of endangered biodiversity just prior to the 1992 Earth Summit at Rio in Brazil. But it did not take long for the enthusiasm to die down. Realizing that this trend in reporting and analysis will affect profits and see a slump in the Wall Street accounts of big companies, media conglomerates soon pushed environmental concerns to the background. As a result, environmental destruction no longer evokes the same kind of spirited response.

However, a new issue has emerged that has seen the media take its own independent editorial line. Concern with industrial pollution has now been overtaken by fear of what was dubbed in the British tabloid newspapers as 'Frankenstein foods'. The media has refused to blindly accept the new genetic products and the hypotheses about safety and 'substantial equivalence' with natural products. Perhaps the fact that genetic manipulation and biotechnology have the potential to shock people has allowed the media to generate broad public awareness of issues which have great relevance for present and future generations.

True, the transfer of genetic information from one organism to another, even across species boundaries, represents the most powerful tool for the 'improving' of plants and animals. After all, nature had not allowed the movement of genes and DNA across the species. Yet, any tinkering with the genetic make-up is certain to raise eyebrows, to raise questions and to provoke people to ask – why are you doing this?

The answer is simple. The stakes are high. For an industry which spent an estimated US$8 billion on biotechnological research in 1996 alone, the urgent pursuit of immediate economic returns is understandable. At the same time, the growing concerns in the media over the grave risks these genetic foods pose to human health and the environment have forced many governments to rethink the need to introduce such designer crops.

AN ENGINEERED MEDIA?

Often, the biotechnology industry has asked, 'Who is engineering the media to report negatively on a promising technology?' It is the spate of 'negative' reporting in the Western media that has forced the industry to tread cautiously. Such has been the media uproar in the UK and other parts of Europe that 1999 will go down as the year the media returned to its role as the mirror of society. It returned to older rules of journalism, with professional, independent and intelligent reporting: skills that we had forgotten in this age of the market economy.

It is difficult to conclude whether the consumer backlash against genetically engineered foods in Europe was fuelled by media reports or vice versa. But it remains a fact that faced with consumers' ire, major European retail chains have responded by forming a consortium to ensure that no genetically modified (GM) ingredients get into their own-label products. Britain's J Sainsbury's supermarket worked with six other European companies to weed out possible GM foods at any stage of production. Activists have regularly destroyed test field trials of GM products in Britain, France, Germany, The Netherlands and in India to regular and lavish media coverage.

Geneticists have had no problem in joining the chorus in favour of GM foods. Many of them have come out openly in support of altered soyabeans, or in spraying frost-resistant bacteria on California strawberries, or in introducing some alien genes in salmon fish. But governments have been forced to respond to public concern over the safety of such food products. Greece is the latest to have banned the import and marketing of a gene-modified rapeseed developed by AgrEvo Gmbh of Germany for reasons of potential risks to human health and the environment. Earlier, Austria and Luxembourg banned the sale of GM corn developed by Novartis AG of Switzerland. Following an unprecedented consumer backlash, the European Union has finally imposed a de facto moratorium until the year 2002 on approving any more GMOs (genetically modified organisms).

For the first time, the European Commission's scientific advisers have recommended that a genetically engineered potato be withheld from the market because they cannot guarantee its safety. And worried about the growing acts of vandalism against the genetically engineered crops in Britain, where over 300 incidents of uprooting and burning of GM crops have shaken up the biotechnology industry in the recent past, Environment Minister Michael Meacher has gone on record in saying that the UK government is considering imposing a three-year ban on transgenic crops grown for commercial use.

In the same period, several chief executive officers (CEO's) of Europe's biotechnology companies have been sacked in the recent past, having failed to substantiate the exaggerated claims about GM crops and products. The boom in the stock market for biotech products is also on the wane. British Biotech, Europe's flagship biotechnology company, for instance, has lost its share value by 70 per cent. The London Stock Exchange, the London-based European Agency for the Evaluation of Medicinal Products and the House of Commons have also launched separate inquiries into fraudulent dealing on the US stock markets. The financial bubble has also finally burst.

The British daily *The Independent on Sunday* published an exclusive report showing how the US had threatened to call off a potential free-trade agreement with New Zealand over its plans to label and test genetically engineered food. Publishing the New Zealand cabinet's documents, made possible by New Zealand's Freedom of Information Act, the newspaper report revealed how the US, the world's biggest producer of GM food, had been 'bullying' governments into protecting the economic interests of the seed multinational Monsanto. The New Zealand cabinet note, dated 19 February 1998, states:

> '*The United States, and Canada to a lesser extent, are concerned in principle about the kind of approach by ANZFA (part of the Australian New Zealand Food Standards Council), and the demonstration of the fact this may have on others, including the European Union. The US has told us that such an approach could impact negatively on bilateral trade relationship and potentially end a New Zealand US free-trade agreement.*'

Angered by this revelation, several British MPs were quoted as saying that the documents gave them the first clear evidence of the lengths to which the US will go to defend the American biotechnology industry.

As if this is not enough, *The Telegraph* (11 July 1999) revealed in a report that CIA agents have been secretly investigating the British Environment Minister Michael Meacher, adding that the US government confirmed that the CIA keeps a file on him. It is believed to contain details of Mr Meacher's reservations about GM foods. Although the CIA later refused to release details of the contents of its file, described by another department as a 'biographical profile', inquiries by newspapers showed no other files compiled by the CIA on British ministers.

With the US pressing for GM products to be allowed more freely in Britain – despite British consumers' worries – GM food has emerged as a potential source of conflict between the two countries. President Clinton is known to have had several conversations on the subject with UK Prime Minister Tony Blair, and US diplomatic missions abroad have been ordered to promote the GM industry. According to Bill

Lambrecht of *The St Louis Post-Dispatch*, when the French were reluctant to allow Monsanto's seeds to sprout on French soil, US Secretary of State Madeleine Albright and US Trade Representative Charlene Barshevsky intervened on Monsanto's behalf. When the French still refused to yield, President Clinton personally took up the matter with French Prime Minister Lionel Jospin and gave him 'an earful'. And when that did not work, Vice President Al Gore followed up with a phone call to the French prime minister. Ultimately, the French gave in to the steady high-level pressure.

Developments in biotechnology over the last decade have been accompanied by often exaggerated claims as to their likely impact on agriculture. As a result of the excitement about the scientific possibilities of genetic engineering, there was a considerable loss of perspective in some quarters. Some prophets of the new technology have underestimated the pace of technical innovation, and overstated the probable flow of useful end products to agriculture. Much of the basic scientific knowledge originated in laboratories where scientists had little knowledge of the existing systems and technology of food production, into which new technologies must fit, and with which the new technologies must compete.

UNDERSTANDING BIOTECHNOLOGY

The media's understanding of the aggressive marketing of GMOs is based on the assumption that since biotechnology is likely to emerge as one of the biggest commercial enterprises of the next century, vested financial interests are pushing technologies which have not been adequately tested for environmental risks. Already, the biotechnology industry has earned a special name for its dubious claims on environmental benefits: greenwashing. In the past, for example, biotechnology's promoters have promised that fertilizers will become unnecessary as crops are engineered to fix their own nitrogen, and that pesticides will become obsolete as crops are engineered to resist insects and other pests. While the first promise failed to materialize, we now have herbicide-tolerant plants which, in fact, results in more usage of herbicides. These unrealistic claims have spurred general caution about new biotech products.

Journalists find it much easier to shock readers. But often, they themselves have an inherent limitation in understanding the nuances and complexities of the cutting-edge technology. And it is here that the voluntary agencies and the non-governmental organizations

(NGOs) have come to the rescue of the media. Briefed adequately by these advocacy groups, journalists have found it much easier to communicate with the public. In turn, the media has provided support by way of unearthing the political linkages and exposing the politics of biotechnology. The synergy of the media–NGO alliance has so far paid dividends.

The media realizes that progress in biotechnology is being targeted in the agriculture and food industries. The focus, for instance, is on commercial opportunities for tomatoes that stay firm and fresh (having a shelf life of somewhere between 40 to 90 days), on improving the strength of cotton fibres, and on products such as GM bananas, potatoes and tomatoes that may provide edible vaccines as replacements for injected ones, and so on. Biotechnology-based products and processes will surely have a significant impact upon the agricultural and food industries in coming years.

Increasing productivity through higher yield crops, and new geographical locations for crops (such as arid areas and marginal soils) is also being attempted, although there still remains doubts about the trustworthiness and reliability of such engineered products. Debate is also raging on the implications of these products for biodiversity. The media has also raised questions about a number of ethical and equity issues relating to: proprietary rights; access for small farmers to new technologies and markets; effects on displacement of traditional products; use of land for non-food crops, and the effect of promoting of non-food crops on the global food supply.

As media coverage becomes more widespread and indepth, there is an increased public concern over the safety of genetically modified plants, within the food chain and within human foodstuffs. And as the British Medical Association points out in its interim report of May 1999, '[at] this stage in the development and application of genetic modification it is not possible to provide any guarantees against, or insurance for mistakes. When we seek to optimize the benefits over risks, it is prudent to err on the side of caution and above all to learn from our accumulating experience.'

These are the sorts of statements, coming from expert and citizen bodies around the world, that have revived the tendency among journalists to dig below the surface to the root of an issue. In the rest of this chapter, the story unfolds of how the media has gone beyond the received wisdom of the GM industries' scientists and US government agriculture and industry bodies to uncover the politics of biotechnology.

THE DEBATE

The debate is by no means limited to food. GM material is being used in a wide range of products, from textiles to pharmaceuticals. Yet, it is food that seems to generate the most emotional response. Consumer advocates say that people must have the right to know about – and thus reject – food that has been subjected to genetic 'tampering'. Proponents of biotechnology say that requiring labels is tantamount to branding demonstrably safe food as inedible and would raise food prices for consumers. Moreover, it is argued that 'genetically enhanced species' are essential to generate the crop yields needed to nourish the world's exploding population and to reduce the use of herbicides and pesticides. They say that the foods have been exhaustively tested and demonstrated to be safe enough to pass muster with the US Food and Drug Administration (FDA) and the Environmental Protection Agency (EPA), as well as with international regulators.

Some journalists were quick to see the role of the US Department of Agriculture (USDA) in all of this. Ostensibly acting as a front for the multinational companies to force open the developing country markets for transgenic plants, it has embarked upon a massive international programme to provide credibility to the American biotechnology industries' untested claims – more often than not using journalists as carriers of the message. Under the garb of accelerating efforts in mobilizing the tools of biotechnology and genetic engineering for improved crop productivity, profitability, stability and sustainability of the major cropping systems in the Asia–Pacific region, the USDA, for instance, is promoting a biosafety protocol that paves the way for smooth entry of transgenic plants, irrespective of the needs of the people. In the Asia–Pacific region, so far countries such as China, Japan, Korea and Thailand are already engaged in field testing and release of transgenic plants. In India, it is still at the field-testing stage.

And yet the wider media in developing countries has generally failed to realize that the USDA's objective is very clear: to push biotechnology products onto developing countries. In the bargain, it refuses to accept responsibility for any environmental mishap that might happen. Since the USDA only accords approval for the transgenic product, it does not certify whether the transgenic is better than the existing plant variety or not.

A minority of journalists have done the public a disproportionately large service in raising key issues. They have, for example, raised doubts about the environmental risks, such as those potentially introduced by the '5345' tomato (a transgenic tomato, with a gene from the soil bacterium *Bacillus thuringeinsis* (Bt), genetic characteristics of which are introduced into tomato to produce a natural insecticide against pests, reducing dependence on chemical pesticides). They have also raised doubts about the economic performance of some of these products, such as Monsanto's Flavr Savr tomato, or Bt-induced transgenic cotton crop which has seen crop (and hence stock market) losses in the US.

In my own reports and analytical articles, I have often questioned the role of the USDA in promoting an untested technology. What the USDA, as well as the multinational seed companies, do not reveal is that several of the transgenic cottons in the US are restricted in usage due to fears of accidental release of the toxin gene into the environment. Such is the rapid breakdown of the technology that the EPA has now ruled that new Bt varieties can only be planted on part of a farmer's corn acreage. And yet, this GM cotton and corn is being promoted as completely safe for developing countries. The USDA has also been insisting that the transgenic plants do not pose any appreciable environmental risk worth mentioning.

At the same time, USDA accepts that it has so far not conducted any biological risk assessment. Nor does it have any plans to do so. While it lays down well-defined procedures for introducing transgenic material, it is not at all willing to be held responsible for any environmental and biological mishap. Since the USDA itself is not conducting any research to produce GM plants, it has taken on itself the initiative to push and protect the commercial interests of the American multinational companies.

Most farmers in the Asia–Pacific region are poor and cannot afford risk, particularly since no effective crop insurance mechanisms are yet in place in several countries of the region. Therefore, a careful cost-benefit analysis should be done before they are asked to switch over to new material resulting from recombinant DNA experiments. Critics say that a beginning can be made by adopting the polluter pays principle, making it obligatory for the biotechnology companies to compensate the farmers for any losses suffered.

The growing fears over the release of genetic material into the wild are not unfounded. The media has been quick to highlight these lapses. There exist numerous cases where alien genes introduced into a crop have escaped into the wild. Herbicide-resistant transgenic oilseed rape, for instance, has already hybridized with several wild relatives. Cornell University researchers have established that GM corn could induce mortality in monarch butterflies. In fact, the chances that such escapes will be frequent in developing countries are high for the simple reason that these countries are the repository of rich plant and animal biodiversity; therefore, developing countries will be more open to biological pollution.

TAKING SIDES

Journalism schools teach trainees to look for the counterpoint to 'balance' the story. Yet, in the context of an increasingly dominant, globalized market economy, 'balanced' journalism became tilted towards the concerns of the rich and powerful.

Nevertheless, media reporting and the critical analysis of genetic engineering have broken the trend. By more often than not taking the side of consumers, the media has clearly demonstrated its ability to spread clarity about the new technology and its socio-economic relevance in the developed and developing world economies. Unconstrained by economic interests, much of the media has played the role of opposing GM technology, and in turn supporting sustainable development.

To report on these global issues and relate them to local actions presents major new challenges for journalists. There is an urgent need for journalists who understand and appreciate science, and who are at the same time deeply concerned about the environmental crisis and the future of the human society. Unfortunately, not many of the journalists in the electronic and the mainstream print media have a scientific or technological background. They also need to be able to explain the implications of the new technology expressed in global treaties, legislations and undertakings. For instance, it is important that they understand biotechnology, but perhaps even more important that they analyse it in the context of the emerging free-trade paradigm, erosion of biodiversity and debates about intellectual property rights.

Some of the official accounts of the nature and implications of these technologies are highly technical, cool in tone and apparently neutral, making the journalist's job of 'spotting' and making the story more difficult. The US Office of Technology Assessment defines biotechnology as 'any technique that uses living organisms, or substances from these organisms, to make or modify a product, to improve plants or animals, or to develop microorganisms for specific uses'. Biotechnology, therefore, includes 'traditional biotechnology', covering well-established technologies used in commercially useful operations. These include the technologies today used in brewing, biological control of pests, conventional animal vaccine production and many other biotechnological applications. 'Modern biotechnology' encompasses the use of more recently available technologies, particularly those based on the use of recombinant DNA technology, monoclonal antibodies and new cell and tissue culture techniques, including novel bioprocessing techniques.

The media has given a fair amount of representation to the claims of the biotechnology industry. It has been widely reported and known, for instance, that as of May 1997, in the US alone there were about 5000 field tests of genetically engineered plants, 100 to 200 field tests of genetically engineered microorganisms, and two field tests of genetically engineered fish. A number of crops are now being engineered to produce pharmaceuticals, polymers and industrial enzymes, and to alter oil, starch and protein contents.

Rapid progress is being made in refining the techniques that allow a gene from one species to be transferred and expressed in another species. The potential for improvements of crops from genetic engineering is immense. Current research and development is concentrating on the commercial applications: herbicide resistance, insect resistance, improved protein composition and improved post-harvest handling among other traits. As yet, however, agriculture even in the industrial world, with all its resources, has not benefited greatly from biotechnological applications.

NOT FOR THE DEVELOPING WORLD

Certainly there have been significant media successes in raising the level of debate about these important issues, but one of the biggest implications has been underreported in both the developed and developing world. GM technologies promise major implications for food security and the eradication of hunger and malnutrition in the South. This is essentially because of the scant understanding that the media has about the prevailing issues that confront developing world economies. This is crucial because, for all practical purposes, the global decision-making authority, or power, rests on either side of the Atlantic.

My own perception of agricultural biotechnology is that it is essentially being developed for the Western markets. Nowhere in the biotechnology laboratories in the developed world is the focus on meeting the growing food needs of developing countries. There is a huge gap between reality and perception that needs to be filled. The biotechnology industry is developing novel products which have wider applications in the North. These products are also being pushed in the South to maximize investments, despite the fact that these GM products were developed with no reference to developing world political, economic or environmental settings.

For instance, the controversial recombinant bovine growth hormone (rBGH) was developed for the American and European dairy farmers. Repeated injections of the genetically modified hormone are given to boost milk yields artificially by up to 15 per cent. It was only after the European Union imposed a ban until the year 2000 that the multinational industry which developed the product started looking for markets elsewhere. The ban is likely to be extended in the light of clear evidence of serious adverse impacts on the welfare of the cow, notably increased foot problems, mastitis and injection-site swellings.

With animals being treated as factories, the resulting health hazards and the ethical and religious considerations are being pushed to the background. Although the data on potential risks to human health from products made from rBGH-treated milking herds has been disputed, the Canadian Scientific Committee on Veterinary Measures relating to public health has reported to the European Commission that there is a possible 'association between circulating insulin-like growth factor (IGF-1) levels and an increased relative risk of breast and prostate cancer'. Levels of IGF-1, which also occurs naturally in milk, are substantially increased in milk from rBGH-treated cows.

The hormonal drug rBGH is being pushed onto developing countries, including India, Brazil and Argentina, without adequate scientific tests. First of all, it has to be understood that the drug was an outcome of research on the exotic cattle breeds which are quite different from the hardy and comparatively low-yielding cattle breeds of developing countries. And, more importantly, the media has often asked: even if developing countries are to accept rBGH, where is the assurance of a simultaneous increase in the market for milk? This is for the simple reason that people who are hungry and malnourished do not have the means to buy it. And in any case, the drug is being marketed at a time when the US, the European Union, Australia and New Zealand are waiting to deluge the South with highly subsidized milk and milk products once trade barriers are lifted.

Incisive analysis into the games the biotechnology industries play to garner more profits can help clarify the issues in the public's mind. Take the case of cassava highlighted in a recent article in *The Hindustan Times*, published from New Delhi: it serves as a staple food for at least 300 million Africans. And yet, no biotechnology company made any effort to improve the crop yield and production. It was only after cassava was found to be a feed substitute for the growing pig industry in the US that four food and biotechnology companies began research on cassava, amply indicating how animals take precedence over humans when it comes to economics.

With a major shift from public to industrial funding, and with current intellectual property-protection strategies narrowing, the nature of private research relating to biotechnology is without much regard for its impact on food security. Moreover, in a hurry to market agricultural biotechnology, farmers are not only the last to be considered but are never consulted. Biotechnology is a science which has gone beyond the control of society or the farming community. Half a dozen executives of a biotechnology company, sitting comfortably in air-conditioned board rooms, take decisions that affect millions of farmers. The media certainly has the right to question the collective wisdom of these executives.

These cutting-edge technologies have often been advertised and promoted as a way of providing consumers with a greater choice of food, as well as a possible way to solve global problems of hunger and food shortages. Unfortunately, what is being conveniently over-looked is the fact that hunger and malnutrition exist not because of a lack of production, but rather a lack of access. Millions of poor people (including 200 million in India alone) go to bed hungry every night because they cannot afford to buy food. The Indian media has clearly established that biotechnology cannot make food cheaper. In fact, all indicators point towards still higher prices for food in the coming years.

How will biotechnology solve the problems of access and distribution of food grains? In fact, given the high seed cost, royalty and the cost of other inputs that farmers will have to use for precision farming (for instance, more herbicides in the herbicide-tolerant plants), the cost of cultivation will go up and so will the market price. Food will then go out of the reach of still more people.

THE DEMON SEED

Another classic example of how the media can influence policy decisions, and in the process create hurdles in adopting a genetically engineered technology that does not benefit society at large, is reflected in the debates about seed sterilization techniques (or 'Terminator' seeds).

In a recent development, the USDA together with one of the biggest cotton seed companies, Delta and Pine Land Inc, have patented a jointly developed technique that enables seed companies to switch on and off a plant's reproductive processes. This means that farmers will get a good crop in the first year of sowing. But if they try to save the harvested seed for replanting, the crop would be sterile. In other words, farmers will be left with no choice but to buy seed afresh for every sowing.

Still more worrying is the fact that the genetic engineering technique can be easily manipulated to reduce crop harvest in any given year. Depending on what the commercial interests of the seed company and its food exporting allies are, crop production can be programmed – thereby threatening the food security of the country. Seed company AstraZeneca's patent can create plants that need continuing exposure to a particular chemical not only for germination, but for the plant's healthy growth. Novartis has at least 12 terminator-type patents, which will depend upon herbicides or even fertilizers to trigger the suicide sequence within the seed.

Delta and Pine Land have already announced their intention to apply this technology – aptly named 'Terminator' – to staple food crops such as wheat, rice and sorghum by the year 2004, primarily targeting markets in developing countries. Considering that in countries such as India, where only 10 per cent of the 400 million farmers buy seed every year, 'Terminator' will rake in a massive windfall for the seed companies. Crops that are difficult to hybridize, mainly self-pollinated crops such as wheat and rice, generally ignored by the seed companies because of the low profit potential, will now receive utmost attention.

The USDA accepts the downside for farmers since they may be forced to pay more for seed stocks every year. For the USDA, what is of paramount concern is an adequate protection of its emerging multibillion-dollar biotechnology seed industry. Although the seed multinational Monsanto, which is likely to buy Delta and Pine Land, has repeatedly said that the fears over 'Terminator' are misplaced since the patent is only a concept, the fact that the company has already applied for a patent in 87 countries makes its intentions clear.

The Indian media was quick to react on this issue. Soon after reports of the 'Terminator' seeds appeared in early 1998, both print and electronic media were quick to react. And such was the uproar in the media that the Indian government was forced three months later to impose a ban on the use of the 'Terminator' gene in Indian crops. *The Hindu Business Line,* published from Madras/Bombay and New Delhi had this to say:

> *'The battleground for biological warfare has now shifted. It is now the turn of resource-poor farmers in the developing countries to face the fury and onslaught of genetically engineered seeds.*

Exercising complete monopoly control through patent rights, the multinational seed industry is now poised to unleash its latest weapon.'

THE FUTURE SHOCK

Lester Brown of the US-based Worldwatch Institute said of the environment crisis: 'We don't have generations, we have years.' Biotechnology has an even shorter timespan before its serious implications begin to emerge. The media, therefore, cannot wait for years to sway public opinion and through it bring about a change in public policy. Biotechnology industry claims to provide the answer to growing food needs, to improving the health of millions and to providing a low-cost solution to most of the vexed problems relating to energy use. What it does not explain is that the same cutting-edge technologies hold the potential to create major social dislocations, to threaten the social fabric of developing countries, and to bring disastrous consequences for the food and livelihood security of millions of resource-poor farmers in the South.

The US Office for Technology Assessment calculates that with the help of biotechnology, the total production of corn, soyabean and wheat in America will increase by 21 per cent, 68 per cent and 35 per cent by the year 2000, respectively. Journalists have to explain that this will obviously result in an increased overproduction of these crops and, consequently, greater pressure to dump the surpluses on developing world markets. The worst would be the genetic impoverishment that is expected with the increased use of biotechnology.

One of the potential areas of negative impact from biotechnology on developing countries is the development of new methods of producing commodities or their industrially important constituent chemicals. More worrying is the possibility of producing the desired compound, such as cocoa butter, in tissue culture rather than by traditional means of field production. Alternatively, there may be ways to alter the quality of a temperate crop so that it is able to substitute for a previously imported tropical commodity – for example, rapeseed could substitute for imported coconut oil. The list of such product substitutes is endless.

This chapter has shown how some aspects of the GM issue have been covered well by the media. Indeed, the dramatic issues, and the equally dramatic public responses around the world, have been seen to have revived independent and critical editorial voice. But before the media praises itself too loudly, it is important to recognize that there are still many questions that require the sharp eye and probing questions of the professional journalist. Above all, it is crucial that the media in developing world countries moves away from its preoccupation with politics and glamour. Its analysis of politics must be expanded to include step-by-step scrutiny of corporate behaviour on questions that will, in the near and medium term, affect the lives of millions.

REFERENCES

British Medical Association (1999) *The Impact of Genetic Modification on Agriculture, Food and Health,* an interim statement, May

Cox, C (1995) 'Glyphosate, Part 2, Human exposure and ecological effects', *Journal of Pesticide Reform,* vol 15, no 4

Cunningham, E P (1990) 'Animal Production', in Persley, G J (ed), *Agricultural Biotechnology: Opportunities for International Development,* CAB International, Wallingford, UK

Dixit, K (1997) *Dateline Earth: journalism as if the planet mattered,* Inter Press Service, Pasig City, the Philippines

Ho, M W, Meyer, H and Cummins, J (1998) 'The biotechnology bubble', *The Ecologist* vol 283, pp146–153

Hobbelink, H (1991) *Biotechnology and the future of world agriculture,* Zed Books, London

Lambrecht, B (1998) 'World Recoils at Monsanto's Brave New Crops', *The St Louis Post-Dispatch,* 27 Dec

MacDonald, J F (ed) (1995) *Genes for the Future: Discovery, Ownership, Access,* National Agricultural Biotechnology Council, New York

Mackenzie, D (1998) 'Gut reaction', *New Scientist,* 30 Jan, p4

Persley, G B (1990) *Beyond Mendel's Garden: Biotechnology in the Service of World Agriculture,* CAB International, Wallingford, UK

Sharma, D (1995) *GATT to WTO: Seeds of Despair,* Konark Publishers, New Delhi

Sharma, D (1997) *In The Famine Trap,* The Ecological Foundation, New Delhi and UK Food Group, London

Part III

Understanding Environment, the Public and the Media

8 MEDIATING GLOBAL CITIZENSHIP

Bronislaw Szerszynski, John Urry and Greg Myers

Are there any signs of a new kind of citizenship emerging, in which people see themselves as bearing responsibilities and rights that stretch beyond national borders? Some such notion of 'global citizenship' seems to be implicit in many political appeals from governmental and non-governmental institutions, such as those requesting that people act locally in some way on behalf of the environment, or recognize the disparities between lives in richer and poorer countries. Such appeals might try to get us to reduce our fossil-fuel use to avoid global warming, to use wood only from sustainably managed forests, or to buy coffee that has been produced by farms that provide fair pay and conditions for their workers. They rely on, or try to instil, a sense of responsibility and belonging that goes beyond people's own locality, even stretching to the world as a whole.

But do people think of themselves as 'global citizens' in this – or any – way? Has the increased availability of experience brought by improved travel and communications initiated a broadening of moral boundaries, so that problems of global distance or global scale are seen as 'our' business? If so, what kind of role has the mass media played in this development? These are the sort of questions we tried to answer in a recent two-and-a-half-year research project, Global Citizenship and the Environment.[1] Using interviews with communications professionals, a survey of broadcast television output, and a series of focus group discussions, we sought to understand better the dynamics through which global imagery, narratives and appeals are produced and circulated within the mass media, and the effect this might be having on people's senses of themselves as bearers of rights and responsibilities in an increasingly globalized world.

THE CONTEXT OF THE RESEARCH

One of our starting points was the set of debates about globalization that has grown almost exponentially since around 1989 (see Held et al, 1999; Urry, 1999). We took certain points from this emerging 'globalization paradigm' for granted. For example, we presumed that the media and other industries increasingly involve globally interlocking ownership patterns, that there are multiple forms of 'global governance', and that overlaying this is a proliferation of images and brands, from Coca-Cola to Greenpeace, that circulate around much of the globe. While we do not presume a single global society, we thus took as our starting point the importance of powerful, interconnecting global processes.

In particular, we have been interested in how such processes might be transforming the nature of contemporary citizenship. 1989 was also when the Berlin Wall came down, symbolizing the emergence (or re-emergence) of national identities and new national states. And yet, in the 1990s there has also been the development of a post-national citizenship, not so much imposed from above by transnational forms of governance as created below by the actions of individual citizens and consumers, refugees and activists, acting in the context of increasingly global flows of migrants, tourists, environmental risks, information and images (see Albrow, 1996; Soysal, 1994; Yuval-Davis, 1997). We have elaborated elsewhere the outlines of this post-national citizenship in terms of global risks, global rights and global duties, especially in relation to the environment (Urry, 1999, Chapter 7).

One way of describing what we were doing in the project was trying to identify the cultural conditions for such a putative post-national or global citizenship. In relation to the emergence in earlier centuries of *national* citizenship, Benedict Anderson has brought attention to the crucial 'cultural work' that needed to be done before people could begin to feel part of such large political and civic units. Printed books and newspapers, radio and public service television, flags and civic rituals all played important roles in this process – not just by making possible the circulation of information about the life of the nation, but also by providing ways in which people could feel part of an 'imagined community' made up of people they would never meet in places they would never visit (Anderson 1989). We argued that the formation of anything like global citizenship in the 21st century would require a comparable amount of cultural work to generate what is, after all, a far more extensive 'community in anonymity'.

What role might mass media play in generating such a sense of global responsibility? One way to understand this might be in terms of the media's capacity to carry information – about distant places, peoples and problems, and about the operations of cause and effect, such as through markets and pollutions, that connect distant places in relations of responsibility. However, such information is only likely to be of significance to people if they have ethical horizons that already reach beyond their immediate family, community and nation. In the project, therefore, we wanted to study the media less as a carrier of information and more as a potential vehicle for the production and circulation of cultural materials out of which globalist identities, sensibilities and values might be fashioned.

Television clearly has a problematic reputation in relation to citizenship, and is blamed by writers such as Robert Putnam for almost singlehandedly causing the erosion of civic awareness and action in contemporary societies. Yet a number of characteristics commended it to us as a useful medium to choose for our study. Television carries not just facts and opinions, but also images and narratives – images of places, brands, peoples and the globe itself, and narratives of various figures, heroes and organizations (see Alexander and Jacobs, 1998, on the narrative structure of national civil society). Besides such content, television also has certain formal characteristics – of collage and 'flow' – that might just have the effect of displacing unreflective identification with local and national cultures. By placing particular places and ways of life within a wider context, television could assist in creating the cultural preconditions for meaningful emotional and moral encounters with various 'others' (contra Bauman, 1993).

Furthermore, the very pervasiveness of television in modern life means that its cultural effects – whether benign or otherwise – can only be of great importance. 'Televisual flow' has become a constituent part of the texture and rhythm of everyday life for much of the world's population (Williams, 1974; Allan, 1997; Scannell, 1996). Indeed, the very banality and unremarkableness of television's place in contemporary life may actually make it a more powerful shaper of moral and political sensibilities. Michael Billig has argued that perhaps the most important symbols of national belonging are what he calls 'banal nationalism' – the almost unnoticed symbols of nationhood that pepper our everyday lives, from coins and maps to the very use of the word 'we' (Billig, 1995). In a similar way, we wanted to explore whether televisual images and narratives might be developing a global equivalent, 'banal globalism', which could help create a sensibility conducive to the cosmopolitan rights and duties of being a 'global citizen'.

We broke down these theoretical questions into three specific research objectives. Firstly, we sought to establish how global images were generated in the media industry and how they were used within environmentally oriented NGOs (non-governmental organizations). Secondly, we wanted to determine the empirical scale and distribution of 'global images' within the outputs of the contemporary mass media.

And thirdly, we wanted to see how such images were received and interpreted within the everyday lives of very different social groups of people living within contemporary Britain. Through these methods, we hoped to determine whether there was a banal globalism operating within Britain, the role of the mass media in generating this, and its consequences for people's actions in relation to global issues.

Firstly, then, we conducted lengthy telephone interviews with communications professionals about their use of global images and narratives. Secondly, we recorded 24 hours of broadcast output of four terrestrial and satellite television channels, logging all images and actions related to globalism, and organizing the clips into a computer-based visual images database. We added to this collection, in a separate category, other documentary and advertising images collected opportunistically. Thirdly, we discussed the relation of media images to global citizenship in 18 focus group discussions held in the north-west of England between November 1997 and January 1998 (on focus groups, see Barbour and Kitzinger, 1999). In the next three sections we summarize the findings of these three stages to explore: the production and mobilization of global images in relation to environment and development issues, their distribution on broadcast television, and their reception and interpretation by the public.

PRODUCING AND MOBILIZING GLOBAL IMAGES

We interviewed about a dozen communications professionals working in the public, private and NGO/voluntary sectors who developed or deployed 'global images' in one way or another, and supplemented these by a number of shorter interviews, in both cases using the examples of global imagery from our survey as a starting point. We were particularly interested in finding out the reasons for their organizations' use of global images and narratives, and how they understood the effects of this on the public. All of the people we interviewed argued that media images are centrally important in developing social and political relationships within contemporary society and hence the global media has irrevocably transformed the nature of contemporary consumerism and citizenship. In describing the contemporary role of the mass media, they all deployed a media-literate discourse and were familiar with ideas of 'global citizenship', cosmopolitanism, global brands and icons.

The interviewees readily talked about the media as a kind of 'public stage'. It was seen as crucially important to find ways of getting images appropriate to their organization onto that stage and that those images should exert a powerful impact upon dominant discourses and narratives. It was also recognized that consumers respond in complex and unpredictable ways to the advertising of brands and organizations (such as the 'complete . . . rejection of commercialisation' by young people, according to an advertising accounts director). It was also recognized by those working in campaigning NGOs that they had no choice but to get appropriate images onto that public stage, and that their own organization was itself contributing to the development of a global media industry. All interviewees used the language of contemporary consumer advertising to analyse the respective impact of their organization on the mediatized global public stage.

The interviewees were well able to discuss the consequences of globalization. The advertising accounts director described 'groups of people that run across Europe . . . If each of the local countries were horizontal bands, there are vertical bands running through them of specific groups of . . . different product users' (such as Sony cameras, Nike running shoes, Coca-Cola, the consumers of which are 'completely separate from any sort of regional boundaries in any way'). This is connected to what he saw as some decline in the power of 'American' images and the much greater use of European images in contemporary advertising.

Interviewees also discussed how globalization both weakened individual states and forms of resistance to the global marketplace, and enabled campaigners to connect issues of individual consumption to their global environmental impacts. The press officer for a national environmental NGO stated that: 'there is an opportunity there because we are becoming more globalized. There are opportunities to understand more about the impact you are having as a consumer.' Other environmental press officers similarly argued that 'there are features of globalization which make consumer and citizen action really powerful', and that 'the media has an incredibly powerful role to play in terms of making people aware about the role they have as global citizens'. Indeed, most interviewees readily used a general notion of global citizenship to characterize the contemporary social world. One of the press officers talked of the 'shared idea of global citizenship and that we are all in it together and perhaps what you see today has an impact tomorrow'.

Most interviewees also agreed that images play a very significant role on TV, partly because of what was perceived as the 'dumbing down' of recent TV output. So although TV companies are desperate for stories, these were increasingly entertainment based and organized around life styles. The director of One World Online (a consortium of

260 NGOs using the Internet for political organization and dissemination) suggested it is precisely because of this televisual dumbing down that the Internet has developed as an attractive alternative to the broadcast media for detailed analysis of environmental issues (One World apparently receives four million hits a month).

For 'environmental stories' to work it is argued that they need a human face, so that images of local disaster can connect to global transformations. As an NGO press officer suggested: 'if you want to do climate change then you know it becomes a really good story when the camera is on somebody whose village is disappearing under water or whose house in East Anglia is falling over the edge of a cliff'. In more complex fashion, the director of a BBC2 documentary on the global food trade tried to make a 'film about connection' between those involved in food production in the developing world and its consumption in Britain. Thus the film was said to be about: 'how we are all alienated from the world that we live in, about disconnectedness' and to show striking parallels between the everyday aspirations of African farm producers and British middle-class consumers. The importance of recognizing such 'shared experiences' was also emphasized by the media manager of a development charity.

Interviewees were critical of how the 'human face' had been presented in the past. Thus the documentary maker, like the other interviewees, was determined to 'make a film about Africa that wasn't about starvation, death and rotting and plagues and flies and all that'. The head of press at an aid charity claimed that as an organization they spent much time agonizing over appropriate imagery of poverty and environmental degradation, in the light of a constantly reviewed moral and ethical code. According to another charity's media manager, Oxfam's ideal was of people 'being presented in a dignified manner, of being seen as individuals rather than a mass of faceless people'. More generally, an environmental press officer strongly emphasized the importance of 'citizen action, positive alternatives, the choices that people can make, consumer choices, political action they can take', rather than pity or despair (interviewees were specifically asked about Clare Short's views on how especially 'Africans' should be portrayed on the media).

Finally, these interviewees were well aware that iconic individuals, especially those known for their cosmopolitan life style, could well offset 'compassion fatigue'. The development charity media manager talked of 'using celebrities an awful lot more to front up media work and to get coverage in more popular broadcasts and print media'. While the head of media affairs for another charity maintained that: 'in a world where you have moving images, a photo of a [logo] probably doesn't have that kind of authority, whereas someone speaking on television and moving around a land mine does have significance'. In the next section we summarize our findings concerning the distribution of such 'moving images' on television.

THE DISTRIBUTION OF GLOBAL IMAGES ON BRITISH TV

Three categories of images, and actions associated with them, were found to be particularly significant in our 24-hour survey of broadcasting output on four channels (BBC2, ITV/Granada, Channel 4 and CNN). These images provided an unremarked-upon 'global' context for various kinds of action. We identified over 100 substantial examples of the following:

- Images of the planet as a whole, and actions involved in travelling across it, which make us think of the planet as a unified *globe*;
- Images of places as particular emblematic *environments* associated with reporting on, and from, such places;
- Images of representative *people* which are associated with actions of care and helping and which raise issues of wider planetary responsibility (see Toogood, 1998; Urry, 1999, Chapter 7).

We found that these images of the planet, environments and peoples pervade broadcasting output, not just in documentaries, advertisements and direct appeals. They are ubiquitous within links, trailers, station identifications and logos, within the globalized connecting tissue of contemporary broadcasting. Below, we discuss each of these three groups of images in turn.

Globes

One obvious way of suggesting that we all belong to the same planet is to show a globe (Ingold, 1993; Cosgrove, 1994). A common version of this image is the 'Blue Globe': the Earth seen in dark space, as a whole defined against threatening emptiness, with no lines or political colouring, freezing a moment in time. But our research shows that the globe appears in many other forms. The globe can function as a symbol of authority, organization and coverage of global information, particularly in news programmes – the graphic news globe, for instance, shown at the beginning of the BBC's or CNN's regular news broadcasts. These representations draw on the image of the Earth seen from space, but altered to incorporate other conventions: the land may be yellow and sea green; or the globe might be translucent, and weather formations absent. This sort of globe suggests a universal perspective in which physical processes do not obscure the view of the outline of continents – everything can be seen.

The Blue Globe is associated with a perspective from outside the Earth, from the point of view of an astronaut or satellite. But the shift need not be so dramatic; any vast panorama, especially seen from above, and especially with a curved horizon, can suggest that it is the Earth itself that we are looking at, not the particular local place and people. Scenes of travel evoke global citizenship, especially when they are linked to a cosmopolitan sense that everyone can and should be able to travel anywhere that they want to, and to 'consume' such places (Urry, 1995; 1999). Space is seen in terms of the endless possibilities of travel and the potential consumption of many other places and cultures across the globe (see Toogood and Myers, 1999).

Environments

Over the last 30 years the global media has been central in generating images of threatened and risky environments which are symbolic of the wider threat to life on Earth (Allan, Adam and Carter, 2000). Some places are seen as settings for action in relation to the whole Earth. For example, an overhead shot of a rainforest canopy can be framed as standing for the environment in general, while football pitches can stand for global enjoyment. In the broadcast data surveyed, this generalizing move was signalled by treating shots of unnamed places as representative of generic categories, such as desert, ice or beach, by linking the visible image to an invisible threat, or by presenting the place as a habitat for animals. For instance, in a Compaq advertisement, spots of light pass over generic environments of desert, cornfield, tropical atoll, coastal beach and ice flows. These images constitute a kind of rhetoric (see Myers, 1999a, Chapter 4).

We found that a key practice linking these environments is report-age, the witnessing of a distant place and of the action occurring within it. The reporter speaking live about the setting behind him or her, at the scene but not part of the scene, has become one of the most easily recognizable and adaptable forms of broadcast address. A CNN promotional spot for the work of its war correspondent Christiane Amanpour has at the bottom of the screen quoted tributes to her fame and skill, while the top of the screen shows medium shots of her against a wide variety of chaotic, war-torn backgrounds. But it is not just news reporters who take on the reporter's voice. Homepride ads for their curry sauces are presented in mock news form, as reports showing people of various ethnic groups in their kitchens around Britain ('Enjoyed around the world . . . and in Liverpool'). As with images of the globe, images of places as environments are open to multiple interpretations, sometimes as symbols of concepts, sometimes for affective associations (Toogood and Myers, 1999).

People

People are also be made to represent and to speak for the 'human race'. This can occur through juxtaposition, making them representative of other cultures, or by focusing on particular people whose lives are taken to stand for global action, responsibility and cosmopolitanism. There is a conventional iconography for presenting the cultural differences between peoples within a deeper shared humanity (the 'Family of Man' [sic]), with diverse people seen as engaging in the same universal activities, whether getting married or playing football (the global game) or drinking Coca-Cola (see Toogood and Myers, 1999). Or a single exemplary person can be presented as taking on responsibility for humanity and/or the globe as a whole. Advertisements and news reports very frequently use images of 'global figures', such as exemplary heroes (Mandela), global celebrities (Jagger) and global figures of hate (such as Saddam Hussein) (see Szerszynski and Toogood, 2000). We found that such figures can be ambiguous in their meanings. Princess Diana functioned both as a cosmopolitan 'clothes horse', as well as an exemplary 'citizen of the world' in campaigning against land mines. She appears in the broadcast data, conducted six months before her death, in both guises.

In summary, the use of global imagery was perhaps not as insistent or overt as we had expected. However, we found that it was often there, in the background, in globes (as on the news), representative environments (such as rainforest or the Antarctic ice shelf) and representative people (such as Nelson Mandela). This imagery occurred not just in programmes devoted to global issues, but also in graphics for the networks, in trailers and in advertisements for a wide range of products. Otherwise ordinary images were framed as global – for instance, with soaring, gliding camera movements, through the juxtaposition of comparable images from around the world, by certain types of music, or by a reporting voice. These constant reminders of the accessibility and relevance of other parts of the world are usually the unremarked background to the main message, forming what we have called 'banal globalism'. Such images are common, routinely taken for granted and enter into the intimate, personal and local concerns of people's lives (Toogood and Myers, 1999).

Globalization imagery proposes possible relations to other people and the Earth as a whole, and such new sets of relations can carry powerful feelings of helplessness or responsibility, distance or engagement. We explored the power of these various sentiments in our focus group discussions.

RECEIVING AND INTERPRETING GLOBAL IMAGES

The nine focus groups were chosen to give a good distribution of occupational group, age and gender, as well as of different kinds of local–cosmopolitan lives. The three groups that met in Blackpool were chosen to explore different kinds of activity that people pursue in their leisure time (local citizenship; consuming the globe through travel; consuming the globe through the media). Three groups were convened in Manchester to explore comparable sets of options in different professional working domains (caring for local places and people; producing the global mediascape; travelling the global corporate world). Finally, three Preston groups were chosen to explore how notions of citizenship might play out within recognizable, existing 'subcultures' (local businesspeople; 'Old Labour' internationalism; global flows of labour). The nine groups each met for two two-hour sessions, with a facilitator and an assistant. In the first session we discussed their activities in the community, and used four television advertisements to lead into a discussion of wider responsibilities. For the second session, we asked them to collect instances during the week of people whom they would consider to be examples of 'global citizens'. These lists provided the starting point for a discussion of possible global citizens; we then showed documentaries that related citizenship to environmental issues.

Our first key finding was that few participants in the groups wanted to claim an identity as a 'citizen of the world' or to challenge existing conceptions of national identity (for much more detail, see Myers, 1999b). Whenever notions of abstract or formal rights or responsibilities were introduced into the conversation, the discussion tended to proceed along national lines, exploring what the nation can and cannot demand of its citizens – and what non-citizens can demand of it.

However, what our respondents did manifest to a considerable extent was what we would rather call cosmopolitanism (see Tomlinson, 1999; Beck, 2000). By this we mean a practical and subjective awareness: of global flows of money, commodities and pollution; of extended relations to other peoples, places and environments; of blurring boundaries of nation, culture and religion; and of a diverse range of social experiences. Such a cosmopolitanism was evident in all groups, not just amongst those who travelled or had international links as part of their work, but those whose lives were lived almost entirely within small local communities. Sometimes (as with the New Europeans) this cosmopolitanism took quite strong forms, with individuals manifesting a loosening of commitment to purely local forms of life, and the embracing of a more culturally mobile sense of identity. But more often the form of cosmopolitanism we encountered was of a weaker but significant kind, involving a broad openness to others and an awareness of 'distant' and 'different' lands, peoples and ways of life.

Especially in those latter instances, concepts of global connect-edness and responsibility were nevertheless firmly rooted in a sense of local citizenship and belonging (see Berking, 1996, pp192–194, on the extraordinary scale of local gift-giving especially within the US). Most, if not all, of the respondents had some kind of active and compassionate commitment to an immediate community as an actually existing way of life, as a lost world of the past, or as an ideal for the future. But participants are not necessarily tied to a community that is based upon geographical propinquity or family. They also conceive of wider, dispersed communities based upon shared interests in football, scouting, work, the environment, student unions, caravan-ning, car racing, short wave radio, or even tortoise protection (see Szerszynski, 1997; 1998a).

However, people clearly had problems with simply trying to extend the taken-for-granted sense of moral connectedness that pertains in their more local communities to a larger and more abstract global community, since the latter seemed to lack the immediacy and genuineness ascribed to the former. This problem appeared to be one of the reasons that the respondents seemed much happier talking about specific figures than they did discussing abstract concepts of duty and belonging. This was the case in discussions both of the moral 'patient' (to whom do global citizens have responsibilities?) and the moral 'agent' (who are global citizens and what should they do?).

In relation to the question of moral consideration, at times comp-assion seemed (as might have been predicted) to decrease with distance – to be directed first at family and friends, then at one's immediate community, and only then provisionally extended further. But at other times the emphasis seemed not so much on the near but on the particular, the problem being not distance but abstraction. People felt numbed by choosing between the huge range of moral demands that the world confronts them with, whether local or distant. They also felt numbed by the very abstractness of many moral demands, often preferring to fill a shoe box with gifts to send to a particular child, rather than donating money to a charitable cause and an anonymous, general beneficiary.

This particularization also manifested strongly in the respondents' talk about moral agents. Participants clearly had different interpretations of what 'citizen' might mean in relation to the local, national and the global. But they found talking about citizenship as an abstract concept difficult and unnatural, preferring to talk about specific figures – such as Mandela, Mother Teresa and Greenpeace – who might be able to serve as exemplars of global citizenship. Our focus groups were held in Britain in late 1997, and the discussion often turned to Princess Diana. She was used to show the extension of the local sense of personal responsibility and immediate face-to-face contact. For many participants, she could stand for the personal and affective relations needed for global community, and she could be contrasted to politicians, with their political programmes and apparent self-interest. The very simplicity and directness of her concern were taken as evidence of its authenticity.

Although the respondents seemed to need to refer to these global exemplars, there were nuances in their discussion of them. They repeatedly made distinctions between:

- representing and doing (some figures are world famous, others are less known but have more profound effects);
- action for oneself and for others (powerful business leaders could be dismissed as pursuing their own interests, while the selflessness of campaigners or charity workers could qualify them);
- sincere and insincere action (for nearly every exemplar proposed by a participant, others questioned the consistency of their public and private, or past and present, actions).

In relation to other contrasts, however, the groups were less sure of distinctions between:

- local and global care (despite all our prompts, participants seemed unwilling to distinguish between good neighbours undertaking local actions, and those acting on a global scale);

- good and evil (groups were undecided whether powerful world figures could be considered 'citizens of the world' if the effects of their actions were deemed bad).

The overall choice of people chosen to stand as exemplars of global citizenship confirmed that the respondents conceived their wider moral obligations less in terms of abstract rights and duties and more in affective terms of care and compassion (Gilligan, 1982). However, the global exemplars were clearly not regarded in a straightforward way as examples that one ought simply to copy. The respondents seemed to operate with an implicit division of moral labour between the extraordinary morality exhibited in many highly mediated lives, and the ordinary morality of everyday private lives. The global exemplars were overwhelmingly what Blum calls 'idealists' – people who have a mission in life, and who consciously choose and affirm their ideals and look for ways to implement them in their own lives and the wider world. In their own lives, however, the participants felt that it was enough for them to be what Blum calls 'responders' – people who, although they have no clearly articulated moral vision, nevertheless try to respond to the situations that confront them in a morally appropriate way (Blum, 1988, pp208–209; Szerszynski, 1998b).

The focus group discussions showed that insofar as the term 'global citizenship' applies to what we found, it is 'global' more in the sense of being morally and culturally open to other peoples, environments and cultures, rather than in the sense of being shared and universal. Ideas of global connectedness, belonging and responsibility are clearly as 'banal' and taken-for-granted amongst the public as they are in the media, but they are given particular meanings within different cultures. Amongst younger and more mobile groups, it can appear as a cosmopolitan openness to the new and the culturally different (although this too has its limits). For older and more settled groups, ideas of responsibility and intervention beyond national boundaries are interpreted in relation to received notions of British character and the fulfilment of duty – familiar from the days of Empire and the two World Wars.

Global identities and actions also seemed to find a different articulation at different stages in the lifecycle. Young people will talk about travelling and working around the world, but still expect to return to the locality of their origins to settle down. Adult responsibilities bring a greater salience of ideas of duty, responsibility and care – ideas that can then be extended to other places and peoples. Retirement can reopen a sense of wider connectedness. But these life phases also bring their own situated justifications for not being 'good' global citizens. Young people frequently said that its not their job to care or to be responsible, but to enjoy themselves while they can. Parents and workers explained how wider experiences and loyalties, while still important, take second place, contracting the circle of care to the family, or to certain professionally circumscribed limits. The retired could fall back on a sense that it is now time to think of themselves for a change.

Finally, considering the media per se, we noted above that the imagery of 'banal globalism' was widespread, appearing as a ubiquitous background to daily broadcast viewing. We argued that it underpinned taken-for-granted conceptions of space and community. The focus groups showed that this kind of imagery is indeed familiar to a wide range of viewers. But when they considered it analytically (as focus groups call on them to do), they were highly sceptical about its uses. Participants were aware of the rhetorical deployment of global images by corporations, charities, entertainers and politicians, and offered competing interpretations of a range of imagery. There was a clear awareness that global citizenship could constitute good public relations. This meant that the use of the rhetoric of global citizenship in even charitable appeals was often regarded as manipulative. Claims to global citizenship by a person or a company were thus repeatedly scrutinized in a singularly 'knowing' way for the interests that such notions might be serving. This constituted another reason why the participants may have been reluctant to make such claims for themselves.

CONCLUSION: COSMOPOLITANISM, CARE AND GLOBAL CITIZENSHIP

As we explored the production, circulation and reception of the 'banal globalism' of the media, we found that we had to look beyond the televisual genres more usually regarded to be of 'civic' significance – news, current affairs and documentary – to include others, such as advertisements, logos, music videos and soap operas (see Szerszynski and Toogood, 2000). Of course, we have not been the first to question the drawing of too stark a line between consumerism and consumerist images on the one hand, and citizenship rights and responsibilities on the other (eg Meijer, 1998). Nevertheless, we were aware that this approach implied a different and perhaps counterintuitive picture of the 'public' in contemporary societies – one in which the visual and the 'imaginary' is as important as the textual and the 'real'.

In Habermas's account of the emergence of the 'public sphere' in late 18th-century European society, the salon, coffee house and the periodical press provided the spaces in which private individuals could meet together as citizens and debate political issues (1989). Central to this influential understanding of what the public sphere once was and should be like are a number of conditions: copresence and face-to-face encounter; dialogue and exchange; and the dominance of reasoned argument. But the 'mediated' character of contemporary social life transforms all such conditions: we can have encounters without being copresent. Many if not most encounters are not strictly dialogues; and images and juxtaposition are as important as verbal argument as carriers of meaning (for example, as seen in the current spate of *verité* documentaries that abandon 'talking heads' and voiceovers in favour of the powerful editing together of fragments of contrasting lives).

The emerging, if fragmented, sense of global citizenship that our research has found has been profoundly shaped by this mediated nature of the contemporary public sphere. In particular, we have found that:

- there is an exceptionally high level of global imagery on contemporary TV, both directly of the globe and indirectly through images of exemplary individuals and peoples and through various iconic environments.
- the media has developed and frequently uses various techniques by which different places and people are framed as either representing, or speaking on behalf of, the globe.
- this 'banal globalism', and especially the importance of global icons, constitutes a major consideration which those in environmental and related NGOs have to routinely address, develop and deploy.
- most people do not widely use a discourse of formally constituted global rights and responsibilities since citizenship is still seen as involving national rights and duties.
- there is a shift from the kinds of political abstractions used in citizenship debates to a more embedded vocabulary of feeling, emotion and localized care; across very different kinds of social group there are strong expressions of particularistic care and a commitment to various kinds of compassionate and charitable 'local social action'.
- most groups demonstrate a mundane 'cosmopolitanism' within their daily lives, even where these are lived in geographically proximate communities. There is a practical and subjective awareness of the global flows of images, money, commodities and pollution, some openness to other peoples and cultures, a blurring

of national boundaries, and a broadened range of social experiences involving images, places and peoples from different cultures.
- media professionals are reflexively aware of this cosmopolitanism and are endlessly seeking ways, through brands, icons and narratives, of extending it, often in ways which unintentionally enhance the sense of global 'connectedness'.
- such a cosmopolitanism is based upon an ability to move, culturally and ethically, between local and global domains, something which the various focus group members were ambivalently and hesitatingly able to envisage.

Following writers such as John Thompson (1995) and Joshua Meyrowitz (1985), we are suggesting that there is a visual and narrative 'staging' of contemporary citizenship, as the public sphere is being transformed into a 'public stage' (Szerszynski and Toogood, 2000). The emergence of such a public stage also implies that the global media may be transforming associational life within contemporary societies. Multiple identities and associations seem to be developing, producing a kind of civil society that is less nationally organized and instead reaches out, across, through and beyond national boundaries (Rotblat, 1997; Keck and Sikkink, 1998). A 'global civil society' may be emerging which draws upon the cultural resources of 'banal globalism' and depends upon extensive corporeal, virtual and imaginative mobility. How profoundly these transformations might affect the possibilities of political and civic action in the 21st century remains to be seen.

REFERENCES

Albrow, M (1996) *The Global Age: State and Society Beyond Modernity*, Polity, Cambridge

Alexander, J and Jacobs, R (1998) 'Mass communication, ritual and civil society', in T Liebes and J Curran (eds) *Media, Ritual and Identity*, Routledge, London

Allan, S (1997) 'Raymond Williams and the culture of televisual flow', in J Wallace and S Nield (eds) *Raymond Williams Now: Knowledge, Limits and the Future*, Macmillan, London

Allan, S, Adam, B and Carter, C (eds) (2000) *The Media Politics of Environmental Risks*, Routledge, London

Anderson, B (1989) *Imagined Communities*, Verso, London

Barbour, R and Kitzinger, J (eds) (1999) *Developing Focus Group Research: Politics, Theory, and Practice*, Sage, London

Bauman, Z (1993) *Postmodern Ethics*, Blackwell, Oxford

Beck, U (2000) 'The cosmopolitan perspective. On the sociology of the second age of modernity', *British Journal of Sociology* (forthcoming special edition on 'Sociology Facing the Millennium', edited by J Urry)

Berking, H (1996) 'Solitary individualism: the moral impact of cultural modernisation in late modernity', in S Lash, B Szerszynski and B Wynne (eds) *Risk, Environment and Modernity*, Routledge, London

Billig, M (1995) *Banal Nationalism*, Sage, London

Blum, L A (1988) 'Moral Exemplars: Reflections on Schindler, the Trocmes, and Others,' in P A French, T E Uehling Jr and H K Wettstein (eds), *Midwest Studies in Philosophy*, vol XIII, University of Notre Dame Press, Notre Dame

Cosgrove, D (1994) 'Contested Global Visions: One-World, Whole-Earth, and the Apollo Space Photographs', *Annals of the Association of American Geographers*, vol 84, pp270–294

Gilligan, C (1982) *In a Different Voice: Psychological Theory and Women's Development*, Harvard University Press, Cambridge, Massachusetts

Habermas, J (1989) *The Structural Transformation of the Public Sphere*, Polity, Cambridge

Held, D, McGrew, A, Goldblatt, D and Perraton, J (1999) *Global Transformations*, Polity, Cambridge

Ingold, T (1993) 'Globes and Spheres: The Topology of Environment', in K Milton (ed) *Environmentalism: The View from Anthropology*, Routledge, London

Keck, M and Sikkink, K (1998) *Activists Beyond Borders*, Princeton University Press, Ithaca

Levinas, E (1969) *Totality and Infinity: An Essay on Exteriority*, Duquesne University Press, Pittsburgh

Meijer, I (1998) 'Advertising citizenship: an essay on the performative power of consumer culture', *Media, Culture and Society*, vol 20, pp235–49

Meyrowitz, J (1985) *No Sense of Place*, Oxford University Press, New York

Myers, G (1999a) *Ad Worlds*, Arnold, London

Myers, G (1999b) *Cosmopolitanism and Care in Everyday Lives*, Working Paper, Centre for the Study of Environmental Change, Lancaster University

Rotblat, J (ed) (1997) *World Citizenship: Allegiance to Humanity*, Macmillan, London

Scannell, P (1996) *Radio, Television and Modern Life*, Blackwell, Oxford

Soysal, Y (1994) *Limits of Citizenship*, University of Chicago Press, Chicago

Szerszynski, B (1997) 'Voluntary Associations and the Sustainable Society', in M Jacobs (ed) *Greening the Millennium? The New Politics of the Environment*, Blackwell, Oxford

Szerszynski, B (1998a) 'Communities of Good Practice', in I Christie and L Nash (eds) *The Good Life*, Demos, London

Szerszynski, B (1998b) 'Saints, Heroes and Animals: Life Politics, Emancipatory Politics and Moral Responsibility in the Animal Rights Movement', paper presented to *Alternative Futures and Popular Protest IV*, Manchester Metropolitan University, April

Szerszynski, B and Toogood, M (2000) 'Global citizenship, the environment and the mass media', in S Allen, B Adam and C Carter (eds) *The Media Politics of Environmental Risks*, Routledge, London

Thompson, J (1995) *The Media and Modernity*, Polity, Cambridge

Tomlinson, J (1999) *Globalization and Culture*, Polity, Cambridge

Toogood, M (1998) *Globcit Image Database: Description and Categorisation of Images*, Mimeo, CSEC, Linguistics, Sociology Depts, Lancaster University

Toogood, M and Myers, G (1999) 'Banal Globalism and the Media: Images of Belonging, Responsibility, and Citizenship', journal paper submitted March

Urry, J (1995) *Consuming Places*, Routledge, London

Urry, J (1999) *Sociology Beyond Societies*, Routledge, London

Williams, R (1974) *Television: Technology and Cultural Form*, Fontana, London

Yuval-Davis, N (1997) *National Spaces and Collective Identities: Borders, Boundaries, Citizenship and Gender Relations*, Inaugural Lecture, University of Greenwich

NOTES

1   The project ran from November 1996 to April 1999 and was supported by the Economic and Social Research Council (ESRC – award number R000236768). The authors would like to thank Mark Toogood, who worked as research associate on the project, carried out much of the television survey and 'producer' interviews, moderated some of the focus groups, and contributed to the emerging analysis.

9 THE GREENING OF THE PUBLIC, POLITICS AND THE PRESS, 1985–1999[1]

Ivor Gaber

We are currently witnessing a period when the environment, as a news category, has once again moved up the news agenda after almost a decade in the media doldrums. The question I intend to address is: what causes these movements? Is there any discernible pattern? On the face of it there seems to be very little relationship between media coverage and the actual ebb and flow of environmental events. Obviously, the media does respond to disasters or potential disasters, such as dramatic changes in weather patterns or industrial catastrophes such as the Bhopal catastrophe in India; but, in general, there is no doubting that the media's interest in the environment is cyclical. As Anders Hansen (1993) has observed:

> *'The ups and downs of public and political concern about the environment are a poor indicator of the state and nature of environmental degradation.'*

Compare the way that other subjects move in and out of the media agenda; if we take, as examples, the economy or politics, it is possible to track how interest, or lack of it, in these areas might appear to be equally cyclical. However, on closer inspection it can be seen that coverage does, in fact, bear some passing relationship to external events – economic developments are always taking place; but depending upon the state of the domestic economy, these events attract more or less interest. Similarly, the political process is continuous – though media interest will reflect certain external realities such as the prospects of a party leader being replaced, a government being toppled or the proximity of elections.

The environment, however, is different. Environmental degradation is, presumably, a continuous process – global warming, the growth in the hole in the ozone layer, or the increase in pollution, to take three obvious examples, are facts of life. Yet media interest in these topics has demonstrated dramatic shifts – moments of significant intensity, followed by, perhaps, years of drift, and then, perhaps, another surge of interest.[2] So if external environmental events are not causing these shifts, what factors are?

At the core of this question is the notion of agenda-setting, a much discussed concept in the media studies literature (Gans, 1979; Schlesinger, 1990; Schudson, 1989 and 1991; Soloskis, 1989; Strentz, 1989 and Tuchman, 1978). It is one of a number of paradigms that enables scholars to analyse and expose the processes that lead one particular category of news stories to be favoured over any others. But in seeking to explain the presence or absence of environmental issues in the news media, the concept of a single news agenda is only of limited utility. This writer, based on his own professional experience, would argue that it is more useful to characterize the agenda-setting (or building process) as multilayered: a process of three competing yet intertwined agendas – the media's, the public's and the politicians' – which together form what could be described as the 'national' agenda.[3]

However, within these three broad categories there are important distinctions to be made. Firstly, the phrase the 'media agenda' conceals as much as it reveals. The agendas of the press, television and radio differ, sometimes radically; and within these media there are also great differences. It would be fallacious to argue, for example, that the agendas of the tabloid press and the broadsheets represent anything that could usefully be described as a consensus. Similarly, it would be difficult to see a vast overlap of common interest between, say, BBC2's late night current affairs programme *Newsnight* and ITV's morning news magazine *Good Morning Television*.

The notion of an identifiable 'public agenda' is a concept perhaps most identified with the work of the German social theorist Jurgen Habermas. In *The Structural Transformation of the Public Sphere* (1989) he developed the notion of the 'public sphere' as an autonomous set of ideas and values circulating outside the mainstream political and economic institutions, and reflecting the concerns and interests of the general public (although critics would argue that only the concerns of certain strata of the general public are reflected and that Habermas's analysis excluded the marginalized, such as women, the poor, ethnic minorities and so on). The environment is particularly pertinent as far as the public sphere is concerned; opinion polls, both those undertaken for the research project upon which this chapter is based and by a range of other researchers, demonstrate that environmental concerns stand high in the public's list of priorities, even at times when the issue is barely visible above the media's horizon.[4]

So why should it be the case that only at very specific moments does the issue of the environment come to prominence in the mass media and then just as suddenly disappear from view? One possible explanation lies in the activities of the environmental pressure groups and scientists who, as Anderson and others have demonstrated, are key sources for environmental journalists (Anderson, 1991 and 1997; Cracknell, 1993; Hansen, 1993 and Friedman, 1991). However, it can be argued that sources, important as they are, are in fact only a subset of the public agenda, since while they clearly do have membership of, and are active participants in, the public sphere, they are not members of, and are not active participants in, either the politicians', or arguably, the media's internal spheres of activity (though that is not to deny their demonstrable abilities to influence and impinge upon these areas). So the question remains, given that environmental campaigners are constantly trying to attract the media's attention, why does their success, or lack of it, tend to vary so greatly from one time compared to another?

This writer would argue that to understand this media phen-omenon, an understanding of the third agenda referred to above – the political one – is required. As is being argued, it is politicians, or rather the political class (which includes senior civil servants, press officers and, of course, the ubiquitous spin doctors) who play the crucial role in determining the media's agenda, the public's agenda and hence the national agenda. The expansion of the activities and influence of political 'spin doctors' has been well documented elsewhere (Jones, 1995 and 1997; Kavanagh, 1995; Rosenbaum, 1997; Scammell, 1995 and Barnett and Gaber, forthcoming). Their activities, and their supposed ability to dictate their own news agenda to the media, have even been the subject of a major House of Commons Select Committee Inquiry in 1998. The assertion of their virtual control of the news agenda can never be 'proved' as such, and certainly it is in both the politicians' and the media's interests to deny it. However, the testimony of the respondents to the original research project, which is quoted below, seems to provide some significant evidence in support of the contention, first proposed by Hall et al (1978), of the notion of 'primary definers' – certain individuals and groups, because of their positions in society, having privileged access to the news media.

> 'The history of environmental coverage in this country illum-inates this point – never more so than in the period between 1988, when environmentalism made its first impact on the British media, and 1992 when, following the Earth Summit at Rio, the environment disappeared from the UK media's collective radar screen.'

In the late 1980s, as the general level of public knowledge around issues such as global warming and the hole in the ozone layer rose, two specific stories grabbed the media's attention. Firstly, there was the mysterious 'seal plague' in the North Sea in the summer of 1988 – this was dramatically brought to public attention by a campaign spearheaded by *The Daily Mail* (see Anderson, 1997). This was followed in September by an incident involving a freighter, the *Karen B*, which was trying to find a port in the UK where it could unload its cargo of nuclear waste. After a great deal of public pressure, the government announced that it was refusing the ship permission to dock, thus forcing it to search for a country willing to accept its cargo. This was a particularly difficult decision for the Thatcher-led government since it involved intervening in Britain's lucrative export trade in nuclear waste reprocessing.

According to the 'folk memory' of environment reporters, these two issues, particularly because they were given such prominence by newspapers that had a long record of supporting the Conservative government, played a key role in forcing Mrs Thatcher to turn her mind to environmental issues – this she did in a speech to the Royal Society in London in September 1988. Amanda Brown, the environmental correspondent for the UK's national news agency, the Press Association, observed:

> '. . . what really did it as far as greenery is concerned is Mrs Thatcher going public at the Royal Society . . . unquestionably she made it her issue and put it on the political agenda.'

However, the transformation, as one of our original interviewees put it: 'of the iron lady into the green goddess' was, as the memoirs of Lady Thatcher (1995) reveal, a more complicated process. Firstly, she claims that her interest in environmental issues predated the seals campaign and the *Karen B* by a full year. In 1987 she claims to have taken measures to respond to growing public (and her own personal) concern about the environment by reorganizing government funding of scientific research (Thatcher, 1995, p639), and secondly, on an explicitly political level, she was troubled that what she saw as legitimate concern about the environment was being used 'to attack capitalism, growth and industry' (Thatcher, 1995, p640). In other words, she saw her mission as one of reclaiming the environmental issue for the Conservatives. It is also worth noting that this speech, now seen as so important, passed by at the time, barely noticed. Lady Thatcher amusingly recalls the problems caused by lack of television coverage of the event (pp640–641):

*'It [the speech] broke new political ground. But it is an extra-
ordinary commentary on the lack of media interest in the subject
that, contrary to my expectations, the television did not even
bother to send film crews to cover the occasion. In fact, I had
been relying on the television lights to enable me to read my
script in the gloom of the Fishmonger's Hall, where it was to be
delivered; in the event, candelabra had to be passed up along the
table to allow me to do so.'*

Following the positive reception given to her speech in September 1988,
she returned to the environmental theme a month later in her speech
to the annual Conservative Party Conference. The effect of those two
speeches was dramatic, both in terms of their impact on the amount
of coverage the environment received in the national media and on
the timing of the appointment of a whole new raft of environmental
correspondents.[5] It was all a far cry from the situation described by
one of the veterans of environmental reporting Geoffrey Lean (*The
Independent on Sunday*, 23 April 1995), who wrote:

*'For many years the subject [the environment] went so out of
fashion that I would meet the entire press corps in the shaving
mirror each morning.'*

For a year this politically induced shift of interest towards green issues
sustained the media's new-found environmentalism. However, the
elections for the European parliament in June 1989 saw the Green party
capture no fewer than 2.3 million votes, representing almost 15 per
cent of the poll. At this point, perhaps frightened by the green genie
that they had released from the political bottle, the environment
suddenly became a 'non-issue'; none of the main political parties took
any initiatives in this area and the results can perhaps be seen in the
sudden decline in environmental coverage in the media over the next
12 months.[6] The ranks of environmental correspondents on the non-
broadsheet press were decimated. In May 1989 there were 12 dedicated
environment correspondents working in the national press; within two
years the only remaining correspondents were on the broadsheets
newspapers – even Independent Television News (ITN) decided it no
longer required an environmental specialist.

Andrew Veitch, environment correspondent at Channel 4 News,
who was formerly at *The Guardian*, described the changing political
environment thus:

> *'There was the realization in Conservative-supporting newspapers that you could report the environment massively as long as it was perceived in the ranks of the Conservative party that the environment was important . . . When green issues came to be seen as a threat to financial interests, then the enthusiasm declined suddenly. In other words, as soon as the environment correspondents dug in and started looking for the real causes of things, then Conservative editors became rather less keen on running these stories.'*

Michael McCarthy, who was environment correspondent for *The Times*, and was himself a victim of the demise of environmental reporting, perhaps surprisingly defended his newspaper's decision:

> *'I think an environment correspondent, for lots of papers, has just been a totally unnecessary luxury because its not justifiable in terms of the numbers of stories that they would produce which would be considered of sufficient public interest.'*

However, the notion that either Conservative-leaning newspapers took fright when environmental issues seemed to threaten the Conservative's electoral support, or that the mainstream politicians feared the electoral impact of the Green party, are not sufficient explanations in themselves. What, our respondents believed, finally drove environmental issues off both the politicians', the media's and the public's agendas was the onset of the recession of the late 1980s and early 1990s. Amanda Brown of the Press Association , for example, rejects the notion that either the media, or Mrs Thatcher, simply lost interest in the issue:

> *'We didn't lose interest. What happened was there was a change of prime minister [John Major] and the economy took over. Mrs Thatcher led interest in the environment. I think she was genuinely interested, as a scientist . . . The trouble was that the recession came along and she went and the economic agenda just took over.'*

This is a point made strongly by many of our interviewees – that the ebb and flow of interest in green issues is directly related to the state of the economy. Michael McCarthy of *The Times* recalled a conversation with a senior Conservative:

> *'In September 1989, the height of environmental concern, I interviewed Michael Heseltine who was then the prince over the*

water out of office and he said that he believed that if prosperity disappeared environmental concern would disappear with it. And he has proved absolutely right. It was a subject that played no significant role in the 1992 general election. There were no votes in it and I think that environmental concern is a distant issue; it's about things that are happening to future generations and they may be happening a long way away or perhaps in a distant future. Its not an immediate concern.'

Amanda Brown argues that the environment came to be seen as:

'[a] luxury item . . . that people can afford, they like to talk about recycling and doing green things when there is no threat of the old man losing his job. But I am afraid that when the economy is in a muddle it just goes down the pecking order of events.'

The theme of the environment as a 'luxury item', as part of the 1980s 'yuppie culture', was also taken up by Grant Mansfield, who edited BBC TV's environmental series *Nature*:

'. . . during the 1980s the economy was booming and people had quite a lot of money to burn and I think that, if one wants to be slightly cynical about it, people driving round in their GTIs also wanted to have their Greenpeace stickers on their windscreens.'

However, one of the most interesting points raised by our respondents was the notion that the onset of recession not only pushed interest in environmental issues down the public's agenda (a notion that is not sustained by an examination of polling data for the period), but also made those in key editorial positions ponder a little more deeply on the complexity of the relationship between environmental concerns and economic development.[7] Alex Kirby, the BBC Radio's environment correspondent observed:

'I am fond of saying, very boringly, that there is no such thing as an environmental free lunch and I think that realization is coming home to more and more of us now . . . for every environmental solution there is another problem.'

He was supported by his colleague Michael Buerk, one of BBC TV's main news presenters, who has had a long standing interest in both environmental and development issues:

'. . . the deteriorating economic situation has led the audience to believe, and I think the journalists themselves to believe, that a lot of the decisions that appeared to be clear cut in times of prosperity are no longer clear cut. That, for example, there are trade-offs between a protected environment and jobs. Significantly, in this recession middle-class people in middle management jobs have been losing their jobs and environmental concern has been predominant with such people . . . They too have been feeling vulnerable about their jobs. And I think that people have come to realize that there are fine judgements to be made between wealth creation and job creation on the one hand and protection of the environment on the other.*

A decade on from the first major surge in media interest in the environment, it is possible to represent the current situation as almost a mirror image of that which has been described above. At the time of writing (mid 1999), the economy has been undergoing a sustained boom and the Labour government, elected in 1997, has been giving the environment a higher priority than its predecessor – this was evidenced by the fact that the secretary of state who was given general responsibility for the environment (John Prescott) is also the deputy prime minister, and the minister of state with specific responsibility for environmental affairs is the most senior minister outside the cabinet (Michael Meacher). Between the two of them, over a series of issues, environmental affairs were, in the first hectic year of the new government, highlighted.

At the time of the original project, among those journalists and editors interviewed there was a distinct sense that the 1992 Earth Summit in Rio had received, on the one hand, a high degree of media coverage and yet, on the other, had largely failed to deliver any significant global change. This led to a further decline in environmental coverage which was accounted for by so-called 'antisappointment' – a condition brought about when an event is given a substantial build up only to produce minimal results – a phenomenon explored more fully in Anderson and Gaber (1993). However, the amount of coverage given to the follow-up to a major UN climate change conference, held in Kyoto in 1997, indicated that environmental issues could still command broadcast airtime and newspaper column inches if backed up by political punch. In this case, the role of the Deputy Prime Minister John Prescott, in forcing through the final climate control agreement at Kyoto, dominated the UK media.

The Labour government made the environment one of the major themes of its 1998 presidency of the European Commission, and figures for the number of press releases issued by the government between 1995 and 1998 reveal a similar story. In 1995 the ministries covered by the Department of the Environment, Transport and the Regions (John Prescott's department which was created by Labour when it came into office) issued 1283 releases; by 1998 this figures was up to 4718 – an increase of 368 per cent (almost 20 press releases every working day). There was also an increase across all government departments but it was half this rate. This writer has been told (in private conversations) by both members of the government and Whitehall press officers that the new government saw the environment as one of its priorities. Government sources revealed that qualitative research undertaken by the Labour party indicated that the environment was one of those key issues for so-called 'switchers' (voters who moved directly from having voted Conservative in 1992 to voting Labour in 1997).

This greater prominence for the environment has, not surprisingly, been reflected in the media, with levels of interest now approaching those which were seen ten years ago when Mrs Thatcher first 'discovered' the issue. All the national newspapers and broadcasters reinstated their environment correspondents, and a search of four broadsheet newspapers covering the period between 1994 (which represented a low water mark for environmental coverage) and 1998 indicates significant increases in coverage.[8] For example, articles found to contain the phrase 'global warming' rose in frequency from 77 in 1993 to 144 in 1998.

However, just as the 1988–1999 'boom' in environmental coverage was short lived, so too appears to be the current one. A comparison of the flow of press releases from the Department of the Environment, Transport and the Regions in the first half of 1999 indicates that the volume of press releases being issued is running at roughly half the level of the previous year. And the government's positive green credentials have clearly been damaged by its apparent support of large-scale field trials of genetically modified organisms. The environmental lobby was very active in 1999 in campaigning against the government. And there are indications that both the media and the government are showing signs of losing interest in the environment. The indicative review of the broadsheet newspapers, earlier referred to, reveals that mentions of 'global warming', 'ozone layer' and 'pollution' peaked in 1997 and evidenced a small decline in 1998.

And the 'cause' of environmental coverage received a further setback in the 1999 elections for the European parliament in June 1999. Just as the elections ten years earlier had seen the Green party hitting a record 15 per cent of the vote and scaring mainstream politicians away from environmental issues, 1999 was also a good year for the

Greens. For while their overall share of the vote did not reach 1989 levels, the new system of proportional representation being used meant that the Greens, for the first time ever, succeeded in getting two of their number elected to the European parliament. The 'green genie' is once again out of the political bottle and it won't be long before the main political parties collectively seek to put the cork back in.

REFERENCES

Anderson, A (1991) 'Sources, strategies and the communication of environmental affairs', *Media, Culture and Society*, vol 13, no 34, pp459–76

Anderson, A (1997) Media, Culture and the Environment, UCL Press, London

Anderson, A and Gaber, I (1993) 'The Yellowing of the Greens', *British Journalism Review*, vol 4, no 2, pp49–53

Barnett, S and Gaber, I (forthcoming) *The Westminster Tales: the Production of Political News*, Cassell, London

Chapman, G et al (1997) *Environmentalism and the Mass Media: the North–South Divide*, Routledge, London

Cracknell, J (1993) 'Issue arenas, pressure groups and environmental agendas', in Hansen, A (ed.) *The Mass Media and Environmental Issues*, Leicester University Press, pp3–21

Gans, H (1979) *Deciding What's News: a Study of CBS Evening News, NBC Nightly News and Time*, Random House, New York

Habermas, J (1989) *The Structural Transformation of the Public Sphere*, Polity, Cambridge

Hall, S et al (1978) *Policing the Crisis*, Macmillan, London

Hansen, A (ed.) (1993) *The Mass Media and Environmental Issues*, Leicester University Press

Henley Centre (1993) *Media Futures 93–94*, Henley Centre, London

Jones, N (1995) *Soundbites and Spin Doctors: How Politicians Manipulate the Media and Vice Versa*, Cassell, London

Jones, N (1997) *Campaign 1997: How the General Election Was Won and Lost*, Indigo, London

Jones, N (1999) *Sultans of Spin: the Media and the New Labour Government*, Gollancz, London

Kavanagh, D (1995) *Election Campaigning: the New Marketing of Politics*, Blackwell, Oxford

Rosenbaum, M (1997) *From Soapbox to Soundbite; Party Political Campaigning in Britain since 1945*, Macmillan, London

Scammell, M (1995) *Designer Politics: How Elections Are Won*, St Martin's Press, London

Schlesinger, P (1990) 'Rethinking the sociology of journalism; source strategies and the limits of media centrism', in Ferguson, M (ed.) *Public Communication: the New Imperatives – Future Directions of Media Research*, Sage, London

Schudson, M (1989) 'The Sociology of News Production', in *Media Culture and Society*, vol 11, pp262–282

Schudson, M (1991) 'The Sociology of News Production Revisited', in Curran, J and Gurevitch, M (ed) *Mass Media and Society*, Edward Arnold, London

Soloski, J (1989) 'News reporting and professionalism: some constraints on the reporting of news', *Media Culture and Society*, vol 11, pp207–228

Strentz, H (1989) *News Reporters and News Sources: Accomplices in Shaping and Misshaping the News*, Iowa State University Press, Ames

Tuchman, G (1978) *Making News: A Study in the Construction of Reality*, The Free Press, New York

Worcester, R (1993) 'Are Newsrooms Bored with Greenery?', *British Journalism Review*, vol 4, no 3, pp24–26

NOTES

1 This paper is an updated version of part of the chapter 'The view from the newsrooms of the UK and international agencies' in *Environmentalism and the Mass Media: the North–South divide*, G Chapman et al (1997) Routledge, London. The book represents the culmination of the research project, 'The Mass Media and Global Environmental Learning', part of the ESRC's Global Environmental Change Programme, Phase 2.

2 This is borne out by an indicative research exercise undertaken for the original research project. A word search using three key environmental phrases – 'global warming', 'ozone layer' and 'pollution' – was undertaken in five UK national newspapers (*The Times, The Guardian, The Daily Telegraph, The Independent* and *Today*) covering the period April 1987 to March 1995. It revealed a very distinctive pattern. Coverage between 1987 to the end of 1988 was minimal. It then began to climb, peaking in the middle of 1990 and, apart from a brief upturn at the time of the Earth Summit in 1992, fell back, not quite to its 1987 levels but to something like half the level achieved early in 1990. Some of the reasons behind this trend

are explored in Anderson and Gaber (1993). This research was updated by reviewing the frequency of the appearance of these terms in the period 1994 to 1998 in the pages of *The Daily Telegraph*. The results indicated a very distinctive pattern demonstrating a continuation of the initial low levels of interest in 1994 with a gradual upturn resulting in a 300 per cent increase by 1997. Indeed, interest in these phenomena, judged on this crude but effective measure, was in fact running at a projected level for 1998, even higher than it was in 1988.

3   Between 1994 and 1997 the writer was a news editor and programme producer at Westminster – initially for BBC Radio and then latterly for ITN and Channel Four. Prior to that the writer had senior experience as a producer, reporter and programme editor for BBC TV, ITN and Sky News.

4   Gallup undertook a national quota sample in November 1993 involving some 940 respondents. In response to the question: 'What do you think is the most important issue affecting the world at the present time?' 28 per cent responded 'war' whilst 26 per cent identified environmental issues. This, at a time when the level of coverage of the environment, in the national press, was running at a level of barely one quarter of its 1990 high point. And research undertaken by Research International for the Henley Centre in the same year revealed that in a national quota sample of 1500, environmental issues came out as the number one priority in terms of respondents' interests in local and national news items. See also Worcester (1993) in which he demonstrates that the general public is getting ever more 'green'. He quotes from a survey of Members of Parliament in which nearly a quarter (25 per cent) quote the environment as one of the issues about which they receive most letters from the public (p26).

5   For example the indicative research quoted in note 2 reveals that references to 'global warming' were three times as frequent in the 12 months after Mrs Thatcher's speech as compared with the 12 months before the speech.

6   By the beginning of 1991 references to 'global warming' in the five newspapers quoted in note 2 were back to the same level as they were prior to Mrs Thatcher's first intervention in the debate.

7   See note 4 and Worcester (1993).

8   *The Times, The Guardian, The Daily Telegraph* and *The Independent*.

10 'Other' Cultures, 'Other' Environments and the Mass Media[1]

Graham P Chapman

Introduction

This chapter situates the mass media's role in commenting on 'global environmental problems' in an intercultural or intercivilizational perspective. The chapter therefore explores the triangle formed by the three points of humanity, the mass media and the environment. This simple triangle becomes vastly more complicated when looked at in detail, because the triangle is the product of reflexivity. Firstly, common humanity is uncommonly divided by language, culture, sex and wealth, to name but a few obvious dimensions. Secondly, the media is not objectively differentiated from the societies within which it is embedded. Yet it has a mammoth responsibility. As individuals, we know very little of our world from personal experience: most of what we 'know' – even if we think we 'objectively know it' – is based on what epistemologists call testimonial knowledge (Schmidt, 1999). Thirdly, whether the environment is viewed as a singular entity or as a myriad of separate perceptions is the result of social construction, and in many if not most accounts the environment has no separate objective existence. To attempt to say anything of value, all these complexities have to be faced, even if it means venturing into a labyrinth in which there are more dead ends than paths of enlightenment.

The chapter is based in part on cross-cultural empirical research into the mass media and environmentalism in India and Britain – reported on in Chapman, Kumar, Fraser and Gaber (1997) and augmented by a workshop held at Lonavala outside Pune in India in December 1997 – and in part on delving further into the philosophical issues which that work encountered. The conclusions show why, at the international level, different civilizations around the globe do not treat the global environment as an equally significant 'problem'. The West has a tendency to equate hegemony with universality – in other words, what ranks as important in the West is too often assumed to rank equally importantly in all other corners of the globe. This is because Western civilization assumes a single global consciousness, whereas in fact there are many. This is a general finding, which probably has importance for many other issues, and it poses perhaps the greatest challenge possible to the global role and global functioning of the mass media. It is also a reflexive finding because it reifies a civilization and its capacity to know itself, raising questions about how society is consciously self-aware.

HUMANITY

Self-Consciousness and Culture

The Holy Grail of much current science and philosophy is the understanding of human consciousness (the list of contemporary gurus writing on this topic is legion: an interested reader can start with Dennett (1992), Greenfield (1997), Pinker (1999), Penrose (1994), Blackmore (1999) and Rose (1999). Consciousness is the reflexive capacity to be self-aware. The self then is both subject – the agent with initiative, the causer – and object – the recipient upon which the actions of others impacts. For the self to be aware simultaneously of both viewpoints, it is necessary to be able to see this self in some respects as a third party, an outsider, would. Understanding this outsider's view requires a person to accept the social norms such a view embodies:

> 'The consciousness that emerges is at one and the same time the consciousness that makes the human behaviour rule governed, the shared consciousness that makes people behave as social systems, and the consciousness that forms the essence of self.'
> (Kaye, 1982, in Mollon, 1993)

In this sense the social norms which are incorporated within the superego are an essential part of self-consciousness. No one can have self-consciousness without their cultural norms. This implies that the line which divides the conscious from the non-conscious need not actually be 'drawn' inside the head of each individual, but somewhere higher in the social realm.

Consciousness, Serial Speech and Parallel Pandemonium

Descartes's conception of a dualism of mind and body, Cartesian dualism, has long been a major reference point in Western philosophy. In this view there is a central 'I', the 'I' who wants things, means things, does things, denies things. Most businesses and governments follow this model – with more and more information wanted at the top, to be reviewed, to 'get an accurate picture', in order to execute good policy decisions. At its most extreme, this model is best represented by communist central planning, where there was a central 'I', a big boss, or by a rigid company with a domineering boss. Such assemblages respond slowly to their changing environments. They are sometimes called hierarchical and sometimes 'centred'.

Dennett's (1992) account of consciousness rejects dualism. There is no central 'I' at all which, intuitively, sounds like nonsense. The stream of consciousness that is identified with self is mostly expressed in linguistic terms – language being a central (but arguably not necessary) element of consciousness. Although language above all would seem to need a central 'I', the subject of verbs like 'want', 'mean' etc, Dennett suggests that language is generated in another way – that it is the product of an iterative process invoking the generation (quite random but historically constrained by recent and older experiences) and selection of candidate attentions, foci, phrases and words. And even while they are expressed they feed back into the stream of selection – so that meaning emerges rather than is ordained. He calls his model the multiple drafts model. There are always, bubbling in the brain, multiple drafts of different reports on different topics, the vast majority of which have a very short shelf life, but some of which achieve maximum 'attention' and current dominant expression. I put 'attention' into commas for the obvious reason that one must not fall into the trap of an attender.

So attention in this context means evolutionarily successful. That is to say, Dennett invokes the idea of *memes* (a unit of concept, idea, thought, word, construct etc), which multiply and replicate, compete, die, mutate, so that the final solution is the most successful one. (The fullest explication of *memes* is in the more recent book by Blackmore, 1999.) So, from this pandemonium, this maelstrom of replication, mutation, infection, a message struggles up to the level of consciousness. Dennett makes an analogy with contemporary academic writing and publishing. When is a paper finished – when it is actually published? There are many drafts on paper, on e-mail to colleagues, on copies to referees, revisions which occur on copies not yet seen by referees who read older drafts, and at some stage *samizdat* release at a conference, followed by, last and least perhaps, a printed and outdated version in a 'respected' journal.[2] For my purposes it is a happy circumstance that Dennett uses a publishing analogy. The analogy may hold its own truths and apply well to the mass media too.

Another analogy can be with conferences, which meet in plenary mode and reception mode. The former is more centred, more Cartesian. Only one person speaks at a time, either the chair or a speaker or a member from the floor. This is clearly serial speech, controlled by or going through a gate. (In correct English meetings one member may only speak to another 'through the chair'.) In two hours there is, by definition, only two hours of speaking. In (cocktail) reception mode there ia parallel communication, within and between many shifting groups. If people are on average in groups of four and each speaks for an equal time, then in two hours there will be 30 minutes × Y communication, where Y is the number of people involved. With 200 people instead of two hours of communication, there will be 50.

The ideas of parallel processing and pandemonium convey the idea that there is no captain, no boss, no central source of meaning. This does not mean that there can be no coordination. It is a bit like watching a herd of antelope with sentries posted. The herd browse haphazardly, foraging here and there; but if a sentry barks a warning, the whole herd rivet their attention in the direction indicated, until such time as the danger passes or they all stampede together. However, for most of the time our brains can happily bifurcate endlessly into all sorts of parallel competitions and cooperations, while making patterns like uncoordinated termites make intricate termite mounds.

Consciousness is therefore an emergent property of parallel massive information-processing devices that have multiple-purpose components, and pandemonic architecture. It is a product of the shifting and evolving emergence of dominant foci from the work patterns of uncentred networks.

Although it is simple to take this model and apply it to a group of human beings to imply emergent group consciousness, it is also clear that humankind is divided between different groups, some of whom have very little capacity to communicate with each other. These different groups may have different consciousness.

The Clash of Civilizations

To what extent is our singular intelligent species actually fragmented by its languages, cultures and civilizations?

I have deliberately taken the title of this section from *The Clash of Civilizations and the Remaking of World Order* (Huntington, 1997). In this age of globalization, industrialization and urbanization, it might be tempting to think in terms of one culture and one hegemony – essentially the Westernization of the globe. But Huntington's lengthy analysis suggests otherwise. He suggests that it is possible for modernization to occur without Westernization, and that – to take an example – Islamization may strengthen in Pakistan at the same time as Pakistan develops shopping malls and atomic bombs. The same point is made by Khilnani with respect to India (1997, p8):

> 'Nehru wished to modernize India, to insert it into what he understood as the movement of universal history. Yet the India created by this ambition has come increasingly to stand in an ironic, deviant relationship to the trajectories of Western modernity that inspired it . . . the 'garb of modernity' has not proved uniform, and Indians have found many and ingenious ways of wearing it.'

Huntington does not claim that his model is the only model of international relations, nor the best in any objective sense. He sees it as the most revealing in understanding the contemporary world. He believes the primary divisions of the world are civilizational – which other authors may refer to in terms of high-level cultures. These civilizations/cultures are the highest levels at which individuals understand their own identity – and these are the highest levels to which they can appeal in understanding the worth of their own behaviour, providing the triangulation mentioned above. For Huntington, the primary civilizations are Western, Orthodox (ie Eastern Christian orthodox churches and predominantly Slav areas), Islamic, Hindu, Sinic, Japanese, and Buddhist, with emergent roles for African and Latin American. He concludes that it is imperative for the West to realize that its civilization is but one of several, that it is neither universal nor universalizing, and that the best hope for a more peaceful future is not for the imposition of one civilization's values on the others, but for dialogue to find and reinforce whatever intercivilizational values exist, and for understanding of alternative perceptions.

Strangely, for a book that is premised on the idea of separate civilizations, it says very little about how the cultural norms of these civilizations differ. There is no discussion of how culture works at a deeper subliminal level, to colour the whole world view of individuals. What is it in Japanese culture that makes the Japanese (to the Western outsider) singularly unconcerned with the extinction of animal species? Why is Western culture obsessed with finding causes, and pinning down blame and individual responsibility, where Hindu society accepts accidents as accidents and fate as fate?

Everett Knight (1959), a socialist political philosopher, complained at length about the inherent fascism of the Western objective view of the world – everything seen in terms of otherness – things subordinate to, not in reciprocal relationship with, the observer – and in the consequent valuation of its utility. In proposing a subjective alternative he confronts the meaning of self. The definition of self that he ends up with is a definition that is tantalizing for obscuring its own meaning. The point of self is not existence, but becoming, changing, evolving. But what guides that trajectory? Is any self simply the product of the forces acting upon it? Knight's definition is that the self 'is the most sustained, deeply rooted and carefully concealed of our intentions' (1959, p3). At the civilizational/cultural level, perhaps this gives us a clue as to how to conceive of the hidden meaning of culture. It is what, at the most fundamental level, guides the trajectory of social becoming.

THE MASS MEDIA

The Mass Media and Parallel Pandemonium

The world is in continuous cocktail party/reception mode. The pandemonium is, however, very far from being completely random. Differential access to different means of communication, language competence and diversity, as well as a host of other factors, mean that there are clearly discernible and less clearly discernible clusterings. Some of these clusters will be associated with mass media channels – that represent something akin to the Descartes theatre – except that the audience is not one but many. The mass media – and this is its distinguishing characteristic – works in plenary mode. It does so while the world around it continues to function in cocktail mode. Therefore it does not and cannot relay all the views of its audience simultaneously to all others. Its function is to broadcast/report/publish in serial mode, to select an infinitesimal fraction of all that could be recorded in the current pandemonium, and to highlight it in whatever compressed and simplified form for current attention. To do this effectively the media has to be able to market its messages – which means that it has to preserve the attention of its audience. In the broadest possible sense, it has to speak in the audience's language. It has to communicate.

There are many Western theories of communication, but they tend to focus on the technical questions of whether or not the message received was the message transmitted. At the extreme this reduces to Shannon's measures of information, and the technical problem of how to use a given channel capacity to optimum effect. Carey has proposed that in addition to the dominant Western tradition of studying communication as transmission, we ought to reconsider the model of communication as ritual (1992, p18). Such an approach:

> *'. . . exploits the ancient identity and common roots of the terms "commonness", "communion", "community" and "communication" . . . It sees the original or highest manifestation of communication not in the transmission of intelligent information but in the construction and maintenance of an ordered, meaningful cultural world that can serve as a control and container for human action.'*

In Hindu philosophy, communication is not complete until mood has been conveyed (this is elaborated in proper depth in Kumar, 1981 and 1994), and mood is often not conveyed until mood is harmonized. Anyone who knows India will recognize the first phase of the day in, for example, the superintendent engineer's office (see Chapman, 1998). Everyone simply sits around the boss's desk, drinking tea. Conversation may be limited, or spirited, apparently off the point or on the point. The meeting may go on for more or less time – the more or less that it takes to harmonize mood.

In my opinion, the transmission accentuated by the transmission view is actually dependent upon the culture noted by the ritual view. Culture is the deepest and most concealed harmony. It is the wave that is modulated, used as the basic signal carrier of the most basic information – that of mood.

Knowledge: Correspondence and Coherence through Communication

In standard epistemology, to say that one knows something requires the satisfaction of conditions of both correspondence and coherence (Sen, 1995). To the extent that there are any objective facts about an objective external world – perhaps called an environment – then what we know is based upon correspondence. Knowledge then corresponds with the facts. In the experimental sciences the strength of the correspondence is reinforced if results are replicated in repeated experiments.

But knowledge also requires tests of the subject, to see the extent to which other beliefs cohere with one's own. The tests of knowledge therefore add to the idea of 'correspondence 'the idea of 'coherence' – that the ideas of two or more observers confirm each other. Coherence provides justification for belief. Since there is more than one observer, both have to be able to communicate, and 'coherence' is thus intimately concerned with communication.

Different sorts of environmental knowledge fit unevenly into this epistemological model. Eyesight and correspondence alone may persuade one individual to know that one tree has been felled. Perhaps coherence is added when a neighbour agrees that this was an act in contravention of a tree preservation order. But to know that the Himalayas are suffering from deforestation requires more coherence than correspondence (see Thompson, 1995, for a discussion of the range of estimates of reforestation and deforestation in the Himalayas.) The 'correct' identification of subatomic particles from the observation of tracks left in bubble chambers requires coherence. One observer with his thermometer may have a record of atmospheric temperature change at a location – and observe what he believes to be knowledge by correspondence of a warming trend. But coherence is necessary for this trend to be established as part of the knowledge of a global trend in warming. This requires faith in many social systems and individuals and their monitoring equipment – hence the necessity of peer review, and the usual inclusion of caveats about uncertainty.

It follows that the quantitative strength of the coherence is at least in some measure associated with the reach of the communications system. The scientific community internationally is seemingly quite well connected on issues of climate change, and the size and spread of the community that coheres is part of the strength of the knowledge of climate change. This a case where prophecy – which by definition cannot be tested by correspondence – is 'proved' by coherence alone.

LIVING IN THE ENVIRONMENT

The environment is not just something defined by and studied by scientists; more importantly, it is where people live their daily lives. On that basis, although all individuals have different daily experiences from each other, it is also possible to talk in broader terms about the different experiences likely in, for example, hunter–gatherer or industrial society.

In Britain most people appropriate nothing directly for themselves from the environment other than oxygen, which they inhale in their lungs and their vehicle engines, and visual and aural signals which may give pleasure (such as aesthetic landscapes – an increasingly important environmental demand) or pain. Everything else – water, food, clothing, and many visual and aural signals – comes indirectly by pipes, cables and supermarket shelves. For the vast majority of people, therefore, even though they all live and act totally within their own environment, whatever that is, it is possible to conceptualize something called an environment which is far off and separate and abstract, from which their physical needs are satisfied indirectly. The human experience of existence becomes smeared over regions of the planet. Virtual reality becomes more real.

In India 61 per cent of employment is provided by agriculture. For the majority of the population, fuel is something collected by the family, be it wood or dung. The rural population is dependent upon local wells, pumpsets and small reservoirs for water, collected in pitchers and head-loaded home. Half of the 25 per cent who constitute the urban population, and all of the 75 per cent who constitute the rural population – because they have no toilets – defecate on open ground, something readily discussed in our interviews. In other words, the majority of the population is involved on a daily basis with physical exchange with a local lived-in environment.

> 'In India, and probably in other [developing] world countries as well, environmentalism is linked a lot more with livelihood issues rather than these global concerns, global warming or greenhouse effect or whatever ... The environmentalism that people are concerned with in India is very closely linked to livelihood issues, not just a fashionable trend that people are latching on to.'
> (Vinod Pavarala, University of Hyderabad, at Lonavala)

To summarize crudely, in Britain the local roots are few and shallow, and distant linkages are strong and getting stronger, both in resource use and information. In India local roots are many and strong, and distant linkages are weak – though getting stronger. What we have discovered is that in Britain for many people the environment (= problem) 'happens' somewhere else – in developing world countries, in rainforests, and in eastern Europe (because many of the media stories with an environmental slant are on these topics). The environment (= nature) 'happens' in Africa and North America. This is a logical extension of the belief that nature is to be found in nature reserves and national parks. Then cockroaches in warm buildings and legionnaire's disease in air ducts are not nature. In India people's local concerns are often expressed in terms of civic issues (rubbish problems, water problems, sanitation problems); and to the extent that some of the élite recognize a category of the environment (= problem) in the first place, and know anything at all about global ones in the second place, they too happen somewhere else (summarizing from Chapman et al, 1997, p67: '[the] industrial countries suffer terribly from global warming and their ozone holes').

EMPIRICAL

Consciousness as a Social Hierarchical Property

What we require here are examples of the extent to which the media does represent a central attention of the current serial narrative, and examples of how that current serial narrative differentially shifts its attention. The former can be illustrated by the strange phenomenon by which someone seen on TV or in the press gets promoted to a different level of existence – more 'real' than before – because its is intuitively known that they have been seen simultaneously by many others and may be a common reference point.

In environmental terms, there is the example of rising concern over the level of arsenic contamination (from natural sources) in what should be clean water from deep tube wells in West Bengal. The issue has hardly registered in official minds, despite (by 1995) at least 2000 deaths. It took a dedicated freelance journalist Usha, Rai, to print the story:

> 'I just happened to be sitting with one of the senior officials in the Rural Development Ministry under which drinking water comes . . . And then he talked about arsenic, so I asked for more information. Then I went back to him twice, thrice till I got the information that I wanted. I suppose if you have been in the profession for 30 years, you know your senses get hardened to 'here is a story.'[3]

One of the problems of raising these stories to the level of social consciousness is that they do not often scream 'attention'. Many journalists pointed out that environmental stories are about long-term processes, not about short-term events. Dina Vakil (editor, *The Times of India*, Bombay, English) observes:

> 'The news we carry is of the day, event related, and of course a lot of environment issues tend to be stories that really are talking about process not necessarily tied to an event, and for those kinds of stories there is even less space . . . when you are fighting for space those stories have to get less space than they deserve.'

Another blockage is the cost-effectiveness ratio of environmental news, specifically on TV, something which is true both in the UK and India even if at very different scales of expenditure:

> 'Everyone knows about killing whales. That story always makes and if it's in the UK we'll cover it; but, for example, this year the story was in Japan and it was going to cost PA a lot of money to send me, perhaps up to UK£3000, so we just picked up the story from Reuters.' (Amanda Brown, the Press Association: in Chapman et al, 1997, p49)

In response to a question: 'What would you say are the major constraints on environmental issues getting more coverage?', Ivor Gaber got this reply:

> 'Money. It's simply money, to go and film. Obviously if I want to go, as I am doing, and film in the middle of Russia next week, its thousands and thousands and thousands of pounds and that is a big consideration.' (Andrew Veitch, environmental correspondent in Chapman et al, 1997, p49)

Consciousness as a Cultural Property

This is the level at which cultural norms are incorporated within the superego. When Westerners and Indians say 'environment' do they appeal to the same meaning? However, there is no easy way of rendering environment (= nature) in Indian vernacular languages, because nature is not 'other'. To come down to Earth for the moment, how well can the English word 'environment' be translated into Hindi? Given that there are so many connotations of the word in English in the first place, we cannot presume this to be an easy task. In any case, we cannot presume a priori that there are exact and synonymous meanings for words in different languages, because that is a presumption which leads to the erroneous search for a perfect language (Eco, 1997). But let us ask what we think are the nearest ways of saying a similar thing in Hindi. According to Dhole (1997) there are two words which come close. The first is *paryavaran* and the second *nisarga*. There are two, because the philosophical content behind the two is different. *Paryavaran* means the multiple or complete (prefix '*pary*') envelope (*avaran*). This word is specifically used when it denotes a system devoid of life or divinity (the two are also nearly synonymous):

> 'Paryavaran *is the word used in contemporary India to translate the scientific environmentalism of the West. The word is made popular by newspapers and is understood by most literates, and even semi-literates, but its actual usage is restricted mainly to the élite and academic groups. The less élite people tended to interpret the word (ie from less familiar to more familiar terms in Hindi) as forests, rivers and the air in general.'*

On the other hand, *nisarga* has its nearest meaning in the English word nature, but only nature imbued with life and divinity. The word is ancient, dating from Vedic times, and includes humankind within the realm of nature. The word is used extensively in common conversations, prayers and literary writings. Dhole (1997) reports the comments of a roadside cobbler interviewed during our project:

> '*This whole being (the totality of nature) emerged out of a balance between the* pancha-maha-bhutas *(the five divine elements of earth, air, sky, light and water). The "being" is the "chaitanya" (the living spirit) in nature. [If] you disturb the balance it will tamper with the "chaitanya".'*

Dhole concludes that many if not most people in India have an ecological perspective, but are not aware of 'environmental' problems.

I have asked my (geography) students to define 'the environment'. I suspect the way that Lancaster University has divided knowledge by academic departments has had an impact on their assumptions, because the most usual definitions given are vague, but refer 'to something physical and chemical'. The students lack the *nisarga* point of view.

The cultural differences are not based solely on different conceptual backgrounds, but also quite obviously on different experiential backgrounds too. Children and adults may lack the experience, language and hence knowledge to make sense of some messages they receive. For example, the remoteness of rural India is also reflected in these remarks by Bipin Chowgule who works for Children's Educational TV in Pune:

'Because, you know, the language differs from place to place. We use the standard Marathi language which is mostly spoken in Pune. But whatever language is spoken in villages is different; whatever concepts and whatever associations we have with the things are a bit different with whatever they have.

. . . But the environment as you have defined it – no, we don't make any films on that concept. Somewhere the topic might come but we never directly mention these things because our targeted group is very limited. Up to 11 years of age the child doesn't know who chief minister is or what the problem with the Bombay beach is; he hasn't even seen a beach. He hasn't – most of the children in Maharashtra haven't seen the sea or photos of coastal areas. Many of them haven't seen a train . . . We introduce them to the natural environment as created by the nature.' (Chowgule in Chapman et al, 1997, p70)

Society, however, relies to a great extent on indirect knowledge – what in the terms of social epistemology is called testimonial knowledge – testified by parents, teachers, peers, and even the mass media. This raises questions about the effectiveness of words and pictures in inculcating the idea of a beach in, for example, the mind of a child in rural Maharashtra. Suppose that some image is conveyed, that image may become more 'real' than an actual experience of the beach. When taking geography students on a field course into Berber villages in the High Atlas Mountains in Morocco, I have met with resistance from quite a few, who think the exposure unnecessary because they have seen such places already on TV – despite the facts (maybe because of it) that on TV they cannot smell goat dung and they do not have to interview the villagers in embarrassingly bad French.

Ivor Gaber, coauthor of the main book and project behind this chapter, visited India for the first time when he attended the Lonavala dissemination workshop in December 1997. After the workshop we visited a rural village, and sat by the roadside watching women in saris carrying water from a spring in pots on their heads. He observed: 'Gosh, it is just like watching a TV documentary.'

Coherence and Language

Although ultimate meaning is probably embedded in civilization or culture, language is nevertheless the most important carrier of communication-as-information. Figure 10.1 is an attempt to show graphically the world significance of major languages. The horizontal

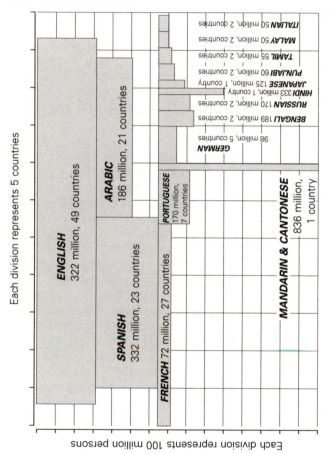

Figure 10.1 *A graphic representation of world significance of major languages*

Note: Encarta aggregates Mandarin and Cantonese. If a second language is included for those who are bilingual, English becomes the second most spoken language with 418 million speakers.

Source: data from *Encyclopaedia Britannica Yearbook 1997 and Microsoft Encarta CD*

axis shows the number of countries in which the language is an official language of communication (there may be more than one, and official national languages – such as Urdu in Pakistan – may in fact be spoken by a minority of the population). The simple count does not reflect on the size of the countries – English has both big states (eg US) and small Caribbean states. For other languages (eg French) and Spanish, there are also skewed distributions. The vertical axis shows the number of speakers.

The languages have been ranked by the area of the rectangles – an area which has no objective meaning but which reduces the two dimensions to a single-dimensional ordering of some sort of 'importance'. The ranking is from top to bottom and left to right. The arrangement into three tiers is arbitrary, based on not allowing the total width of the second tier to exceed that of the first. However, the results suggest clearly that English is the preeminent world language, and that Spanish and Arabic follow. 'Chinese' (here a composite of Mandarin and Cantonese: see the note attached to the figure) and Hindi are 'deep' languages, but not broad. All of this seems to accord with intuition.

The biggest media companies and the most important news agencies operate mostly in English – though there are some non-English players such as Agence France Presse. English, therefore, is the main carrier for the international conveyance of information between civilizations. But in the specific terms of news carried internationally by mass media, there is not much of that:

> '. . . so newsroom editors tend to adhere to the principle that there is only one kind of news. In short, the value of international news is low, except in the case of exclusives of major events and these are pretty rare.' (Papathanassopoulos, 1999, p19)

> 'People appear to want more news, but in their own language, by news people who look and sound like them, and with an emphasis on local and national coverage.' (Parker, 1995, quoted in Papathanassopoulos, 1999, p21)

A very similar finding is arrived at in Chapman (1992). In Chapman et al (1997), before introducing an analysis of news in India and the UK, we caution that we should remind ourselves of what was happening 'in the world' in November 1993. This is, of course, a fairly bizarre idea, because it all depends on whose 'world' we are thinking about, and the argument is circular since we rely on the news to provide the plenary serial mode attention. So here is a random but quite representative sample of the TV news stories of one week in November 1993:

In India

Bomb Blast At Dimapur Railway Station Assam

Iran Extends Full Support To India On Kashmir Issue

Assembly Elections Polling In Harayana Tomorrow

Militants Will Not Bend Until Demands Are Met: Hazratbal Crisis (Kashmir)

Rupee Will Be Fully Convertible Within A Short Time: Finance Minister

One Village Adopted By Coal India In Earthquake Hit Area (Latur, Maharashtra)

Indo–US Relations Not As Good As Expected: Commerce Minister

Tamil Tigers Attack Sri Lankan Military: More Than 300 Soldiers Killed

Black Jawar (a millet food grain) To Be Purchased By Government At 190 Rs Per Quintal

Kerala, Andhra Pradesh: Cyclone, 36 Killed

Mr Ahmed Lenghar Selected As Pakistan's President

Well Known Gandhian Leader Manibhai Desai Dead

India's First Prime Minister, Nehru: Birth Centenary Celebrated

Himachal Pradesh Polls Tomorrow

Efforts Continue To Resolve Hazratbal Shrine Issue

First Ever Multi-Party Elections In Jordan

Over 60% Polling In Himachal Pradesh

Major Fire Breaks Out In Pakistani National Assembly Building In Islamabad

Heavy Rains Claim Many Deaths

Repolling Ordered In 81 Polling Stations In Rajasthan

26 People Killed In W Bengal In Trawler Capsize

Iran Has Appreciated India's Policy Of Restraint

30 Persons Feared Killed In Landslides In Tamil Nadu

Government Has Permitted Indian Companies To Raise Money From Global Markets

PM Says New Delhi Favours Free & Equal Trade For Benefit Of All Countries

In the UK

Princess Of Wales Says She Will Sue Over Sneaked
Photos
Miners See All Hope Fade As Closures Loom Again
Row Over Seat Belts After 10 Die In Coach Crash
Trade Improves But Unsold Nissans Tell Another Story
Mystery Over Popstar Michael Jackson's Whereabouts After
He Cancels His World Tour
Iraq: Saddam Hussein Resumes Executions In Baghdad
Britain Prepares Compromise With China Over Hong
Kong
President Menem Tells C4 News Falkland Islands Will Be
Argentina's By 2000
PLO Chairman Condemns Killings Of Jewish Settler
Head Of RAF Accuses Some Government Ministers Of
Campaign To Undermine Services
Head Of RAF Apologises For Speech In Which He Made
An Attack On Chancellor & Chief Secretary
First Evidence Of Widespread Massacre In Burundi
UN Security Council Voted To Enforce Tougher Sanctions On
Libya
UN Troops Help Mentally Ill Abandoned In Bosnian
Hospital
Back-To-Basics Speech By John Major & Home
Secretary
Should Education Aim For Excellence
Single Mothers Persecuted
EuroDisney £4 Million Loss A Week

This ought to dispel any idea that there is overall agreement on the significant news items, even supposing that the channels in each country were presented with the same list from which to make a selection in the first place. Our analysis, then, shows that major international 'events' such as war in Yugoslavia may feature in both countries. Stories about processes (eg rising unemployment) or values (eg single parenthood) are usually local and stand no chance of being shared. 'Environmental' stories are also few in both countries, and very rarely are on the same events (in our samples Australian bush fires were a rare exception – almost certainly taken up in part because of cheap and dramatic visuals), partly because there is no agreement on what is environmental, developmental or civil.

English is the prime language of Western civilization, the prime language of international connection, and also the *lingua franca* in many countries where the majority may even speak an unrelated language – India for example – but where it remains the dominant *lingua franca* in the mass media, in commerce, in academic publishing, and in much else. There is a Hindi news service but it is growing slowly and is far behind the English language service.

The 'knowledge' of the West is therefore more likely to dominate the coherence in international communication than non-Western knowledge, even if that is expressed in English. In India the situation is complex. The élite 2 to 2.5 per cent who function in English are at an advantage in understanding Western knowledge, and they become the vehicle through which some foreign ideas may penetrate into the local civilization. The ideas that have really penetrated within the culture are the big ones, and they are few: they include self-determination, democracy, development and science. But all have been dressed, as Khilnani put it in the quote above, in Indian garb. The domesticated ideas are now part and parcel of the coherence in the vernacular press. More recent Western thinking on environment has so far only penetrated the élite. For the masses the debate about environment and development does not exist. For them the debate is development and clean-up. In fact, in our research it became impossible to disentangle environment from development (Chapman et al, 1997, p124). Finally, we proposed the hypothesis that the English press is more pro-environment, and the vernacular press more pro-development.

Usha Page of AIR (All India Radio) Pune/Ahmednagar said of TV documentaries:

> 'The one main reason is television programmes – the (greater) percentage of television programmes I found is in English. Actually the programmes should have been broadcast in regional language. So they should reach to the cross-section of people and to the grassroots. But they are not reaching. There are some programmes on awareness, conservation, environment; they are broadcast in English and for affluent audience only. It is in English and the level of the programme is rather ... it is for intellectuals. It is not for the common viewer.'

Shri Raut (*The Independent*, Bombay, English) talking of the highly controversial major Narmada dam scheme, said:

'When I see the coverage on the Narmada, I have a different opinion on this. There is a clear divide between English newspapers and language newspapers. All English newspapers are generally unanimous on anti-Narmada agitation, while the language press in Gujarat or Maharashtra is very pro-dam. So that shows a complete divide in that. In my opinion, both the sides are not fair, because the English people are not giving enough coverage to pro-Narmada, while the language people are just not printing anything about what Medha Patkar [a leading protester] and her people are saying. Both are having a monologue.'

Coherence and Correspondence

In the preceding section the examples were of cases where there was agreement on what was being talked about – the Narmada dam, for example – but disagreement about values – for example the costs and benefits of the dam scheme. I said above that one of the problems journalists have with future global environmental problems is that there is no correspondence – that 'truth' rests with coherence alone. This leaves journalists in a difficult position. Journalists are sceptics – they want correspondence as well as coherence, but on predictions of climate change they cannot have correspondence – unless their correspondence is with the beliefs of the scientific community, so that wherever they test 'facts' by asking members of the scientific community around the world, they get similar answers. This is treating subject as object, and changing the rules. It leaves journalists feeling uncomfortable. They have to fall back on phrases such as: 'Scientists say . . .', 'The consensus of scientific opinion is . . .'. Christian Wolmar (UK journalist, Lonavala) argues:

'There is a difference between good journalism and bad journalism. . . As Friends of the Earth point out: "Many scientists say. . .". I know when I'm writing an article and I write something like: "Many scientists think . . .", I think that it's dishonest, that it's wrong.'[4]

But coherence in the media can, to an extent, be bought by the powerful:

> '*There are huge amounts of time and energy spent in the US by a few scientists who take money from those kind of sources to prove that global warming is not really a problem . . . So . . . of course, big financial interests always make sure that they get their message across and I think that we should remember that.*'
> (Sue Inglish, TV news executive, Lonavala)

Lack of coherence can be used to debunk unwanted messages. To the extent that there is an idea of environment as problem, in India its roots are in Indian experience, particularly the post-Independence famines of 1965 and 1966 – and not in abstract models of global warming. Darryl D'Monte, formerly editor of *The Times of India*, a committed environmentalist and president of the new International Association of Environmental Journalists, put it this way:

> '*Climatic change . . . this is not a problem India is going to worry about, because we have already experienced that. We've been suffering droughts for a long time. We've been suffering famines. We know what change is all about. Nobody can threaten us with any greater change than we've already had.*'

D'Monte is one of the 2 to 2.5 per cent of Indians who regularly converse, read and write in English, and he has no problem with the Western conception of environment. But most of India does not share the same comprehension. Most overseas news has to be translated into local context if it is to mean anything. Bhimla Bhatta (DoorDarshan Public Service TV) states:

> '*You see, basically we try to relate it to the viewership. If there is an international event as I mentioned earlier, news is related to events and developments; then we try to relate it to the national or the regional level also. So, to that extent, if statistics are given, if there are [international] statistics given at a conference, we try to also bring in the regional, the national statistics for that . . . People can understand the enormity of the problem nearer home, rather than as an abstract situation.*'

In both these quotes, from D'Monte and Bhatta, we can see the explicit way in which the viewpoint that they espouse has been implicitly validated by contrast with the alternative viewpoint that they reject. That is, they use another culture (in this case the hegemonic West) to triangulate their own relationship with their own environment.

CONCLUSIONS

Understanding what it is to be a human living on this Earth requires an understanding of what forms the 'self' in human beings. The highest level at which we can understand the formation of self is probably at the level of major civilizations/cultures. This level, in part, reflects the near identity of communication with culture. Contemporary mass media – as one would expect from this model – communicates ritually with its own cultures far better than it communicates between cultures. This means that the (cultural) selves do not develop a mature understanding of their own relationship with their own environment – because they remain bi-polar and untriangulated. The least mature of such views is that of the most hegemonic civilization – in this case the West. The post-modernism of the West is at best a chaotic search for triangulation.

It is the values that infect global pandemonium that matter most. Any attempts to solve 'the environmental problem' by central planners are doomed to fail, as at Rio and Kyoto. There can be no big boss to consciousness, for the sensory array of observant agencies will all be reporting different, and sometimes contradictory, 'facts' – of hunger versus conservation, of potential versus cost, of spurious simplification versus multiple cause and effect. Meaning emerges from networks of thought patterns. If the Western 'hemisphere' of the planetary cerebrum is sincere about planetary health, its first job is to find out how to listen to the silent majorities of the South. Their senses of 'crisis', of 'before' and 'after', are not the same as the North's. At the deepest cultural levels, the trajectories of 'becoming' may not be the same.

I leave the last word to a newspaper essay, 'Eco-politics: a case for equity', by a senior Indian Administrative Service officer:[5]

> 'Meanwhile the rich countries have developed other ways of exploiting them [the developing countries]. The new plan works through environmental phrases, and global warming is the latest bait. . . One does not have to reel out figures to show that the developed countries have been the biggest energy-guzzlers and pollutant-emitters. . . It is equally obvious that during the past decade or so significant success had been achieved by the developed world in reducing the pollution levels in their countries. . . The most obvious explanation, of course, lies in new technologies which help in curbing pollution.
>
> Industrialized countries cannot deny they have been dumping proportionately outrageous levels of pollutants into air, water

and even space. Now it has been accepted that these were and continue to be the common heritage of all humanity, that poor countries must retard their development to save it. Therefore, the debt which the industrialized countries have incurred by utilizing the oceans and atmosphere as a dumping-ground for their high levels of waste must be recognized. While no industrialized country will be in a position to repay the debt it has incurred to the rest of humanity by abusing the common heritage, it should not prevent us from demanding what it is possible to repay.

As stated earlier, the use of energy in the early phases of development is unclean. If the per capita output of pollutants in India or China reaches the levels that pertained in the US in the 1960s, it will be disastrous for the health of their citizens. However, it will be equally disastrous for the rest of the world, the rich countries included.

In their own interests the rich countries should transfer to the poor nations, the technologies required for a cleaner utilization of fossil fuels ... The message is simple. The developing countries shall undergo the process of growth irrespective of the discomfort it causes to them or anyone else. It is up to the rich countries to decide whether they have something at stake in this transition.' (Prasher, 1995)

REFERENCES

Blackmore, S (1999) *The Meme Machine*, Oxford University Press, Oxford

Carey, J W (1992) *Communication as Culture: Essays on Media and Society*, Routledge, London

Chapman, G P (1992) 'TV: the World Next Door?', *InterMedia*, special issue 'The Global News Agenda', vol 20, no 1, pp30–33

Chapman, G P (1998) 'A Short Walk in the Jungle', *Geography*, vol 83, no 359, part 2, pp123–138

Chapman, G P, Kumar, K, Fraser, C and Gaber, I (1997) *Environmentalism and the Mass Media: the North–South Divide*, Routledge, London

Dennett, D (1992) *Consciousness Explained*, Allen Lane, London

Dhole, V (1997) 'Environmentalism and the Mass Media in India: Diffusing North–South Divides', paper presented to the workshop International Communication and Environmentalism, Lonavala, India

Eco, U (1997) *The Search for a Perfect Language*, Fontana Press, London

Greenfield, S (1997) *The Human Brain: a Guided Tour*, Phoenix, London

Huntington, S (1997) *The Clash of Civilizations and the Remaking of World Order*, Simon and Schuster, Dhaka

Kaye, K (1982) *The Mental and Social Life of Babies*, Harvester, London

Khilnana, S (1997) *The Idea of India*, Farrar Straus Giroux, New York

Knight, E (1959) *The Objective Society*, Routledge and Kegan Paul, London

Kumar, K (1981) *Mass Communication in India*, Jaico, Bombay

Kumar, K (1994) *Mass Communication: a Critical Analysis*, Vipul Prakashan, Bombay

Mollon, P (1993) *The Fragile Self: the Structure of Narcissistic Disturbance*, Whurr Publishing, London

Mowlana, H (1996) *Global Communication in Transition: the End of Diversity?* Sage, California

Papathanassopoulos, S (1999) 'The political economy of international news channels: more supply than demand?', *Intermedia*, vol 27, no 1, pp17–23

Parker, R (1995) *Mixed Signals: the Prospects for Global Television News*, Twentieth Century Press Fund, New York

Penrose, R (1994) *Shadows of the Mind*, Oxford University Press, Oxford

Pinker, S (1999) *How the Mind Works*, Penguin, London

Prasher, R N (1995) *The Tribune*, Chandigarh, 25 August, p8

Rose, S (1999) *From Brains to Consciousness*, Allen Lane, London

Schmidt, F (1999) 'Social Epistemology', in Greco, J and Sosa, E (eds) *The Blackwell Guide to Epistemology*, Chapter 15, pp354–382, Blackwell, Oxford

Sen, P (1995) 'Knowledge, Truth and Scepticism', paper presented to the Indian Institute of Advanced Study, Shimla

Thompson, M (1995) 'Policy Making in the Face of Uncertainty: the Himalayas as Unknowns', in Chapman, G P and Thompson, M (eds) *Water: and the Quest for Sustainable Development in the Ganges Valley*, Chapter 2, pp25–40, Mansell Publishing, London

NOTES

1   This chapter reports on work supported by ESRC Grant L320253059, Phase 2, of the Global Environmental Change Programme, and an ESRC Dissemination Grant for the workshop International Communication and Environmentalism, held in Lonavala, India, December 1997. This support is gratefully acknowledged.

2 The phrase used in the Soviet era to denote unapproved 'grey' literature circulated by Xerox and duplicator machines.
3 All interview quotations are from transcripts of interviews carried out in 1994 for the project noted in note 1, except the quotation from Wolmar, a participant at the Dissemination conference in Lonavala.
4 See note 2.
5 The Indian Administrative Service, is successor to the Indian Civil Service, which recruits high-fliers into the top ranks of the government bureaucracy.

11 MAKING THE ENVIRONMENT NEWS ON THE *TODAY* PROGRAMME

Julian Darley

The following chapter presents some recent previously unpublished research into the way global environmental change issues become news on the BBC Radio Four *Today* programme. The programme is the longest and arguably most important news and current affairs programme in the domestic BBC output. It also has the largest radio audience and reaches more decision makers than any other single source – almost everyone involved in the highest levels of state activity listens to it. In addition to its normal terrestrial broadcasting, from 6 April 1999 the *Today* programme has been available both live and on demand via the Internet, which can only increase its reach both globally and locally.

INTRODUCTION

This chapter does not set out to be unduly critical or polemical, but in outlining the way environmental issues are developed and treated on one particular and important programme it will reveal institutional, cultural and structural barriers to producing a better understanding of global change. It will be argued that though the *Today* programme has more environmental stories than any other programme, because of the way items are usually treated as normal news stories the programme cannot advance beyond a certain level or depth of coverage. Environment issues on the programme are probably treated more generously, sympathetically and carefully than any other type of item, by a production team clearly motivated and concerned to produce a high-quality service of use to public and policy maker. However, at least three generic problems still apply:

1 Journalism, as currently practised, is the collection and ordering of surface data of events, perceptions and utterances regarded as

objective knowledge, immediate and non-mediated. Of course, this knowledge is filtered by the prevailing news values and the cultural biases of the reporter and reporting institution. Furthermore, even upmarket present-day journalism is driven less by an idea that it is the 'search for information of use to the public' (Fallows, 1996) and more by what will entertain and get ratings.

2   While it is important to treat environmental stories as fundamentally political and mainstream issues, the more this is done the more likely it is that the issue will be turned into a shuttlecock for the usual construction of public life as a game or a squabble between 'venal and scheming' politicians.

3   While *Today* programme reports are of a superlative standard, as story construction and data-gathering exercises they are still more likely to focus on a descriptive 'who, what, where and when' rather than on a causative 'why'. Furthermore, reports are usually presented in a decontextualized way. They are left hanging with no discussion to follow them unless the issue has clear and present political, though not necessarily policy, resonance and relevance. Ironically, if reports are embedded within a discussion, problem two still applies so that though often informative, the discussions are nevertheless still driven by the underlying and primary decision parameters, to be conflictual, divisive and personalized even where this is wholly inappropriate.

The cumulative effects of these three problems do not naturally induce much greater public understanding, especially when the issues are compounded by being ambiguous, complex and characterized by process rather than event – precisely the features of many aspects of an environmental agenda which looks set to dominate the early decades of the next century.

The evidence for the above conclusions is contained partly in the interviews undertaken with the *Today* production team and partly from analysing the product. The former is original data while the latter is partly original observation (ie listening to the programme as broadcast) and partly distilled from a wide sweep of analytical literature. While it is intended to focus on the former data, some key filters and influences cannot be understood without reference to the actual product.

Over a period of more than six months in 1997 and 1998, I had the chance to observe key editorial meetings, and interview producers, editors, journalists, reporters and a leading presenter. The aim of the research was not to see how the specialist correspondents (such as Roger Harrabin, author of Chapter 5) dealt with environmental stories, but how the daily production team handled them. Much of the questioning and observation was aimed at trying to understand as fully as possible the forces, filters and drivers which shape news and current affairs production in general, while at the same time attempting to map this understanding onto the field of environment. If news production is seen as the result of a set of dynamic and interrelated filters, it suggests that consideration be given not only to what gets through but what does not. Considering what might be excluded, and why, is important when challenging prevailing norms. The filters will include some of the news values categories which have been developed by Galtung (1965), Bell (1991) and others, and some elements which are less often considered.

This chapter is rich in previously unpublished interview data, though none of it will be attributed to an identifiable individual beyond the simple, though artificial, division of producer and senior producer. The former category denotes broadcast journalists and reporters, while the latter categories denote editors, presenters and some day editors.

Three main filter groups will be considered here: time, news values, and the need to entertain. None of them is completely distinct from the other, but a temporary categorization can serve useful analytic purposes – though within the groups other themes and framing effects will be brought in which could otherwise perhaps only appear in a longer treatment.

TIME

Changes in scheduling have compressed or altered the 'time budget' for news programming across the BBC's output. One pioneer news programme, *The World at One*, was cut from 40 minutes to 30 minutes, which one *Today* producer argued reduced it from a true current affairs programme to an 'extended news bulletin with interviews' because 'they don't have the scope to do things as they used to do'. The problem had arisen before:

> 'The same thing happened on Newsbeat *on Radio 1 [where]*
> *basically the audience didn't want any news at all, let alone a*
> *half-hour programme or 15 minutes. I think the 15 minute*
> *programme was probably a compromise ... between the*
> *aspirations of the BBC to inform people and the aspirations of*
> *the controllers of Radio 1 not to lose their audience at six in the*

evening. I mean it was fudge to move from a half-hour to a fifteen-minute programme. It ruined the programme.'

How long a programme is and item lengths are key determinants in what kind of items can be aired and how they can be treated.

The *Today* programme has, since April 1999, been lengthened by 30 per cent. This did not result in an increase in the number of different items on the programme by 30 per cent nor expand their length from five to seven minutes. Both these parameters could influence environmental coverage in positive ways. Increasing items would have been difficult given that few new extra financial resources were allocated to the *Today* programme makers, in part because of the financial squeeze caused by the decision to spend UK£60 million on developing digital broadcasting. Instead, following industry 'lean-production' techniques, existing reporters and correspondents are interviewed for the first half hour (from 6:00 am) – in effect acting as trailers or teasers for the main body of the programme from 6:30 to 8:30am. The last half hour tends to be more discursive, and for some time featured a longer three-way debate. This slot has now been dropped.

The second possibility, of increasing the time length of items, is limited by different constraints. A senior producer explains that:

> *'There are limits with* Today *because of its position in the day, because people rushing around listening to it, you can't sustain a ten-minute item on* Today; *unless it is an absolute cracker, you can't really sustain anything over about five minutes, because we just know that people are moving around the house and aren't able to apply that sort of concentration. [Unlike* Newsnight] *. . . we can't possibly on* Today *. . . say, well you know, we're going to take 30 minutes and really get to the bottom of what we feel about the welfare state or something like that.'*

Clearly, at that time of morning (6:00 to 9:00 am) 30 minutes would be impossible to justify – indeed only on very rare occasions (eg in time of war) does the prime minister get more than ten minutes. Yet, time is of the essence when trying to put complex issues in context. One long-experienced *Today* producer said:

> *'. . . you can pin down great moments in [some] interviews for ten seconds in any one seven-minute interview and it's worth the full seven minutes because that's what it takes, and the ten seconds can come right at the beginning but it's only apparent that that was the important ten seconds after six and a half minutes.'*

It echoes Etzioni's (1993) suggestion that 'quality time' only comes out of 'quantity time'. In addition, it has long been accepted by media analysts (Fallows, 1996; Chomsky and Herman, 1988) that the more the quotation or interview is squeezed down to soundbite length the harder it is to say anything new. This increasingly reinforces the 'known' accepted dogma or 'common-sense' view, rather than exploring the 'knowable' – a situation which runs counter to the view of one senior producer who says: 'What you've got to try to do with . . . current affairs programmes is to try to make sure that you are endlessly chasing the knowable as well as the known.'

A startling example of the opposite of 'chasing the knowable' was apparent in a BBC TV news report in 1999 which examined the *Exxon Valdez*–Prince William Sound disaster ten years on. The reporter ended the package by repeating the misleading simplification that the disaster was the fault of a drunken Captain Joseph Hazelwood and it was thus the 'worst drunk-driving incident in history'. No attempt was made to look at the institutional and structural reasons and background behind the story nor to mention that Exxon has strenuously avoided paying all of its US$5 billion fine (Facts On File News Services, 1998). This might have explored a deregulated, globalized, hypercompetitive shipping industry which disregards safety of ship and crew in order to drive down costs and increase profit, while having inadequate measures to deal with oil slicks in confined bays and straits (Hannigan, 1995, p65).

Another difficulty lies in the 'knowable' being hard to explore by using the 'common-sense', 'tribune of the people'-style of questioning favoured by *Today* and BBC TV's *Newsnight*. Another related point reinforces both the time difficulty and questioning style. If, as one senior producer maintains, 'the primary mode of current affairs programmes is interrogative', then it surely matters what questions you ask and what answers you are expecting, since visions of what 'ought to be' inevitably frame or at least colour stories of what is. Furthermore, in the positivist world view of most journalists, questions must produce answers. One senior producer, who is highly aware of the problem, said with irony: 'it's cause and effect and there's a definite answer to everything'.

Some *Today* producers understand well that environmental problems often don't yield answers of the cause and effect variety. They consist, rather, in matrices of human choices and options, and different philosophies of action and decision (Rayner and Malone, 1998). At the same time, that wish for a 'common-sense' view of the world produces a desire for misleading simplicity, 'facts' and monocausal frameworks. The antidote which is seized upon is also illusory, namely a kind of 'reflex counter-intuitivity', which gives airspace to people who hold an opposite view to a prevailing opinion. This occurs even where that view is highly partisan, contains a hidden agenda, or masquerades under a title which is the opposite of reality as with the Global Climate Coalition – a group of global fossil-fuel-producing corporations opposed to action to mitigate climate change. From the current-affairs production point of view, however, it produces an immediate polarization and ensures 'good knockabout stuff' as one producer described it. Another senior producer said: 'We try and get warring parties together on the programme, we want them to war, we want to hear that war aired for the public'.

During the research period, there was little reference to or awareness by any of the general production team that this kind of journalism could be problematic, though there was reference to the difficulty of covering the 'centre ground' UK Liberal Democrat party. Polarization was certainly not discussed in the highly charged professional atmosphere of editorial meetings. One producer talked about how people are selected for interview with regard to structuring the discussion, saying that 'because you have decided how you want to people that particular debate, you will normally know what line you're expecting them to take'. Of course, the production team wants to know what people are going to say in advance – if not, it would be very difficult to make a programme like *Today*. Nevertheless, scrutiny of this key determinant of the discussions (or 'discos' as the presenter-two-participant interviews are known) should be a focus for those interested in the way global environmental change is covered.

At a more strategic level producers are aware of other 'external' framing effects which change with *time*, for instance the effect of a powerful UK government:

> '[I]t is true that it is far more difficult for us now with a government with a majority of 179. We have to be more proactive in taking decisions which appear to attack the government . . . [and we have to be] more careful. . . [I]t then begins to matter where your producers come from, what perspectives they come from, whether they can shift across perspectives to look at stories from various different angles.'

It has long been argued that élite or establishment views dominate serious journalism in the UK. While there is no longer a preponderance of old Etonians at the *Today* programme, there is still an unrepresentatively large number of private-school-educated, Oxford and Cambridge graduates in the production team, many of whom have studied humanities and social sciences, specifically politics and economics. There is also a strong bias towards establishment views in the background materials that are routinely consulted. For instance, almost every production team member mentioned *The Economist* and *The Spectator* as regular sources. While the latter publication was 'balanced' to some extent by the left-leaning *New Statesman*, no alternative views to the uncompromisingly neo-liberal and to a large extent anti-environmental *Economist* were cited. Likewise, reference to foreign journals, especially European ones, was generally unusual. All of these factors tend to feed a myopic, 'pencil beam' journalism rather than helping to 'look for truth but truth in the broader sense of the wider picture', as one producer suggested.

With regard to that 'broader sense' and time, various producers stressed the importance of contextualizing the day's events – 'we're the BBC's first draft of what's happening in the day' – but contextualizing can't always be so easily shoe-horned into the same five-minute-sized box. However, two fairly safe ways of doing this are to use a debating rather than a dialogical technique and to have a preexisting agenda or line that is determinedly extracted from the interviewee. The technique sometimes, but rarely, yields useful pearls. Dialogue has always been a better way of revealing context, but it is by nature open ended and irreducibly unpredictable – which makes it very difficult to pre-plan, pre-time and fit into the production line or sausage machine that late 20th-century news production has become.

The 'preexisting agenda' is a device which further reduces the time available to an interviewee to offer a substantial statement or argument. The need to follow a particular line leads to unwarranted interruptions which break the flow of thought and often forces the interviewee to explain what they are *not* propounding rather than what they are. It is a very easy way of filling up space, especially when deeper knowledge would be required to elicit more profound results; but it is not very illuminating. Yet many journalists proceed as if without a combative line there is somehow no point to the questions – nobody is going to be the winner or the loser.

One senior producer commented that:

> *'I think that in the post-Watergate grandeur. . . a lot of American journalists . . . will believe that if they're not threatening to bring down an administration tomorrow they're not doing their job.'*

While the independent and critical nature of BBC news journalism is widely recognized and valued, the result of this in professional practice has proved an obstacle to a fuller understanding of complex long-term issues.

A further difficulty for the BBC is the highly professional nature of the public relations industry, especially with respect to politics (Michie, 1998). One senior producer expressed the following:

> '[T]here is a real fear that absolutely everything that we get to know about what's happening is the product of a press release and the product of very, very, very sophisticated spin doctors, company PR consultants and so on ... and it's only the ... rather subversive interrogative approach, which has been traditional in current affairs programmes ... that can get under that and hold [politicians] to account.'

However, no producer questioned raised the fact that most PR work, especially for powerful corporations, is about keeping things out of the news (Michie, 1998); nor did any producers mention the problem of economic globalization or the undemocratic, unchecked power of transnational corporations. However, one senior producer did mention one area of corporate power:

> 'We were far, far less aware of that situation [ie bias and credulity] with [other] groups [like pressure groups – see later] and we've sorted that out a little bit ... now I think the one that's left is analysts, City analysts. They also have a perspective, they also have a political perspective.'

The same producer also underlined the sheer difficulty of getting business people to come on the programme. Unfortunately, this aversion to, or avoidance of, focusing on the undemocratic power of the corporate world is a major hindrance to covering the causes of global environmental change issues.

As the BBC conducts continual reassessments of its news coverage, it must be hoped that these wider and carefully hidden issues will be considered more fully.

NEWS VALUES

Over the last few decades there has been a considerable amount of work on news values, though there is not complete agreement on categories and terminology. A few concepts of considerable importance to environmental change issues will be dealt with here. Collating and compressing the work by Galtung and Ruge (1965), UNESCO (1975), Mencher (1977) and Bell (1991) produces the following typology.

'Culturally Independent' Factors

- Frequency – how well a story fits with daily news cycles.
- Timeliness / Proximity / Topicality – the way an item is close in time, or place, or both.
- Threshold – the level at which a story becomes news, eg numbers killed in an accident.
- Unambiguity – issues should be clear cut and contain few 'ifs, buts and maybes'.
- Meaningfulness / Relevance – cultural proximity or how much people care about something.
- Consonance – how well a story fits with news producers' preconceptions or prejudices.
- Unexpectedness – degree of surprise.
- Predictability – extent to which events (of the 'right' type) are prescheduled by PR operatives.
- Continuity / Currency – events and situations that are being talked about; 'news breeds news'.
- Cooption – hanging similar stories on the same news peg.
- Competition – is the story a scoop or an exclusive (opposite of cooption)?
- Composition – balance (eg between social affairs, foreign, crime, politics etc); this includes the idea of 'light and shade'.
- Conflict / Controversy – events that reflect clashes between people or institutions.

'Culturally Dependent' Factors

- Prominence / Éliteness (nations–persons–sources) – eg the US is the most élite nation, the US president is the most élite person, government sources are the most élite; 'names make news'.
- Personification / Personalization – concentration on social and news actors rather than, structural–institutional forces.
- Negativity – news is inherently bad.
- Facticity – number of facts in a story.

The first and undoubtedly deepest difficulty of global environmental-change news coverage is the problem of 'event versus process'. This aspect is well covered in other areas of this book, but one comment from a senior producer illustrates awareness of the problem – and how difficult it will be to tackle it:

> *'Events happen in a different way [from] the way that most journalists think they happen. We see an event start, and we also perceive it to have an end. At the simplest level, process versus event – you have 300 killed in a plane crash, but you know 1000 are killed that week in car accidents . . . it's the nature of news, isn't it. It's drama. And we try and address that, but you can't get away from drama – drama is a part of news, a sense of event. And we always try to put it in context.'*

The rest of this section will look at some other news values and especially their interactions, at least some of which may be less intractable than the *event-process* problem.

Consonance is a complex news value that can be exaggerated by the short time lengths required of items by many news programmes, including *Today*. This is especially true if issues are polarized and treated dualistically, in dramatic black-and-white, goodies versus baddies style. Consonance prefers stories to fit preexisting models and tends to filter out deviance and variation from the dominant 'script'. By its nature consonance helps to telegraph and telescope stories by not needing contextualization because it's there already in the framework supplied, rather like a game – or indeed a TV game show. Known and accepted programme or game formats put reflexive questioning of the nature and shape of their own existence off limits. Thus the format cannot ask: 'why play football rather than play music? or whether game-shows are 'good' or not. The only question is – who will win and how. Thus consonance conspires with conflict to exclude complex and process-oriented environmental stories.

Personalization or *personification* is a normal part of story-telling. Interest in *prominence* and *élite people* is a part of the 'social structure of attention' (Chance and Larsen, 1976). Believing sources of authority which reinforce the dominant world picture – a sense of legitimacy – is something desired by any government whether totalitarian or democratic (Summerton, 1998). These elements are always going to be important in, and to some extent constitutive of, news and current affairs. The situation becomes problematic when *personalization* and an interest in prominent people becomes either an overriding news value, as in the tabloid press when it causes extreme trivialization of public life, or when it becomes an excuse for not looking more deeply into the causative sources of problems, such as legal structures, institutions, corporations and – most intangibly – belief systems. It is clear that when *élite nations* use their power to construct a world view which hides the damage they are doing to others and increasingly to their own people, that is a cause of concern to those seeking environmental and social justice. These areas are some of the most difficult to explore with production staff. They are 'transparent' in the sense that they are part of 'normal' journalism in the same way that facts are 'out there' in 'normal science' (Kuhn, 1962). One producer referred to the reasonable need to be sure of sources:

> *'You need to know that [a report or story] has been fully investigated, that it's academically rigorous, that you can trust it . . . that it would be a report of an august body of some sort.'*

Having authoritative sources saves a lot of time and avoids extra levels of fact-checking for hard-pressed journalists. However, coming to rely on these sources, which are nearly always representative of governments or powerful institutions, as part of the 'news routine' combined with a traditional British 'common-sense' distaste for analytic techniques, militates against exploring the sources for deeper messages and prejudices. An interesting shift in position has happened with a group of sources who started peripherally two decades ago but have slowly moved, in a convection-like process, near the centre in terms of authority if not in éliteness. This group consists of the 'traditional' radical environment NGOs in the UK, such as Friends of the Earth, Greenpeace and the World Wide Fund For Nature (WWF). They have moved so far that in some senior producers' minds (and public opinion – MORI, 1998) they were more trusted than government and other élite sources, enjoying the kind of credulity more often produced by science reports (see later):

> *'There was a time, two or three years ago, when we were perhaps a little too credulous about pressure groups – and not just pressure groups. By and large, we're very rigorous about political bias, we're very rigorous in balancing the politics, and we're very much aware when we have an MP on, that he [sic] represents a political line. We were far, far less aware of that situation with pressure groups and we've sorted that out a little bit . . . We do tend to compartmentalize these things, and until a couple of years ago, pressure groups were seen as being objective people who merely represented, what's the best way of putting it, represented the real world whereas politicians represented a political point of view. A few things happened. We started to address it ourselves.'*

Once again, there is considerable awareness of methodological journalistic problems and a willingness to take remedial action. A question remains, though, as to what that action is. An example occurred on the *Today* programme on 22 April 1999 when a report from the Institute of Economic Affairs (IEA) claimed that many aspects of the environment are much cleaner now than for decades, and that there was much exaggeration of the environmental problems by environmental pressure groups. In an example of lack of contextualization, it was not mentioned that IEA is a right-wing think-tank that vigorously promotes deregulated free-market capitalism. If, as has been shown in recent surveys, many *Today* listeners do not know what a party whip is, and amongst the wider British public very few have any idea of the political biases of the press, then they might easily regard the IEA – which outside think-tank and policy circles is little known – as being 'neutral'. *Today* producers might question whether this kind of political education is part of their job. If not, then whose job is it?

One of the most problematic but subtle news values relevant to the coverage of global environmental change issues is that of unambiguity. The problems to be discussed are anything but 'clear cut', contain lots of 'ifs' and 'buts', but are obviously complex, dynamically interdependent and often require a sophisticated understanding of science. However, one senior producer reported that:

> '. . . when you're in a science class at school, you do biology, chemistry, physics: this happens, then this happens and that happens as a result of it – write it down. That's how we do science at school, or how the people who work on the programme do science at school. It's cause and effect and there's a definite answer to everything . . . and you can see it. And we still think like that when we're faced with scientists now.'

This problem can be alleviated to a considerable extent in correspondent packages, and *Today* has a special correspondent dealing with environmental matters and another who has special expertise in transport and greenbelt problems. However, *Today* is a live interview-led programme, and presenters increasingly find themselves in territory for which many years of political reporting do not give them the kind of analytical tools they need. This situation is related to, and compounded by, a paradoxical attitude to science: a mixture of awe and contempt. Some quotes from senior producers will illustrate this:

> 'Whenever we do science stories, we sound credulous; it's like The Beano *covering science.'*

'We're either credulous, in which case. . . [we talk about] in different half hours of the programme. . . BSE and . . . genetically engineered fruit. The genetically engineered fruit one was: "Gosh, can we really do that? I can't wait to get hold of some of these new tomatoes." Half an hour later. . . "How did we get to this position where, you know, BSE is rampant, and people are getting Kreuzfeld Jacob's disease. It's appalling."'

'[U]sually we pooh-pooh science stories. . . [the] approach is: "This is all rubbish", [which is considered to be] a populist approach . . . that's what the man in the street thinks. But actually . . . from e-mails, we get some virulent criticism.'

These quotations also clearly illustrate that *Today* is very concerned about this problem, though it has as yet been unable to take significant measures to improve it – and indeed it would involve considerable paradigm shifts in a number of aspects.

Another aspect of *unambiguity* is revealed in its combination with *consonance*. It is in certain respects structurally even more serious than the foregoing difficulties with science in that it illustrates the deep problem of dualisms or binary dichotomies which erase the subtle interstices in between. Although this can be shown more clearly with political examples, such as the difficulty of covering centre-ground parties mentioned briefly earlier, nonetheless the analogue with environmental stories is clear – global environmental change stories are not black and white or full of obvious goodies and baddies. One producer suggested that the problem was deep seated and certainly not peculiar to the BBC:

'[The media] still see things in Punch and Judy terms and they like to portray things in these terms; it makes for good copy, it makes for good radio, knockabout politics. But actually, you know, things like [the centrist] Liberal Democrats cooperating with the government on constitutional reform, that is significant.'

News as Entertainment – Turning Programmes into Shows

The need for conflict and preexisting dramatic forms highlights the growth of the news as entertainment, and is one of the developments most likely to hinder coverage of the issues under discussion. The above examples are strongly reinforced by cases from the BBC television's current affairs output. The need for conflict and oppositional dramatization is clear, and critics, analysts and journalists all agree that it is an easy way to increase entertainment value. But it also increases the likelihood of false polarization, 'reflex counter-intuitivity', jumping to conclusions and predictable reactions. Several other producers and senior producers were at pains to underline the need to entertain:

> *'The entertainment value could be dramatic or amusing or maybe because it does have a great influence.'*

> *'What we want to hear is a genuine description of [politicians'] grievances against one another, and something which is entertaining and informative to the audience – there's an entertainment element as well.'*

> *'One job that we must never neglect. It [Today] actually provides entertainment and good company for people at breakfast time.'*

> *'The first thing that any television or radio programme is doing, unless it's sort of the Open University, unless it's something you're switching on, you know, consciously because you're trying to educate yourself, the first thing we've got to be is, companionable and entertaining . . . I mean . . . we must never get away from remembering that we are part of the entertainment business.'*

One senior producer locates entertainment within the public service remit of the BBC: 'an organization like the BBC should have to provide – a level of educational programming, a level of entertainment, a level of sport, etc'.

As in the case of the tabloidization of broadsheet newspapers in respect of foreign coverage and personalization (particularly coverage of royalty and media stars), entertainment in the broadcast media has grown as a value, possibly becoming a news value in itself, though it is certainly not mentioned in 1965 by Galtung and Ruge in their seminal list of newsvalues. In the US, the defining moment for the metamorphosis of news into entertainment, according to Fallows (1996, p55), was *60 Minutes*, simply because it was the first news programme to make money. Before this, network news operations had been 'loss leaders', designed to add prestige to a network. They were given a 'small' budget of around 'US$3 million or $4 million' and left to get on with it, free of the albatross of the audience ratings war.

By contrast, Ted Koppel, one of America's best-known anchormen, claims that now 'network news divisions spend approximately US$0.5 billion on news', (Fallows, 1996, p55), and have developed highly personality-oriented formats designed to keep them ahead in the fierce ratings wars which have inevitably spread to the UK – most recently seen with the removal of the ITN *Ten O'Clock News* which had originally done so much to improve the quality of televisual news. *60 Minutes* achieved the feat of making news pay by presenting 'a lot of "real" news with an interesting veneer. But it also presented a lot of merely "interesting" material as if it were real news' (Fallows, 1996, p55). In the case of *60 Minutes*, by 1994 this had decayed into stories which featured 30 per cent 'celebrity profiles, entertainment-industry stories, or exposés of . . . "petty scandals" [while] barely one fifth of the stories concerned economics, the real workings of politics, or any other issue of long-term national significance'. Halberstam, writing of the history of CBS, said of *60 Minutes*:

> *'The talent level is very high, and the package is very skilfully put together, but the driving force has always seemed to me more about entertaining than informing.'*

News programmes become news 'shows'. Apart from touching tales of rescued furry animals, serious, complex, system-level environment issues can rarely aspire to the levels of entertainment required by such news 'shows'.

Fortunately, as is clear from the evidence gathered from the *Today* production team, and by inference true of the BBC generally, the situation is quite different from the US (though of course the level of production skill is also very high). However, there are a number of powerful forces lining up against high-quality public service news broadcasting, including: the BBC's own 'market reforms' of the 1980s and 1990s that have underlined the importance of ratings; the cutting of analogue news budgets per broadcast minute; the arrival of commercial digital broadcasting (1998 in UK); and the constant pressure from free-market commercial broadcasters to 'let the audience decide what's quality and what isn't' (Bazalgette, 1998). These forces have so far invariably meant lower quality and more superficial reporting and more vacuous discussion. With these factors tending to combine, the BBC will come under heavy pressure to go in the direction of *60 Minutes* and more populist coverage. In the US, where, with the notable exception of C-SPAN (which offers live coverage of

'Senate and House floor action [and] a steady diet of public affairs programming' – C-SPAN, 1998), there is little mainstream indepth coverage of current affairs. Such coverage is confined to the periphery in the form of the ailing Pacifica Radio, the Media Channel, Adbusters, Alternative Views and many other small low-budget organizations, though with the advent of broadband Internet these small voices are increasingly available globally and in rapidly improving reception quality.

Conclusions

Despite the fact that I have identified many problems with *Today*'s news and current affairs production which have a negative impact on covering complex and process-oriented issues, this should not be seen as a criticism of the production team, who aim to be the foremost example of excellence in public service broadcasting. Rather, it is a call for a radical reassessment of the function of broadcast news in relation to public life and argues for a considerable increase in resources for serious news and current affairs programming. This requires a move away from sausage-machine rolling news and 'lean production' processes, with the limited budgets for person-hours spent researching issues. It demands keener and deeper reporting and discussion techniques. Finally, the question should not, indeed must not, be 'will this entertain?' but rather 'is this what we need to know?' Only when the public becomes convinced that serious news and current affairs is indispensable to conducting public – and private – life, will there be the growth in audience figures that every broadcaster is pursuing. These are essential conditions for increased public understanding of global environmental change. They are also, by extension, essential components of broadcasting in a democracy.

References

Bazalgette, P (1998), 'The Guardian Edinburgh International Television Festival Memorial Lecture', reported by Janine Gibson in *The Guardian*, 28 August 1998
Bell, A (1991) *The language of news media*, Blackwell, Oxford
Chance, M R A and Larsen, R R (1976) *The social structure of attention*, John Wiley & Sons, London
C-SPAN http://www.c-span.org

Etzioni, A (1993) *The Spirit of Community – the Reinvention of American Society,* Simon & Schuster, New York

Facts On File News Services (1998) URL http://www.facts.com

Fallows, J (1996) *Breaking the news – How the media undermine* American *democracy,* Pantheon Books, New York

Galtung, J and Ruge, M H (1965) 'The structure of foreign news', *Journal of Peace Research,* vol 2(1), pp64–91

Halberstam, D (1979) *The powers that be,* Knopf, New York

Hannigan, J A (1995) *Environmental sociology: a social constructionist perspective,* Routledge, London

Herman, E S and Chomsky, N (1988) *Manufacturing consent: the political economy of the mass media,* Pantheon Books, New York

Korten, D C (1995) *When Corporations Rule The World,* Kumarian Press, West Hartford, Connecticut

Kuhn, T S (1962) *The Structure of Scientific Revolutions,* Chicago University Press, Chicago

Michie, D (1998) *The Invisible Persuaders,* Bantam Press, London

MORI (1998) *British Public Opinion,* MORI, London

Rayner, S and Malone, E (1998) *Human Choice and Climate Change,* Battelle Press, Columbus, Ohio

Summerton, N (1998) *The media in the public interest,* unpublished lecture given at Regent's Park College, Oxford

UNESCO (1975) *New World Information and Communication debates,* UNESCO, Paris

12 AFTER THE *BRENT SPAR*: BUSINESS, THE MEDIA AND THE NEW ENVIRONMENTAL POLITICS

Joe Smith

'A handful of good-hearted chaps in a lilo taking on the entire Western economy, and with it, the biggest piece of litter in the world: the Greenpeace war on the abandoned 'Spar was an incident crammed with dramatic polarities of the most unsubtle kind' (Simon Barnes, *The Times Review* of the Year, 1995)

News reporting made the *Brent Spar* one of the most recognized industrial structures in the world. The conflict between Shell, owners of this redundant North Sea oil installation, and Greenpeace is one of a small number of incidents and issues credited with transforming business thinking about sustainable development, about decision making, and about the way large corporations relate to their publics.

For most people, the conflict was mediated through television and print journalism. The story offered the media three ingredients it finds difficult to resist: conflict, event and personality. The conflict drew on the general issue of how industries should act with regard to their waste, whatever its nature and wherever it may be. This conflict was distilled in one simple event: should this redundant oil storage platform, the first of approximately 400 North Sea installations to be decommissioned, be dumped at sea? Shell and Greenpeace provided the personality, with walk-on character roles for the British government.

Old enemies; strong positions; good pictures: it's not difficult in hindsight to see why it was a good story. What this summary fails to recognize is that the celebrity of the *Brent Spar*, and the dramatic course of events, surprised all players – including Greenpeace. It also fails to show how, despite the fact that the opposition to dumping the installation was driven by deeply and widely held environmental values, most media coverage insisted on portraying it as a story of conflicting scientific truth claims.

This chapter will summarize the events, emphasizing media treatment of the issue. It will also look at the impact of the *Brent Spar* on both business thinking on corporate responsibility and policy thinking about the representation of 'lay' values in complex decisions. These changes, and the media's performance in reporting the events and its own post mortem, point to the need for new forms of documentation and reporting to complement ambitions for greater public participation in environmental decisions.

MAKING CHANGE: ENVIRONMENTALISM AND THE MEDIA

The early 1990s were a period of consolidation for environmentalism in western Europe. Numerous roundtable processes, stakeholder dialogues, voluntarist and market-based policies had drawn environmental non-governmental organizations (NGOs) into unprecedented levels of dialogue with government and business interests. It might have seemed that environmentalism had lost its teeth.

The *Brent Spar* allowed environmentalism to express something that continued to be deeply and widely felt. Government and big corporations had learned their lines in relation to the flexible concept of sustainable development, yet had not understood the real meaning of the phrase. As Chris Rose, campaign director of Greenpeace at the time, put it (Rose, 1998, p9):

> '*Here in the northern North Sea was the government slipping through the gate at the end of the national garden, and conniving with Shell to dump the '*Spar *at sea rather than reuse or recycle it – behaving for all the world like a couple of bad neighbours who creep out at night and craftily wheel a rusty old car into the village pond.*'

One widely held caricature of the *Brent Spar*'s rise to fame is that the media sophisticates of Greenpeace seized a highly telegenic piece of ocean dumping to boost (flagging?) membership and visibility at a time of more consensual mood between environmental NGOs, business and government (see, for example, Matt Ridley, *The Sunday Telegraph*, 25 June 1995).

This account ignores the long-standing presence and expertise of Greenpeace in the ocean-dumping policy world. Peter Melchett, executive director of Greenpeace UK, noted that: 'as often happens with our campaigns, the historical context in which we work was ignored by all those looking at things in a much more short-term framework' (Melchett, speech to the Royal Institution, 14 November 1997, quoted in Rose, 1998, p18).

The campaign was a natural Greenpeace topic, following over 15 years of work as a catalyst for change in international and domestic policy, including dumping of radioactive and industrial waste, incineration of hazardous waste, dumping of decommissioned nuclear submarines, and dumping of sewage sludge at sea. Most of this activity, and most of the outcomes in terms of changes in the regulatory framework on these issues, had gone on within the slow process of international meetings, with little media attention.

Within this context the *Brent Spar* was important to Greenpeace as a precedent. It built on the previous work on ocean dumping. Yet, it also offered an opportunity to highlight and gauge increasing interest in corporate responsibility issues. The decision would influence thinking about all offshore installations – and, in the context of the more conciliatory setting of the environment–business debate of the early 1990s – offer an important measure of the degree to which big corporations had 'got the message'.

For their part, Shell and the British government were confident that legal obligations and best practice had been represented in the decision to dump the *Brent Spar*. They insisted throughout that science was on their side and that they were pursuing the best practicable environmental option (BPEO). The public case was built on expert risk assessment and an internal view that this was the most economic solution (both for the company and the UK government – specifically the UK treasury).

From the start, however, the media interpreted the conflict quite differently. Indeed there was dissatisfaction on all sides at the media handling of the *Brent Spar* episode. Greenpeace, the UK government, Shell and senior media decision makers were all forced to examine the way the '*Spar*' had been constructed as a story. Certainly, it had developed differently in print and broadcast media, and the same issues and events had been presented differently in the range of countries, papers and programmes that covered it. However there was one feature common to the great majority of initial coverage, particularly in the British media: who had got the science right? What was the view of experts? What was the 'right' decision?

For Greenpeace, the evidence that the *Brent Spar* was, in effect, a test case that might have allowed (relatively cheap) offshore disposal of other installations was persistently underrecognized in the media. Also, the longstanding response of journalism to draw upon the balance of scientific opinion as the core of environment stories was a constant source of frustration. Lengthy assessment and debate failed to throw up one clearly preferable environmental option; but before, during and after the events surrounding the *Brent Spar*, Greenpeace was persistently questioned about its science.

The news media found it difficult to report the story as anything but an adversarial contest between two versions of scientific truth. The media's determined search for 'experts' that might adjudicate over the scientific claims only exacerbated this, and drew the story further away from a debate about the *Brent Spar* as a precedent-setting case of corporate responsibility to the environment.

When the battle was apparently won by Greenpeace, and Shell announced a change of heart, the story was translated into another well-established strand: political leadership. For the UK government, media treatment of the *Brent Spar* episode presented one of the most marked political embarrassments of that term. On 20 June 1995 Shell announced that it was, despite agreement and active support from the British government for dumping, in effect abandoning this as a solution to the *Brent Spar's* decommissioning.

Centre-left papers, which had in some cases expressed active support for Greenpeace, were jubilant at this 'people's victory': *The Daily Mirror's* front page headline 'Glad Oil Over' was matched by an editorial which proclaimed a 'Victory for the People', and which argued that:

> '*Shell's decision not to sink the* Brent Spar *oil rig is a fantastic victory . . . A victory for Greenpeace, a victory for* The Mirror *and other newspapers which campaigned against scuppering the platform. But most of all it is a victory for the people. The people whose boycott of Shell forced it to back down.*'

Drawing a similar conclusion about the key role of popular boycotts, *The Independent* newspaper's editorial suggested that:

> '*Shell's loss is democracy's gain . . . The decision establishes that the purity of the seas must be safeguarded . . . [Popular opinion] has ruled that, whatever destruction may be wrought elsewhere, the oceans cannot simply be regarded as waste disposal sinks. On this issue we have seen the rolling back of values that have until now underpinned the "throwaway society".*' (21 June 1995)

Under the headline 'Shelling out for Pollution', *The Guardian* argued that:

> '[the] decision not to dump the Brent Spar *was right* . . . *Shell*
> *did have some arguments on its side for dumping at sea. Even*
> *so, its decision to bow to public protests and abandon this decision*
> *should be celebrated. People still count. Boycotts can still work.*
> *This is as refreshing for democracy as it is for the North Sea.'*
> (21 June 1995)

In more moderated tones *The Financial Times* had noted that:

> '[although] the widening consumer boycotts were not expensive
> *in money terms, they were doing untold damage to Shell's*
> *public image. Even the German police were refusing to use Shell*
> *petrol.'* ('Company Struggles to Accept Disaster', 21 June
> 1995)

The right-wing press in Britain mostly emphasized the negative political implications for the government and, following the government line, taunted Shell for cowardice (see *The Express*, *The Telegraph* and *The Sun* for 21 June 1999; *The Sunday Express*, *The Mail on Sunday* and *The News of the World*, 25 June 1999). Following the headline 'Shell U Turn Sinks Major – political storm as giant oil platform heads back to Britain', *The Daily Mail* stated that 'John Major was left betrayed and humiliated last night after Shell lost its nerve'. The comment column went on:

> '*Greenpeace's triumph is Downing Street's disaster* . . . *So what*
> *about Mr Major's judgement? Couldn't he see what was*
> *coming? Was the foreign office too dozy to warn him? Was the*
> *president of the Board of Trade otherwise engaged?'*

The Daily Telegraph promoted what became a more widespread line that Shell's and the government's good science had been overcome by sophisticated manipulation by the media:

> '*In this instance there was never very much doubt that Shell*
> *had the best of the argument. Greenpeace, however, had the best*
> *of the publicity* . . . *[this was] a battle environmentalists did not*
> *deserve to win.'*

The right of centre press pointed to the power of the visual images on television news in Britain and the rest of Europe as the source of the problem. Government also attacked the news media, and specifically its reliance for press information, photographs and film images on Greenpeace Communications. *The Independent*'s environment correspondent, Nicholas Schoon, had gone on board the *Brent Spar* and remained until he was taken off with the protestors by Shell. He concluded that:

> '. . . *there was widespread questioning among the UK media, including the BBC, as to whether Greenpeace deserved to win. The suggestion was that Greenpeace had won the day thanks to the continental media, which uncritically broadcast Greenpeace's emotional appeals not to dump the* Brent Spar *in the Atlantic*' ('Covering itself in glory', *The Independent*, 5 September 1995).

The next turn in the *Brent Spar* saga reawakened media interest and further fuelled the debate about the role of NGOs in policy and politics. Greenpeace discovered that they had made errors in sampling and estimating the amount of oil remaining in the installation. Although this estimate (of 5000 tonnes) was barely reported when the information was released to the UK media on 16 June, and had played no evident part in the unfolding consumer boycotts, the announcement was given almost as much prominence as Shell's decision weeks earlier not to dump. While some coverage held that it is 'Better to Blunder than to Lie' (*The Independent*, 6 September 1995), the more widespread reaction was that the media had been spun by Greenpeace's potent mixture of emotive messages, strong visual images and confident defence of its own science. MORI's regular survey of news editors found that:

> '*One commentator spoke spontaneously about the past legacy of Greenpeace campaigns saying "our relationship is very difficult and very tense . . . [Greenpeace] manipulated [us] and the agenda; we felt bounced quite significantly over the* Brent Spar, *they were very restrictive over Moruroa Atoll. We felt manipulated and could not put our own journalism into it. We have been very cautious since then"*' (quoted in Rose, 1998, p151).

While intensely critical of Greenpeace's deployment of scientific claims, the media failed to interrogate science produced by government and industry to the same degree. Assumptions (and errors) were made by all parties (see NERC, 1996; 1998; or ENDS, 1996), yet the sense amongst editors that they had been successfully manipulated by a pressure group seems to have stung their professional pride. A debate about the coverage of the *Brent Spar* at the Edinburgh Television Festival gave insights into the process of editorial decision making, and something of the irritation felt by news media decision makers towards Greenpeace.

The debate was given extensive media coverage. The head of newsgathering at the BBC suggested: 'It was our own fault, the media's fault. We never put enough distance between ourselves and the participants. I'm left feeling Greenpeace was pulling us by the nose . . . The provision of pictures and facilities and information, be it from Greenpeace or anyone else, is a Trojan horse for editorial and political spin. I'm going to be more careful who I let through the gate' (Richard Sambrook quoted in *The Financial Times*, 28 August 1995, *The Independent*, 28 August 1995 and *The Sunday Telegraph*, 27 August). Similarly, David Lloyd of Channel 4 News stated that:

> *'On the* Brent Spar *we were bounced. This matters – we all took great pains to represent Shell's side of the argument. By the time the broadcasters had tried to intervene on the scientific analysis, the story had been spun far, far into Greenpeace's direction . . . When we attempted to pull the story back, the pictures provided to us showed plucky helicopters riding a fusillade of water cannons. Try and write the analytical science into that to the advantage of the words'* (quoted in Rose, 1998, p158, and covered in newspapers as above).

The provenance of the 'pictures provided' became a particular cause for media introspection, prompted by government and business complaint. The *Brent Spar* coincided with debate about the use by television news broadcasters of video news releases (VNRs), short, professionally shot video press releases commissioned by businesses, public relations firms, NGOs and in some instances governments. Increasing time pressures in newsrooms and restricted budgets have seen these used in the preparation of television news programmes (often with a statement of source). In fact, Rose insists, Greenpeace makes very little use of VNRs; however, the fact that Greenpeace footage was used so widely by the news media reflected not only that NGOs now invest considerable resources in communications, but also that news cannot afford to report all stories on the basis of direct reportage and filming by their own staff. Greenpeace's output was sufficient, providing the basis of good picture-led stories, and the *Brent Spar* was not initially considered worthy of investing on-the-ground reporters and crews for any length of time. Rose (1998, p157) suggests that:

> '*Cost was a major factor in determining what got covered and what did not. To go on a Greenpeace ship, or to join the occupation of the* 'Spar *and be on the spot, meant that a news editor had to assign an expensive crew with no good idea of when they might be back, or whether anything 'newsworthy' would happen'.*

The bruised professional pride amongst media decision makers seems to have shaped the way any reference to the *Brent Spar* was covered in the following months. While the episode contributed to dramatic reappraisals of corporate social and environmental responsibility in the mid 1990s, one of the main strands of media reference was an introspective exploration of Greenpeace's unsteady science, and its emotional manipulation of the media. The reporting on the publication of the first Natural Environment Research Council report (NERC, 1996) on the decommissioning of oil installations a year after the *Brent Spar* indicated a high degree of 'over compensation'.

The NERC committee of scientific and engineering experts, set up at the request of Energy Minister Tim Eggar, was carefully evenhanded in its conclusions on the science, and did not take either a British government/Shell pro-dumping line, or support Greenpeace. It qualified some Greenpeace claims about the environmental impact of deep-sea disposal, but also stated that '[nothing] in this report should be taken as promoting the deep-sea disposal of decommissioned off-shore structures, or of any other wastes'. It argued that even if the final cost of onshore disposal is higher, 'when viewed against the many other aspects – social, ethical, legal and environmental – this may mean that the costs should be accepted' (NERC, 1996). One influential specialist environmental-policy journal targeted at business audiences gave the headline: 'NERC embarrasses DTI with report on *Brent Spar*', and went on to note how the report pointed to several major flaws in Department of Trade and Industry (DTI) and Shell decision making, and criticized the level of secrecy (ENDS, 1996). Yet some key news reporting, including the BBC *Six O'Clock News*, pitched the story as supporting Shell's case.

Rose charts the course of a further 18 months of reporting from this date where TV news and current affairs continued to summarize the *Brent Spar* by suggesting that '[the] "environmental campaigners" who played on European emotions against dumping in the Atlantic acknowledge now that they may have been wrong' (BBC *Newsnight*, 5 March 1997). In these cases creative media talent was being expended in an interrogation of Greenpeace and its campaign techniques and style. This is a legitimate and worthwhile story – the environmental movement itself was aware of some of the ambiguities raised by a case where legal processes are overturned by popular reaction, that was in some senses 'managed' by an NGO. However, the media should have given much greater attention to the bigger story that underlay this. The *Brent Spar* reflected, and further contributed to, a major development in the relationship between science, policy and the public.

EXPERT ASSESSMENTS, PUBLIC FEELINGS AND NEW FRAMINGS OF RISK

In the context of more recent debates about BSE and genetic modification (GM), it is possible to forget the importance of the *Brent Spar* in catalysing thinking among government and business about the limits of established forms of (technical) risk assessment and environmental decision making, and the proper representation of 'public feeling'.

A key tool in the British government armoury in this area – the process for assessing the best practicable environmental option (BPEO) – was shown to have serious limitations. Tony Rice, a deep-sea biologist who published a book on *Decommissioning the Brent Spar* (Rice and Owen, 1999) based on his professional involvement in the debate, gives considerable space to discussion of the misuse of the BPEO system: '[much] of this resulted simply from a failure to have relevant specialists check some of the basic scientific and technical information at a sufficiently early stage' (p149). His conclusions support those of the second NERC report (1998) that argued for less secrecy and more peer review of the BPEO, above all to identify issues requiring indepth attention in terms of feasibility. This was deemed particularly important where the environmental impacts of different options are small and difficult to distinguish between. Rice (1999, pp149–150) summarizes:

> 'The implication is that it would be pointless to agonize about small environmental impact differences when the differences in other BPEO criteria might be much more significant . . . Following on from this, although the report does not say so . . . it would be tragic if lives were lost in turning the Brent Spar into a quay extension simply to satisfy the principle of not causing any impact on an already less-than-pristine ocean.'

He found media representations of scientific issues around the *Brent Spar* wanting, and bemoaned the failure to recognize the relationship between scientific uncertainties, risk assessments and decisions. However, this does not result solely in the by now familiar demand for better 'public understanding of science' communicated by a pliant media. Rather, his final conclusion, echoing the first and second NERC reports, is that public acceptability may be, and perhaps should be, the most significant factor in making a decision. A comment by the chairman of the NERC Committee points to how this group of scientists may have understood the real significance of the *Brent Spar* better than government or much of the media:

> '*If people have an emotional response to pristine areas like Antarctica or the deep sea, and want them to remain unpolluted, it is not up to scientists to say this is irrational*' (John Shepherd, chairman of NERC report, 1996, quoted in Rose, 1998, p51).

The same conclusions have been arrived at by some key policy bodies, marking a dramatic break with the established tradition in British environmental policy making. Without referring to these events specifically, the *Seventh Report of the Advisory Committee on Business and Environment* (ACBE) argues that companies should: 'move away from the decide-announce-defend system towards one of genuine dialogue with "interested parties". This can allow companies and "interested parties" to understand each other's values better and reduces the likelihood of direct action by "interested parties".' The report goes on to recognize that, while NGOs might argue on the basis of scientific data, risk and cost assessment, 'they often have other values as well, which may include aesthetic, amenity and symbolic factors' (1997, p18).

More influential and thorough, the Royal Commission on Environmental Pollution's (RCEP) *Report on Environmental Standards* develops the theme:

> '*Environmental regulation has become more and more dependent on the advice of scientists. Governments justify their action or inaction by appealing to the authority of science. Yet the changed character of environmental concerns has highlighted the extent to which there are uncertainties in scientific assessments, and the scope for different perceptions of the issues involved.*'

These observations by scientists and policy experts support insights of social scientists that have explored 'lay' and expert values about environmental issues (see for example, *Environmental Values, Special Edition on Risk* (1999), and the websites of three UK social science groups who work in this area: the Environment and Society Research Group (ESRU), the Centre for the Study of Environmental Change (CSEC) and CSERGE). Apparently influenced by such work, the RCEP report was run through with a critique of the deficit model of knowledge and action, which suggests that people will act if they are given, and accept, information that they do not yet possess. Rather, the RCEP recognizes the range of values that are held in relation to the environment, and argues that:

> *'technical analysis and command and control regulation have either failed to deal satisfactorily with environmental problems, or, in suggesting solutions, have created conflict with other valued social objectives'.*

If one of the most respected UK establishment voices in environmental policy debate, whose membership has predominantly been made up of scientists, was talking in such terms, things had clearly come a long way.

The *Brent Spar* is as much a measure as a cause of these shifts in public attitudes, and in the relationship between science, the public and policy. However, the media failed to represent this shift in public attitudes and values, let alone to give adequate weight to something as tangible, for example, as the RCEP's published account of this new thinking. This is a serious criticism of the media's capacity to keep track of the deeper currents in society and politics. This failure is most clearly illustrated in this case by the inadequate account of the dramatic shifts in business thinking in the wake of the *Brent Spar*.

New Thinking on Corporate Responsibility

Mainstream business journalism initially struggled to understand the Shell climb down. Hugo Gordon, industry editor on *The Daily Telegraph* summarized the initial reaction:

> *'What now? Or perhaps, wherever next? There were many despairing questions facing industry following Shell's astonishing capitulation to Greenpeace and Europe's ecosentimentalists'* (24 June 1995).

The same paper, capturing a tone found more widely in business journalism, later suggested that the *Brent Spar* represented:

> '. . . *a defeat for rational decision making. An emotional camp-aign has forced the oil company into an expensive, hazardous course of action that appears to make less environmental sense than its original plan* . . . *It says much for the maturity of the Shell executives that despite the way Greenpeace bullied, manipulated and misrepresented Shell over [the]* Brent Spar, *they have opened the door to the bunny-huggers'* (7 August 1998).

Greenpeace was in no doubt about the answer to some of these questions: '[T]he real significance of the [*Brent*] *Spar* is all about corporate responsibility, not about oil or steel or the ocean' (Rose, 1998, p95).

Senior Shell figures arrived at conclusions similar to Rose's even before they announced the turnaround, when managing the crisis of continental European public boycotts of the company in mid 1995. One of the startling features of the events around the *Brent Spar* was that Shell had long been recognized as a leader in scenario planning, yet had utterly failed to anticipate European public reaction. Shell had gone through an extensive three-year process to identify the BPEO.

> '*But we found that what appeared to be the best option in the UK was not acceptable elsewhere. We were caught between two different approaches to the environment. The public reacted in a way that we did not expect and the pressure groups used the* [Brent] Spar *as a symbol in a way we did not anticipate*' (Cor HerkStröter, former chairman of Royal Dutch/Shell, quoted in Elkington, 1997, p146).

Shell concluded that two key factors were the communications revolution and the loss of trust in institutions:

> '*Today the world visible to any one person, anywhere on the planet, is becoming increasingly fragmented. The speed and immediacy of modern communications ensures that this process will continue. National governments, political parties, instit-utionalized religions, academic institutions will never regain the authority they used to have – that ability to exclusively define the world view of large segments of the population*' (Herkströter, quoted in Elkington, 1997, p146).

The company had been long respected for its careful nurturing of its trusted global brand. These events woke this complex and slow moving organization out of complacency, leading it to think hard about extending the meaning of a phrase such as 'license to operate': 'The fact that parts of Shell have been in business for 110 years is no guarantee that the future will be okay too' (quoted in Elkington, 1997, p143). In the face of the *Brent Spar* episode, and the devastating publicity surrounding Shell's complicity in human rights abuses in Ogoniland in Nigeria later that year (see Smith, 1998), Shell's first reaction was to work to convince the relevant publics that their practices were acceptable. Rose (1999) recounts a major communications effort by the company to gain media acceptance that its 'science was sound'. However, the scale of public reaction demanded considerably more if the company was to recover trust in its brand.

Among Shell's responses was the 'Society's Changing Expectations' initiative, whereby Shell staff were brought together with senior figures from business, NGOs, academia, and the media in 14 locations around the world, in an open debate of their business practice. Shell also invited environmental and human rights NGOs to take part in developing Shell's thinking about the course of developments in environmentally or socially sensitive projects in the South. Shell executives started to suggest that the increased scrutiny of NGOs might be viewed as 'a tool to strengthen performance' (Judge Institute, seminar discussion, 1997).

One of the most tangible outcomes of the events of 1995 was the decision to develop social and environmental reporting alongside the cycle of standard financial reporting (*Tomorrow*, Nov/Dec 1998). The results included publication of 'Profits and Principles', an annual review of Shell's progress across the 'Triple Bottom Line' (a concept derived from John Elkington and the consultancy SustainAbility, one of a number employed by Shell to aid the rethink). This attempt at an integrated review of the economic, social and environmental performance of a major company marks an astonishing development in corporate self-examination – all the more surprising for the fact that it has been undertaken by one of the largest, and historically most bureaucratic and secretive, of the global extractive industries.

Enthusiasts of new forms of environmental and social accounting within companies, and the wider policy community, see them as no less than the beginning of a new, and very different, sort of capitalism. Yet, business people feel the media's performance on this, compared with the lavish coverage of financial results, has been poor. Interviews conducted with public affairs professionals from major companies show disappointment at the failure (barring a few individual exceptions) of the media to appreciate the scale and significance of these novel and far-reaching activities (Gooch, 1999).

NEW THINKING ABOUT FUTURE CORE BUSINESS

The *Brent Spar* was not solely about corporate responsibility linked to near-term dumping issues. With a major oil company as its target, the campaign, and the linked 1997 Atlantic Frontier campaign against the development of new oil fields, slotted neatly into the wider environmentalist argument about shifting from a fossil-fuel-based to a renewables-based economy. Several chapters in this book have shown how the media has persistently found it difficult to report both the time scale, and extent, of climate change. Certainly this aspect of environmentalist campaigning against oil companies is, given its significance, underreported. Nevertheless, specialist environment journalists, and some of the businesses under scrutiny, lost no time in making the link. In an open letter to Greenpeace, the *New Scientist*'s long-standing environment journalist Fred Pearce wrote that:

> '... by largely ignoring the posturing of governments and targeting the companies, Greenpeace hastens the day when those companies will see the dollar benefits of changing tack. It hasn't worked with global warming yet but you have shown the way ... And anybody who believes that Shell's recent announcement of a US$500 million investment in photovoltaics is unconnected to the Brent Spar fracas is being very naive' (New Scientist, 15 November 1997).

Perhaps more telling is a speech made to a Scottish oil conference by Heinz Rothermund, managing director of Shell Exploration and Production. Referring to Greenpeace's Atlantic Frontier campaign, Rothermund said:

> 'It is important to recognize ... that the specific attack ... on oil and gas developments in the North Atlantic margin, accompanied by the usual exaggerated claims about last wilderness and environmental devastation, with emotional references to whales and endangered species, also raises a key question: "[To what extent] is it sensible to explore for and develop new hydrocarbon reserves, given that the atmosphere may not be able to cope with the greenhouse gases that will

> *emanate from the utilization of the hydrocarbon reserves discovered already?" Undoubtedly, there is a dilemma and I would now like to spend some time analysing it'* (Rothermund, 1997, quoted in Rose, 1998, p195).

Rose notes regretfully that he, in fact, failed to explore the question further, and also that Shell insisted the following day that he had been speaking 'rhetorically'. Nevertheless, such comments pointed to the fact that thinking had started not just on corporate reputation management, but also on what makes up core business, and – even more dramatically – the place of oil companies in a long-term view of the global political economy. In April 1998, in the context of extensive contact with environmentalists and the policy community, Shell pulled out of the Global Climate Coalition (GCC), the grouping of oil and car companies that were campaigning against action on climate change. While this decision lagged some way behind BP's departure from the GCC, this was another sign of an openness to new ways of responding to a changing political, social and environmental terrain.

The *Brent Spar*, and the ensuing Greenpeace Atlantic Frontier and pro-solar campaigns, played a role in opening up fossil-fuel industry debates about future core interests. The industry began to present itself as energy – rather than fossil-fuel – companies, and renewables became a more prominent part of their investments (and even more so, their communications).

CONCLUSION: GOVERNANCE, ENVIRONMENTALISM AND THE MEDIA

Shell's self-examination since the *Brent Spar* saga offers important pointers on how all big corporations might expect to work in coming decades. Innovations such as engaging NGOs and other interests in business decision-making processes, and developments in corporate social and environmental accounting, were catalysed and accelerated by the events around the *Brent Spar* platform. A range of commentators from business, academia, the media and NGOs view these as some of the most significant changes in the way business thinks and works in the last 50 years (see for example, *The Financial Times*, 17 March 1997; Elkington, 1996, 1997; McIntosh et al, 1998; Zadek, 1997).

Yet, with the exception of some individual reporters on various papers and programmes, the wider media failed to reflect the significance of these developments in its reporting. Business reporting remains fixed upon well-established near-term issues of share price and profitability. News reporting has immense difficulties handling long-term science and policy stories that contain high levels of uncertainty and are unsure of how to represent 'subjective' public voices. The changed conditions for decision making about environmental issues needs quality media coverage more urgently than ever before. The reason is contained within Rice's neat summary of the background to Shell's decision to see the *Brent Spar* turned into a jetty in Norway:

> *'The onshore fate of the* Brent Spar, *essentially brought about by public protest stimulated by Greenpeace, may well be the 'right' one. But when we take these decisions, individually or collectively, we should not kid ourselves . . . that they are based clearly and unequivocally on cold, dispassionate rationality. They certainly were not in the case of the* Brent Spar' *(Rice, 1999, p152).*

This observation could be true of a range of pressing local and global environmental issues, and it presents a significant challenge to the media. Robin Grove-White, in an afterward to an important volume of essays on risk (Grove-White, *Environmental Values*, 1999, p282) suggests that:

> *'[most] people have a shrewd (if imprecise) sense of the strengths and limitations of scientific knowledge, as employed by real institutions in real life. By contrast, what is increasingly dangerous is the evident lack of official appreciation of the connection between governments' frequently opportunistic use of scientific insight and reassurance in new and unfamiliar "environmental" controversies, and the continuing growth of public cynicism and mistrust towards political authority.'*

The RCEP *Environmental Standards* report (1997), the *Seventh Report of the ACBE* (1997) and Shell's *Profits and Principles* reports all suggest a dramatic reappraisal in *some* of the relevant quarters of the significance of public feelings – subjective opinions – values – instincts – in decision making.

Faced with strong public reaction against genetically modified (GM) products, business (outside the GM companies themselves) has shown itself to be more sensitive to the fact that the issues represented by environmentalism are not primarily issues about science but about values. A range of authors have accounted for these changes in public attitudes and behaviour. They point to the emergence of global environmental risks, widely felt in society. These are shaped and communicated by environmental NGOs working across scales, and mediated by a range of broadcast and print media. The evolving web of links between global environmental change, new social movements and developments in information technologies represents one of the bigger components of a dramatic reformulation of politics. The media both shapes and is shaped by these forces.

Certainly, media professionals are correct to insist that aggressive editorial independence, and rigorous balance in overall coverage, are necessary for them to play their proper part in this. These attributes will be essential in the working out of the practical significance of the fluid and negotiated concept of sustainable development.

But it will also be necessary to look up from mainstream political and economic reporting. The media must reconsider the relationship between 'expert' and 'lay' claims in decision making, and invest more financial and creative resources in reporting complex stories of long-term significance. This last point is perhaps the key. The best journalism is produced by: asking the right question with persistence; identifying the relevant detail; and illustrating or giving context to a 'wider truth' by means of a well-chosen story. Such talents, focused by the decisions of senior editorial decision makers, will allow publics, business, NGOs and governments to play their part in moving towards environmentally sustainable development.

References

ACBE (1997) *Seventh Progress report to, and response from the President of the Board of Trade and Secretary of State for the Environment*, March, DoE/DTI, London

CSEC: www.lancs.ac.uk/users/csec

CSERGE: www.uea.ac.uk/menu/acad_depts/env/all/resgroup/cserge

Davis and Watts (1998) *A commitment to Sustainable development: World Business Council for Sustainable Development launch of 'Exploring Sustainable Development' scenarios* – 13 March 1998, Shell International Ltd, London

Elkington, J (1997) *Cannibals with Forks*, Capstone, Oxford

Elkington, J and Trisoglio, A (1996) 'Developing realistic scenarios for the environment: Lessons from the *Brent Spar*', *Long Range Planning*, vol 29 no 6, pp762–769 December

Elkington, J, Münzing, T and Stibbard, H (1998) 'Shell in the Goldfish Bowl', *Tomorrow* Nov/Dec, pp56–58

ENDS (1995) *Misreading Public Perception*, no 245, p2

ENDS (1996) *NERC embarrassed DTI with report on Brent Spar*, no 256, pp4–6

Environmental Values (1999) *Special Edition on Risk*, vol 8, no 2

ESRU: www.ucl.ac.uk/esruwww

Gooch, F (1999) Interviews conducted with business people, in support of the Cambridge Media and Environment Programme

Greenpeace: www.greenpeace.org

Grove-White, R (1999) 'Afterword', in *Environmental Values, Special Edition on Risk*, vol 8, no 2, p282

NERC (1996) *Scientific group on decommissioning offshore structures: first report*, April, NERC, Swindon

NERC (1998) *Scientific group on decommissioning offshore structures: second report*, May, NERC, Swindon

Pearce, F (1996) 'Never mind the science, feel the emotion', *New Scientist*, vol 147, p48

RCEP (1998) *Setting Environmental Standards*, 25th Report, Cm 40553, HMSO, London

Rice, T, and Owen, P (1999) *Decommissioning the Brent Spar*, E&FN Spon, London

Rose, C (1998) *The Turning of the Spar*, Greenpeace, London

Shell: www.shell.com

Shell International (1998) *Profits and Principles: Does there have to be a choice? The Shell Report 1998*, Shell International Ltd, London

Smith, J (ed) (1998) *Managing Sustainability Dilemmas in the Developing World*, University of Cambridge, CIES, Cambridge

Zadek et al (1997) *Building Corporate Accountability*, Earthscan, London

PART IV

Making the Environment News

13 COMMUNICATING ABOUT CLIMATE CHANGE: AN NGO VIEW

Cherry Farrow

Hard news and science have never made for easy bedfellows in the daily news media, print or broadcast. The hard sciences of physics, chemistry or biology can too easily get in the way of a good story, and scientists are notoriously conservative and reluctant to engage with the news media, whom they distrust.

Broadcasters, journalists and newsdesks need headlines or soundbites. Imprecise science is no use to them. Once a scientific story has broken they want clear-cut answers. And most news editors, commissioning editors or TV controllers come from an arts background and culture.

Genetically modified organisms (GMOs), climate change and biodiversity have all fallen into the 'problem reporting' category. The complexities and contradictions of media messages, science and politics were highlighted recently by the public and high-profile debate surrounding the potential release of GMOs upon environment, wildlife and humans.

Although media coverage has increased in importance for environmental groups, it can also (as was the case of GMOs) move faster than policy is developed. But that coverage is vital. It is needed to put pressure on politicians and decision makers; it raises the profile of the organization and – hopefully – raises awareness among the public of environmental issues. How to frame the messages, how to relate the issues to readers, viewers and public is an increasing dilemma for the communications specialists within the non-governmental organizations (NGOs) and pressure groups, who are facing increasing pressure from within their own organizations to be out in the lead on an issue.

But to retain credibility, particularly in a society where government and industry scientists are increasingly distrusted, the science and the policy have to be sound. Long drawn-out scientific experiments that have to be tested and peer reviewed do not fit easily with breaking news. Modelling climate change or the accompanying political processes of the international treaty negotiations, with their own lengthy political and legal processes, has meant that environmentalists and environmental journalists have often spent years trying to break these stories without luck. Alex Kirby, long-time environment correspondent at the BBC and presenter of *Costing the Earth*, says:

> '*I think there was a generalized bias against science in the media – it's the hardest thing to get on. It's the person on the day on the desk who will decide what goes on and what goes out –* whatever the editor of the* Six *or* Nine O'Clock News *says.'*

As membership organizations, the environmental NGOs need to bring their members with them. In the early days, the term global warming, like the destruction of the ozone layer, tended to make the public believe that the subject was simply too big to deal with at a local level. This feeling was reinforced as the politicians and world leaders travelled the globe to negotiate the climate change treaty conventions. Public perception was that this was something that could only be dealt with at the global level.

Opinion polls on public attitudes towards climate change, carried out by the World Wide Fund For Nature (WWF) in Washington and the UK (1996 and 1997) revealed that the public thought that action should be taken by governments and industry to control emissions. Yet, more than 25 per cent of carbon emissions come from the household sector. Buying energy-efficient white goods or central heating boilers was not received favourably until the 'message' was broadened out to show that families could cut their electricity and heating bills by buying more efficient household goods. Women were more receptive to the environmental message, but for them it was strongly (and wrongly) linked to health fears – skin cancer, for example. Overall, climate change was (and often still is) confused with the ozone layer, hence the association with skin cancer.

If it was hard to engage the public in climate change and biodiversity, it was harder to try to get coverage in the tabloid press and TV media. We all had to learn how to relate the issues to the public. Previous press and campaigning work within the NGOs had been more black and white: issues such as animal welfare, deforestation, ivory poaching or whaling. Species- and habitats-related issues had been key to WWF's communications work – direct threats of habitat destruction, poaching and hunting. Climate change was something more insidious and the science was imprecise. But as it moved into the political and environmental agenda it became increasingly obvious to the environmental NGOs that communications officers had to take it on board.

There has also been a long history of distrust of the media within the NGOs. Policy officers are always looking for access to government departments and policy makers, and are anxious that a wrong headline or quote could misrepresent their case and result in closed doors. There has been – and still is – an inability to see that the specialist journalists are on the same side and are looking to the NGOs to say the kinds of things that they can't.

The role of the NGO as information broker to the journalists is crucial, not only in terms of explaining the science, but the politics too. Explaining the impacts of climate modelling or the processes surrounding the signing of an international convention is vital to how an NGO is perceived. Credibility is paramount. And opinion polls have shown that the public trust the NGO scientists far more than industry or government scientists.

Adam Markham, head of WWF's international climate change campaign remembers the Sundsvaal meeting in Sweden as being a landmark:

> 'All the UK press came to that. We were a major source of information at that meeting. We could tell the press what the delegations were saying and we proved our usefulness to the UK journalists and helping them get an angle on the story.'

WWF's credibility lay in being a wildlife organization and for the first year of its climate campaign the organization focused on the threats to wildlife and species: the Arctic caribou and bears, migratory birds – together with the Royal Society for the Protection of Birds (RSPB) – and coral reefs. By now the international negotiations process had started and the two were campaigned on together. When WWF launched its climate change campaign it deliberately headquartered it in Washington DC – directed at the US administration – since the US was the biggest polluter and most reluctant to cut back on its greenhouse gas emissions.

But in the US, environment is not a prime beat. Environmental journalists do not stay around long. This, and other factors, made it even harder to develop communications strategies. Adam Markham says:

> 'I can't tell you where the environmental journalists that were on The Boston Globe or The LA Times are now; they've all changed, whereas [UK journalists such as] Charles Clover or Paul Brown, they're still there. . .

> *. . . We did things first and wondered about the audience
> second . . . The objective for me was to show that climate
> change was a problem for our conservation movement. The
> communications strategy was fitted into the international process
> – at that time national governments weren't doing anything.
> Now we're aiming it at the national governments – what they
> are and are not doing.'*

If it was hard for the environmentalist organizations' communications
officers to find their way, it had been harder for many of the specialist
press. Alex Kirby of the BBC remembers Mrs Thatcher going down to
Berkshire to open the Hadley Centre: 'They gave me a leg man. I
remember thinking it must be important . . . She really put it [climate
change] on the map.'

Adam Markham remembers having dinner in the UK with Charles
Clover (*The Daily Telegraph*) and Chris Rose (formerly WWF and
Greenpeace) the night of her speech. 'It was a watershed event and
because of that, environment journalists were taken more seriously
. . . [in the UK]'. Kirby agrees:

> *'Those were heady days – it was virgin territory – in a sense
> you could do anything. But the news editors took a lot of
> persuading. It was a hard story to sell. They were all arts
> graduates and science was foreign to them. Until Rio this was
> cutting edge stuff, but when Major came in he was about
> surviving and so environment went off the boil.'*

Kirby remembers a senior UK government adviser, Sir Crispin Tickell,
saying at that time that one of the problems of communicating climate
change was that editors were arts graduates. He also remembers
offering up a climate change story and his editor of the day saying:
'I'm not going to run that – I'm an arts graduate.'

> *'There is no doubt the jury is in now, but the media have changed.
> Now we are writing for our peers and news editors, for
> management. They're the audience. Whereas the public used to
> come back frequently saying we want more on the environment
> – listeners mainly – they would have liked more on the
> environment'.*

And the science was also a lot shakier then. In the UK the environmental press had been covering the climate change beat longer than
many of the NGO press officers. They knew as much about their

subjects as we did – and were constantly looking for new things to say – new impacts to feature, new science to emerge. The pressure was on the NGO scientists, conservationists and communicators to produce it.

One of those in at the beginning of the climate change debate, and coauthor of Chapter 6 in this book, was *The Guardian's* Paul Brown. Brown went to the Antarctic in 1988–1989, the same time that Mrs Thatcher addressed the Royal Society.

> *'There had been stuff about global warming. The NASA scientist Hansen had given evidence to the senate the same year of the US drought in the wheat belt. Hansen was head of science in NASA and said this was the kind of thing we can expect with global warming. That is what put it on the political stage.'*

Environment was to move slap into centre stage for a while. The Greens had done well in the UK European parliament elections and many of these Green voters were dissatisfied Conservatives. Hence, Thatcher was persuaded that the environment was a political issue. She delivered the same speech to the UN that she had made at the Royal Society. It was this speech (along with King Hussein's impassioned plea for his country) that put climate change truly onto the political agenda. Paul Brown remembers:

> *'After that you couldn't get environment off the front page. Almost everything was carried because it was new: drought, disease, gales, the ozone layer – they were all completely new. People like weather stories – and this was the weather story to end all weather stories . . . Then we had Hadley and the computer – and we were approaching the Earth Summit, so for two or three years, climate was the big story.'*

The Earth Summit in Rio in 1992 was the environmental jamboree to end all jamborees. All the presidents from Bush to Castro in the same room! Mrs Thatcher announced she would be going. As she was still a world leader it was an announcement that people took note of. If she was going they were all going. For the first time the NGOs were linking the different issues. Until then, they had been saying it was too wide, too difficult, too amorphous for them to handle. It was easier to talk about protecting the tiger or cleaning up water pollution. It had taken time for them to realize that they couldn't look at one without looking at the others.

But according to Paul Brown, climate was beginning to go off the agenda even before the Earth Summit. At home the recession was starting. Interest in the climate change story died the day after Rio ended.

> *'My stories went from page 1 to page 3 to page 7 . . . and there was nothing to report. There was no new science – all that had had to be done before Rio, and we were waiting for years for ratification. Then Mt Pinatubo exploded and that brought the Earth's temperature down – there was a worldwide recession'.*

Brown believes, however, that the public's understanding of climate change leapt forward.

> *'In ten years the subject had gone from the scientific uncertainty to political initiative to a subject of everyday conversation. So the public had gone from knowing nothing to knowing a huge amount. The public understands climate change remarkably well – arguably better than many politicians'.*

The story was aided, of course, by the four-year drought. There had also been big Easter floods. Climate change itself was not the story. It was a case of identifying aspects of global warming within stories that emerged from the woodwork – quite literally, in some cases: in the UK there were termites in the South East and malarial mosquitoes in Epping Forest and, on a global scale, there was El Niño. Although to the newsdesks these were weather stories or termite stories, they were, of course, climate change stories and the correspondents and environmental organizations saw that and were able to fit climate comment accordingly.

Increasing globalization, economic pressures and scientific knowledge brought home to the NGOs that pressing the same environmental message to the same hard core of environmental journalists was simply no longer enough. They had been reporting the issues and the arguments for years, but the climate story was not moving and changing sufficiently. However, the new government came in with a new green agenda. The Labour Party manifesto for the 1997 election stated: 'We will put concern for the environment at the heart of policy making'. One of the New Labour government's first moves was to create a new Department of the Environment, Transport and the Regions. There was a sense among the NGOs of new opportunities. Certainly, there was a need to target those journalists who would be following Tony Blair to the G8 Summit in Denver and on to the special session at the UN known as Earth Summit II in New York.

Anticipating that New Labour's commitment to tough new cuts in greenhouse gases would inevitably engage sectoral correspondents from transport, energy and industry – who would 'need to know' about climate change and its implications for the economic and business arena – the NGOs set about producing a whole different series of scenarios and findings. These ranged from the economics of developing new, renewable technologies, to the employment opportunities that would go with that.

The politicians, apart from those in the US, were ahead of the game in committing to emissions reductions. NGO members and public became more aware they wanted solutions. They were fed up with the 'doom scenarios'. From within, policies became less 'utopian', less confrontational, and more pragmatic. NGOs would still fight to protect the environment, but they would now to do so within the framework of economic growth. The new buzz word was to become *partnerships* – working from within to change industry's attitudes. There was an economic argument (and a market) to be exploited in exploring green electricity, renewables and, in WWF's case, the potential for introducing an environmental certification scheme for 'green' electricity.

This followed a very successful partnership that WWF had already undertaken in launching a forestry labelling scheme with some of the large do-it-yourself and home improvement companies, in which wood products and wooden shelves, windows and door frames could be reliably traced back to properly managed forests. WWF aimed to do the same with certifying 'green' electricity, once deregulation of the electricity market came about.

This opened up new opportunities for media coverage: consumer and lifestyle pages, business pages, city pages and the utilities correspondents. *The Financial Times* and the city pages of *The Guardian*, in particular, were open to the economics and possibilities of new technologies, and it was a way for the environmental lobby to counter the arguments (and the advertising accounts) of the lobby against action on climate change.

In the US this lobby had been able to wield great influence. Broadcasters are always helped by confrontation and, unfortunately, before 1991, climate change had been overstated by some of the climate scientists and the NGOs. The anti-climate change lobby – the climate sceptics – spent time and money challenging climate science. Many were scientists themselves who were working as consultants for the coal and oil industry interest groups. Former US Under Secretary of

State Tim Wirth referred to their motives as 'bent on belittling, attacking and obfuscating climate change science'. But it is only now that they are beginning to be seen as eccentric and the scientists are having the courage to come out again. So, for a time – an important time in the climate negotiations – more than 2000 scientists had a smaller voice than the 15 paid for by the oil lobby!

As the scientific evidence became firmer, and it was finally agreed that there was 'a discernible human influence' on climate change, it became necessary to meet the global climate coalition on its own ground. The NGOs started lobbying industry who, being first in the field with the new technologies, could create employment and overseas export opportunities.

There has also been the change on the part of industry from being originally resistant – viewing the issue as a threat – to being proactive and seizing opportunity. British Petroleum and Shell announced sharp increases in investment in renewables. This has changed the political atmosphere and transformed the standard of the business debate.

All of this has meant targeting different journalists – who until now had not been writing on these issues. Within the NGOs the communications officers being hired were no longer from the inside but from the corporate outside, where they could bring journalistic credentials and contacts, and the ability to tune in to public and political opinion and tailor messages accordingly. 'Spin' had arrived within the press offices of the NGOs.

But it is still hard. Going as part of an environmental lobby to the BBC ahead of the 1997 election, and asking the election team how they intended to cover the environment in the run up to the election, we were told that the environment was not an issue. Health and education and economics, yes – environment, no. The links between European Union Common Agricultural Policy (CAP) reform, Common Fisheries Policy reform and the environment were deemed too remote and lay eleventh in the election unit's priorities.

Although the links between environment and sectoral issues are now clearer to some correspondents, why certain organizations are working on them is not. At the time of the Berlin Summit on CAP reform, three of BBC's mainstream news programmes could not see why the RSPB was commenting on the issue. Explaining that the RSPB's interest was about demonstrating linkage between the impacts of intensive agricultural practices (dowsing the countryside with pesticides and fertilizers, digging up thousands of miles of hedgerows and ploughing up woodland) and the massive reductions in farmland bird numbers, the RSPB clarified its involvement in agriculture.

WWF too has similar problems with association. Despite its name change – from World Wildlife Fund to World Wide Fund For Nature – the panda logo can still stretch journalists' and editors' credibility when it comes to endocrine disrupters in animals and chemicals found in breast milk.

The environment and science do not remain static, and the public and consumers have now become more involved in issues surrounding their health and their quality of life. This should help those environmental organizations attempting to make the links to the bigger picture. But we still have to contend with the editors. As Alex Kirby says, 'we're all spinning now. And with the proliferation of outlets whether it's new or not is not important. The media itself has changed.'

References

Kirby, A (1999) interview with author
Markham, A (1999) interview with author
Brown, P (1999) interview with author

14 Media Coverage of Sustainable Development and Local Agenda 21[1]

Heather Voisey and Chris Church

Agenda 21, the document agreed at the 1992 Earth Summit as the blueprint for implementing the concept of sustainable development, saw communication and awareness-raising as vital to that process of implementation. Despite seven years of innovative work since, media coverage of sustainable development initiatives in the UK (and elsewhere) is still minimal, confused and fails to recognize the aims of such work. Environmental topics continue to get good press coverage, but media reporting of sustainable development issues is sporadic, even almost non-existent. This poses special problems for those working on issues relating to Local Agenda 21 (LA21) and sustainable development in terms of accessing resources and support, and innovation beyond the environment sector. This chapter summarizes exploratory research over a two-month period at the end of 1998 looking at why this is, with particular reference to LA21.[2] The chapter begins with a general discussion of problems associated with coverage of sustainable development by the media, then looks specifically at LA21, followed by a discussion and some recommendations on how the situation could be improved.

The Problems of Getting Media Coverage of Sustainable Development and LA21

It is fair to say that presenting sustainable development to the media (and indeed to the public through the media) poses a range of particular problems: we have identified five. Firstly, sustainable development is a new idea, new jargon that needs to be explained. The fact that there is no one definition of this concept hardly helps overcome the barriers to understanding and adopting it. LA21 and sustainable development are complex issues that are difficult to cover briefly or embed in people's memory. Using them in a story each time requires them to be reexplained to the audience; this is particularly so for LA21 which is not in the least self-explanatory. In the media LA21 is referred to, and often explained with reference to, the future and our children, or by reference to the Brundtland definition (WCED, 1987). However, it is just as often not used in the story, or the local name for it is used, disconnecting it from any countrywide activity or global initiative. This is a particular problem for regional newspapers, radio or TV that cover many areas, each with their own name for their LA21.

Secondly, sustainable development came onto the agenda through the 1992 Earth Summit. As such it is seen mainly as an environmental issue, and almost all national news stories in the field originate at the environment desk. The broadsheets and national broadcast media influence not only the public but also journalists in other sectors. As a result, the stories environmental correspondents cover and where they come from is important. Most journalists we interviewed recognized that sustainable development is a broader issue than the environment, but this rarely surfaces. Despite a commitment to sustainable development, the main NGOs get their coverage off single issues – such as traffic or climate change. Few have time to spend on developing stories that sell the broader message of sustainability. Journalists, therefore, do not get a strong sustainable development message from their key contacts. Sustainable development activists are frequently very aware of links with broader social issues, but still focus their media approach on environmental ideas, partly because they perceive the difficulty of getting media coverage for the broader issues. This is negative reinforcement: if it is not news, then it does not get coverage, and if it is not being covered, then clearly it is not news. In addition, many of the more innovative sustainable development stories relate to intersectoral work (such as environment and poverty); these can get lost between specialist journalists, and for many there is still a conviction that sustainable development equals environment and therefore environmental correspondents should be covering it.

Thirdly, the multisectoral process-focused approach that is inherent in sustainability cuts across many traditional approaches to environmental reporting. As one journalist put it, he does not want to 'write for the spike'. Stories on sustainable development have to compete for space with others that may be more topical, with easier messages and less initial explanatory blurb, that report controversy, crisis, significant action or changing circumstances. Adversarial stories make for good coverage: sustainable development stories, where everyone claims to be on the same side, are harder to cover. This may lead journalists to look for conflict and discord rather than the first small steps towards cooperative working. The most common comment from journalists about LA21 activity is: 'It's all very worthy . . . but . . .'. This comment stems not only from the lack of a 'bad guy', but also from the fact that the global nature of LA21 is often ignored – the fourth problem. It can be hard to convince local editors or journalists that this new local initiative has global significance. This is possibly because global level action, particularly relating to the UN, is only reported if it is about wars and more recently humanitarian crisis. Yet, it is the 'global to local' aspect of the process that is among its innovative aspects and this needs better exposure.

Lastly, almost every cause has one organization for which it is the major issue – not so with sustainable development. This not to criticize or ignore the work being done by many organizations on aspects of sustainability; but there is no one organization that is actively promoting and advocating to the media sustainable development as an idea and a way of working. Whether such an agency is desirable must be debated; but at present, given the way in which the media responds to such inputs, there is a gap.

Specific Issues for Media Coverage of LA21

LA21 is a long-term process that needs to communicate a large amount of information to different audiences not just once, but many times over a long period. It should also, ideally, set up feedback mechanisms to enable local people to input their ideas and needs into the process, and to develop and evaluate the success of initiatives. Therefore, successful practice is not just about individual stories, but consistent media coverage of LA21. However, most current practice is ad hoc, with some good examples of individual stories and regular pages on LA21 in local newspapers. This leaves an identifiable gap: newspapers, TV and radio want more 'good' stories; at the same time, LA21 practitioners want more media coverage. This section will look at some of the reasons why this gap has not been bridged.

LA21 initiatives currently are heavily about process, with few concrete outputs. It is difficult to get the media interested in meetings, launches and the publication of documents unless there is an imaginative spin put to the material – such as Tony Blair launching a new publication for Durham County Council. An LA21 initiative does not produce regular action; there are long periods when there is not much to announce. As a result, LA21 is not seen as being generally newsworthy – instead, it is perceived as feature worthy, summarizing old news, or a long process.[3]

There are also issues with regard to the quality of material available. Many journalists feel that LA21 practitioners do not provide them with good imaginative stories, with ideas for action, pictures, local facts and figures, real people to focus stories on – or in the case of LA21 coordinators, contacts to community groups with initiatives to report. This means that potential stories – for example, putting the local angle on a national or international story – are opportunities often missed. Research strongly suggests that stories need to be linked to action: an event, an award (national/international recognition for local people). For television and newspapers there needs to be a good picture opportunity – not just local dignitaries smiling in front of a building, although the exception is national figures and celebrities – visual stimulus that attracts the reader or viewer to the story. Another good component is linking an article to action the audience can take, such as competitions, tips and offers. It is also important to have a 'people angle', to make the message or point of the article more real to the audience – for example, 'the Smith family tried switching to organic food; Mrs Jones cycled to work for a month; and their experience of the change was . . .'. Alternatively stories can form part of a larger or long-running awareness-raising campaign, which is discussed below.

Local authorities are where most LA21 activity is based, and they are therefore the largest potential source of stories. However, this can be problematic. Local authorities have been the targets of a number of NGO campaigns on environmental issues rather than being portrayed as defenders of the environment. In addition to this negative publicity, local authority environmental staff are less trained or briefed on the issues than are other potential sources such as NGO represent-atives; they are less likely to have a story that links to topical national news, and they often lack access to up-to-date research and information on key issues. The mish-mash of material that sustainability practitioners receive through various channels seems to be inadequate in key areas. To change the perception of local authorities as a questionable source of stories on sustainable development will need a long-term targeted initiative, based on real, solid, sellable stories, and the development of a strong working relationship between the media, NGOs and local authorities at national and local levels. But this is not so easy in practice.

The media, particularly at the local level, does not want to be seen as the mouthpiece of government, but rather as the champion of its audience, on the side of communities. Therefore, it wants the freedom to have critical as well as congratulatory stories. This can make developing a working relationship between journalists and local government very difficult.

In turn, local authorities have to be cautious in their approach to the media. Restrictions on their political activities mean that they cannot produce the kind of press releases that NGOs do, and in a competition for space, they may well lose out. Stories often have to be approved by senior officers which takes time and makes it difficult to be responsive to local media requests for material. LA21 officers often do not have the skills or experience to write press releases that will interest the local media. They need support from a good press office, but there are reports of press offices rationing stories that go to the local press, with LA21 competing with 'real local authority work', such as economic development and regeneration. In addition, some authorities, fearing negative publicity, want to put their own houses in order before pursuing an active strategy of promoting LA21 in the local media. This can take time, during which LA21 has a very low local profile outside limited circles, and the local authority is not providing momentum that community-based initiatives with success stories can tag on to.

LA21 is still seen as a local government initiative and often community-based work in this field is perceived as very marginal (and considerably less relevant than community-based protest). This is exacerbated since many community-based organizations have even less resources to get stories into the media than local authorities. Nevertheless, many local authorities are keen to promote good practice by themselves and the wider community, and do so. But a lack of clear criteria for such good practice may mean that local authorities are not clear on what to promote, and some cases may be seen as being selected to fit the PR officer's brief rather than being genuinely good examples of sustainable development.

We found the common experience of LA21 officers and other practitioners is one of frustration at not being able to get stories into the media. Many practitioners find it difficult to find the time to write press releases, let alone set up picture opportunities or arrange for their own photographers. Getting media coverage for stories is seen as important; but other methods of providing information direct to people are given more resources (newsletters, plans and strategies and leaflets), although these are not the most effective and accessible way of reaching a wide audience. One of the criticisms of LA21 is that it attracts only the 'usual suspects', people who are already interested in local issues or the environment. Widening out LA21 to more, and different, people through the media should be a priority for many local authorities seeking to develop inclusive strategies.

Most success, in terms of getting a story in print or on air, was achieved when a working relationship between local journalists and LA21 practitioners had developed over time, and where both sides were seen as reliable; however, as indicated above, this not easy to achieve. We were unable to identify any example of a long-running successful partnership between the local media and LA21 practitioners, although some were emerging. More research may be required on this, especially on the value of a topic-based approach, such as local food production. One potential example is the Turning the Tide (TTT) initiative that began in Leicester in 1996 and went regional in 1998 with the addition of Nottingham and Derby. This initiative is a public awareness-raising campaign on environmental issues, primarily aimed at consumers, encouraging them to think about their consumption activities (see TTT, 1998). The core of this approach is a partnership, coordinated by the environmental charity ENVIRON, between local authorities and other public service providers, privatized utilities, local businesses, local newspapers and regional BBC radio and television. TTT is a purely environmental campaign, but elements of it could be used for local sustainability.

Our research suggests that developing a strategic approach to communicating the issues of sustainable development is needed, while retaining local flexibility. It is this local flexibility within a broader partnership that appears to be a key to TTT's success. The local media knows its local audience and local issues; as a result, it is able to tailor issues in a way that makes it interesting to the local audience. Some of these elements could be taken forward at a national level – such as themed months of media activity. However, any nationally coordinated approach that tries to restrain this flexibility is unlikely to be successful, since it will not have maximum appeal to local people and will not have as much support from local and regional newspapers, radio and TV stations. A number of interviewees also pointed out that even a well-resourced national campaign needs to put in place the right mechanisms at local level first so that people can have a local contact point, a way of becoming involved.

Why do We Want Better Coverage of Sustainable Development and LA21 in Particular?

We have identified three objectives that are met by media coverage of sustainability activities and LA21.

1 Signal achievements to international, national and local audiences; Publicize existing LA21 activity; tell people what has been done to obtain recognition of efforts (and to justify the resources used).
2 Mobilize support and resources for existing and new LA21 work by raising the profile of initiatives to councillors, chief executives, government departments, NGOs, funders, etc.
3 Involve people in the future of their locality and the world through education, and action, to produce a long-term and measurable response to sustainability concerns.

Currently, communication of LA21 is inconsistently attempting to do all three. Different objectives require different methods, and possibly a package of methods to maximize chances of achieving all of these objectives. This leads to the question: should we be trying to meet all of these objectives in a media campaign at different levels – the first two for the national level, all three for the local level? Different objectives also require using different media. Newspapers, television and radio have different styles, audiences and requirements in terms of stories, which alters whether they are national or local. For example, elderly people on limited incomes tend to listen to local radio to get information, while students who will only be in a place for three years do not tend to read local newspapers. Any attempt to increase and improve media coverage of sustainable development and LA21, in particular, has to think about what it wants to achieve, who it wants to achieve it with, and what types of media could be used.

Is LA21 the Right Banner on Which to Hang a Story?

One central issue for work in this field is whether it should be communicated under the LA21 badge. Experience shows that four words that are unlikely to get coverage, if they appear in the first paragraph of a press release, are: sustainable, local, development and agenda. LA21 is not a title that explains what it is; and LA21s across the country have different names. Many journalists and LA21 practitioners feel that it is the message and the issues that were important, not the name, which can ghettoize it and turn people away. If we want to meet the third objective listed above, then 'badging' activity as LA21 is not necessary, and effort is being wasted trying to embed LA21 in the public memory and imagination. However, if the aim is to make UK efforts observable on the world stage, then the LA21 banner should be used. In addition, if the aim is to justify the resources spent on responding to LA21 in the UK, particularly to local authority councillors and senior officers, government ministers and departments, then a LA21 badge is also important. Certainly, it is this latter motivation that seems to have prompted the discussion of a national media campaign at the 1998 conference of local authority environmental coordinators.

CONCLUSIONS AND RECOMMENDATIONS FOR ACTION

A promotional focus for sustainable development is urgently needed if this work is to develop. A campaign for sustainable development and a campaign to promote LA21 will both add value if done well, but would be quite different in focus in their approach to the national and local levels, and to various audiences. However, to be successful both campaigns would need to have clear links and objectives that were thought out and stated. Overall, there is a need to recognize the diversity in and between national, regional and local initiatives and to build on that diversity, while seeking a common framework and some common key ideas and language. This would be aided by a detailed promotional and marketing strategy that would do for sustainable development what campaigns such as TTT have done for environmental concerns.

Importantly, there needs to be more horizontal and vertical integration. Vertical integration would enable a better linking both of national and local stories – for example, fitting local and national stories around the DETR's 'Are you doing your bit?' campaign and therefore accessing its resources and established media interest. This would make the most of its momentum rather than duplicating effort and resources. A national campaign could also round up good local examples of action, giving them a wider audience as examples of innovation and achievements.[4] For these purposes, LA21 badging would be needed, showing concerted effort around a local, national and international agenda. A focus on horizontal integration would develop media coverage for cross-sectoral issues, such as environment and health and the more 'difficult' aspects of LA21, such as poverty and consumption issues. This should be aimed not only at policy makers and professionals in other fields, but also generate interest in local initiatives. It appears that there is a need for an agency or organization to facilitate this vertical and horizontal integration. This body could provide briefings, support training, develop networks of organizations working on similar issues, and develop longer features and briefings. This agency could also coordinate a partnership between the media at national and regional levels, the DETR and other government departments and agencies, the local government association, NGOs, and other interests who work on sustainability issues.

Turning to the specific issue of LA21, initiatives need to put in place a more consistent communications strategy, so that even if a local authority or community organization is not doing anything newsworthy now, it can start developing working relationships with the local media for the future. Such a strategy should: put in place aims and objectives; keep the messages simple but present them in a stimulating way; assess the various local audiences to be reached and suitable media; and fit in with any national-level campaigns. It is clear that a strategic approach should focus on greater interaction between sustainability practitioners and local journalists, aided by training, in order to produce stories that both parties want. A strategic approach, as in the case of TTT, should develop working relationships that are important for pooling knowledge, skills and resources, offering a relatively low-cost way of reaching a lot of people who utilize existing communication mechanisms. This partnership approach can also acknowledge LA21 work by local authorities, while emphasizing the role of the council within the community, perhaps brokering stories between local community groups and the local media. However, it is also important that local authorities, as a key focus of LA21 activity, work on reducing the barriers facing their officers in producing better stories and developing relationships with the media. Crucial to this is seeing LA21 as an opportunity to be proactive rather than defensive in its relationships with the media, community groups and local citizens.

Sustainable development has, since 1992, been recognized by many as a powerful new approach to change. While practitioners have different viewpoints and approaches, the broad commonality of an integrated approach, multisectoral working, and a commitment to public involvement and social justice in that change all provide an operational framework in which much can and is being done. However, there has been little recognition of the value of this approach for the reasons outlined above, and so it may fail to reach its potential. There is a need, expressed by almost all of those who have bought into the approach, to do more to promote these new ideas. Such promotion needs a more strategic approach than anything that has happened so far. If those responsible for sustainable-development work within the UK wish to see the efforts of their colleagues pay off, they need to commit to a development and publicity programme that will show decision makers in every sector why this is important to their work. They need to show professionals in every sector both the challenges and the opportunities of working on sustainable development, and reveal to the public that this is not just a buzz word – but rather an opportunity for action.

REFERENCES

Turning the Tide (1998) *Persuading People that their Actions Count: a partnership approach. A review of Turning the Tide*, ENVIRON, Leicester

Voisey, H and Church, C (1999) *Media Coverage of Sustainable Development and Local Agenda 21*, CSERGE Working Paper, CSERGE University of East Anglia, Norwich

World Commission on Environment and Development (1987) *Our Common Future – the Brundtland Report*, Oxford University Press, Oxford

NOTES

1 The authors would like to thank the Local Government Management Board, the National Grid, Going for Green and the Local Government Association for supporting this research. We would also like to thank everyone and every organization who helped us in the preparation of the research and the report arising out of it.

2 The research involved a content analysis of stories in five national and a number of local newspapers on sustainable development, interviews at local and national levels with selected journalists and editors, central and local government officers, and practitioners in NGOs and other organizations. For the full report, see Voisey and Church (1999).

3 However, this does depend on the definition of newsworthy and any personal interest by editors and journalists: one local newspaper editor felt that 'LA21 is newsworthy because it seeks to involve people in communities'.

4 It is important to note that publicizing local initiatives that have been lauded as examples of good practice widely could generate interest that often cannot be satisfied due to resource constraints within the local institutions. This form of promotion would need to be thought through and backed up at a national level.

15 COMMUNICATING COMPLEXITY AND UNCERTAINTY: A CHALLENGE FOR THE MEDIA

David Gee

INTRODUCTION

As the focus of environmental policy shifts from 'end-of-pipe', point source pollution problems to sustainable production and consumption, information becomes more important in raising awareness and contributing to behaviour change. Information provision becomes a key policy tool as environmental policies 'shift from directing the actions of the few, via regulations, to encouraging the behaviour of the many, via incentives and information provision' (European Environment Agency (EEA), 1999). The media, as an important source of this information, has a key role in responding to two specific challenges: communicating scientific complexity to policy makers and the public, and giving full and careful expression to scientific uncertainty. This chapter briefly describes some of the difficulties for European policy communities and journalists arising from scientific complexity and uncertainty within the current context for environmental debates. This context is characterized by the following features:

- the European public's deep mistrust of governments, companies and experts who make claims about environmental issues;
- the simplistic descriptions of complex risk controversies as issues of 'science versus emotions', with the media often being blamed for encouraging the emotional part;
- the paradox of the environment becoming an increasingly important issue as its news value declines;
- the market place becoming an important source of research funds, with increasing pressures on scientists to become 'famous and funded' and the consequential difficulties of evaluating 'early warnings' of environmental hazards;

- the 'double trouble' from long-term and chronic, as opposed to short-term and catastrophic hazards, which arises from the absence of early evidence of harm, followed by serious and irreversible impacts;
- the 'profligacy' and 'precautionary' approaches to scientific uncertainty and the unequal distribution of costs and benefits arising from being right or wrong with risk assessments;
- the difference between sound science and good public policy making when evaluating controversial risks.

THE ENVIRONMENTAL CONTEXT AND THE ROLE OF INFORMATION

The Carnoules Statement of 1994 quantified the magnitude of the eco-efficiency target required to keep eight to ten billion people within the limits of the Earth's carrying capacity:

> '[In] industrialized countries, the current resource productivity must be increased by an average of a factor of ten during the next 30 to 50 years. This is technically feasible if we mobilize our know-how to generate new products, services, as well as new methods of manufacturing' (Factor 10 Club, 1994).

This perception of the world may have been accepted by a few people and companies, but most politicians, industries and citizens remain oblivious to this challenge, and to the opportunities it brings for innovation, enhanced competitiveness and a better quality of life.

Achieving the eco-efficiency revolution, while remaining within the carrying capacities of the Earth, will require the communication of information about the 'why' and 'how' of sustainable development, involving the integration of complex data, from many sources, into easily understood assessments and indicators that help decision makers, both private and public, to take relevant actions at the right time (WBCSD/EPE, 1999).

The European Union (EU) Fifth Environmental Action Programme 1992–99 recognizes the increasingly important role that information plays in this new context of sustainable development:

> 'The achievement of the desired balance between human activity and development and protection of the environment requires effective dialogue and concerted action among partners who may have differing short-term priorities; such dialogue must be

supported by objective and reliable information' (European Commission, 1992).

The success of this approach will rely heavily on the flow and quality of information both in relation to the environment and between the various actors, including the general public. The EU aims to achieve some of these goals through the work of the Copenhagen-based EEA, created to produce objective and comparable information for European Community institutions and member states that could help them produce sound and effective policy measures. Its range of products and services includes comparable European data on air emissions and quality; on water and soil; wildlife; integrated assessments of the state of and prospects for Europe's environment; summaries of best practices with management tools such as life-cycle assessment; and reports on issues that either require new approaches, such as water stress or chemicals, or new concepts, such as ecological space and eco-efficiency (EEA, 1998; EEA website, 1999).

These activities are designed to contribute to awareness-raising, behaviour change and the implementation and evaluation of environmental policies and associated instruments (regulations, taxes, voluntary agreements, etc). Part of the EEA's role is to reduce the overload and complexity of information by providing 'structured knowledge' or frameworks of understanding; by integrating scattered data; and by making information both more meaningful through the use of indicators, and verifiable through public access to the data bases that support the indicators.

Since the publication of the Fifth Environmental Action Programme in 1992 there has been increasing interest in 'demand-side' environmental measures, such as encouraging public transport use and the take-up of energy-efficiency improvements. These entail the willing cooperation of many more people than was ever needed for the 'supply-side' measures of building roads or power stations. This further increases the need for widely shared public understanding of the reasons for particular policies. Accordingly:

> *'. . . appropriate education and public awareness should be organized as one of the pillars of sustainability, together with legislation, economy, and technology'* (Declaration of Thessalonika, UNESCO, 1998).

There is evidence, particularly from the US, that information provision has helped to generate environmental improvements:

> '. . . the release of environmental data such as that under the Toxic
> Release Inventory programme has led to dramatic reductions in
> emissions and has prompted the regulated community to increase
> its participation in voluntary emission-reduction programmes'
> (Keough, 1994).

There is also some limited European evidence that information
provision helps to achieve environmental improvements (Fouquet,
1997; OECD, 1997; Winward, 1998), but the links between information
provision and associated changes in behaviour are complex and
difficult to unravel (Williams, 1997). Nevertheless, public authorities
are increasingly influenced by the public's attitudes and seek to involve
the public:

> 'Public priority for the environment, in general, and public
> interest in the enforcement of environmental laws, in particular,
> exert a great influence on political priorities. In the Netherlands
> there is a lot of effort to increase general awareness and to
> influence the commitment and attitudes of the public' (Veenman,
> 1994).

The key elements of public-information provision identified in the Fifth
Environmental Action Programme, such as the level of public
awareness, access to information, rights to participation, and the
associated actions of both consumers (such as green purchasing,
boycotting, green investing) and citizens (such as voting, participation
in Local Agenda 21, and planning processes) are linked together.
However, 'there is no simple, one way relationship between awareness,
information and action – each can influence the others in complex and
subtle ways' (EEA, 1999), mediated by people's values. It is often
differences over values, rather than over information and its significance, that explains the different views of scientists and the public
over complex and uncertain environmental problems (Doble, 1995).

REPORTING THE ENVIRONMENT: SOME
DIFFICULTIES FOR THE MEDIA

The media plays a vital role in getting environmental issues onto the
political agenda, and in communicating information to both policy
makers and the wider public. This is a difficult task given environmental complexity, the need to attract audiences and readers, the

pressures on scientists to get research funding, and the 'profound mistrust of governments, companies and experts making claims about environmental issues' which a UK/Dutch research team found among the public in England and The Netherlands (Burgess et al, 1996). Mistrust in public institutions, and in science, seems to vary widely between member states, with low levels of trust being reported in countries such as the UK and Italy, and relatively high levels in Germany and The Netherlands (Jamison, 1998). Yet, trust in the sender of information is a key element in how it is received and used (Macnaghten and Urry, 1998).

Some of this mistrust arises because of the way the media seems to accept the simplistic dichotomy between 'scientific objectivity' and public/NGO emotion', ignoring the:

> 'social and value pre-commitments which tacitly frame "scientific" assessments – and conversely the rational empirical elements of supposedly "emotional" public concerns – (which) tend to be excluded . . . a tendency which arguably acts to compound public disconnection and mistrust' (Macnaghten et al, 1995).

While the combinations of facts, emotions and values within both public and scientific positions are part of reality, they provide only partial insight into what is going on in such high-profile controversies as the *Brent Spar*, BSE, 'gender bender' chemicals, and genetically (GM) modified foods, where different perceptions of interests, costs and benefits help to explain much of the controversies.

The media, however, thrives on controversy – and it continually needs to attract customers. One consequence of this is that once there is basic agreement on an issue, then the media loses interest, as happened with the environment after 1990, when its importance became more generally accepted by industry and politicians. This gives us the paradox, explored elsewhere in this volume, of an issue becoming simultaneously more important, yet less newsworthy.

A similar paradox occurs with polling data, where falling 'front of mind' concern for the environment, following its apparent uptake by politicians, is reflected in falling 'worries about the environment' polling data, just as the issue becomes more generally important.

Life is made more difficult for both journalists and politicians by the increasing dominance of market forces in the funding of scientific research. Finding funding in the marketplace is now much more of a preoccupation for scientists than when long-term government funds provided a more secure base for such research. This has encouraged some scientists to leap into print with controversial hypotheses and preliminary findings which may generate funding. Being 'famous and funded' is more attractive than being cautious and poor – but this creates problems for both journalists and the public in evaluating the truth of scientific reports.

Journalists thus have a difficult task in reporting complex environmental issues. Institutions such as the EEA have been set up to produce integrated and accessible reports from a more independent standpoint than many other sources. It can also help in the wider dissemination of environmental research results that are relevant to policy makers, industry, etc.

However, reporting difficulties are relative. The professional hazards of media reporting on the environment in European countries are minor compared to the restrictions imposed on journalists in many countries, where to report critically on any aspect of the environment is to run the risk of death or imprisonment.

THE 'DOUBLE TROUBLE' OF LONG-TERM HAZARDS

The problems of long-term environmental hazards from persistent exposures, and related issues of scientific uncertainty, pose particular problems for journalists. The history of research and debate over a well-known long-term hazard such as asbestos illustrates some of the problems. Despite an early warning from an astute factory inspector in 1898, who observed that the 'evil effects of asbestos' had attracted her attention, putting asbestos fibres into the occupational and then general environments seemed to have no serious consequences – until ten to 50 years later when first asbestosis then different cancers emerged to kill many of those people who breathed in fibres. Currently, about 10,000 people a year die from asbestos diseases in western Europe, and the toll will get higher as another 250,000 people, who are in the 'pipeline' of previous asbestos exposure, will die of asbestos-induced diseases over the next 35 years (Peto, 1999). Therefore, despite preventative action being taken now, damage from asbestos will get worse before it gets better.

This 'pipeline problem' is common to other environmental hazards, such as acid rain, ozone-layer damage, global warming and nitrates or pesticides in groundwater. This gives us 'double trouble' in dealing with long-term environmental hazards. Firstly, the absence of any damaging effects in the short term gives us a false sense of security so that exposure to the substance can go on increasing, sometimes enormously, before there is definite evidence of harmful impacts. Secondly, by the time we get convincing evidence of damage to ourselves or the environment, there is so much hazardous material accumulated in the 'pipeline' that, as with asbestos, the damage can only get worse before it begins to get better. The 'pipeline' damage comes from both existing exposures that store up latent damage, and from persistent substances that remain in the environment to give higher cumulative exposures. For example, we will have to face continued exposure to banned or restricted substances such as polychlorinated biphenyls (PCBs) and dichlorodiphenyltrichloro-ethane (DDT) because of their ubiquity and persistence in the environment. Although these substances were banned years ago, they are still present in the environment and enter breast milk and other tissues at levels that seem to cause subtle effects on intelligence and behaviour (WWF, 1999).

'Pipeline problems' are made even more difficult to deal with if their damaging effects are not just long-term and irreversible but also unequally distributed in society. For example, asbestos is not only killing thousands of people, it has also helped to nearly bankrupt Lloyds Insurers of London because of the costs of compensation to asbestos disease victims, and the costs of safely removing asbestos from buildings and other parts of the environment which have become contaminated. 'Pipeline problems' thus build up an 'environmental debt' of costs that damages our economies as well as the environment. A recent estimate of Sweden's environmental debt puts it at US$40 billion, rising annually by US$700 million (Symposium on Sustainable Consumption, Environment Ministry Norway, 1994). It follows that the full life-cycle costs of substances must be included in risk evaluations.

Those who pay the costs of long-term hazards, such as asbestos, are minorities of asbestos workers, their families and insurance companies, while the benefits of asbestos have been shared by consumers, and most particularly by the asbestos companies and their shareholders. The costs and benefits of other long-term environmental hazards, such as acid rain, ozone-layer damage, traffic fumes and global warming are also unevenly distributed within society. For example, a majority of people gain from car use, but it is mainly minorities, of children, the elderly and the car-less, who suffer the consequences of the resulting pollution, noise and deterioration in public transport. 'Cars are not Fair' is how one newspaper reported the distribution of the costs and benefits of private transport (*The Independent*, 19 May 1996, reproduced in EEA, 1996).

How should we deal with these pipeline problems, with their serious, irreversible and unevenly distributed hazardous effects? Two approaches can be adopted, both of which can 'shorten the pipeline'. Firstly, it should be possible to improve our capacity to detect early warnings of environmental damage; and secondly, it is reasonable to give the benefit of scientific doubt to people and the planet, rather than to potentially hazardous chemicals or human activities.

Early warnings can come from improved scientific observation and research. For example, monitoring for hazardous chemicals even in remote places like Antarctica can help to track the spread of pollution, while linking together observations across scientific disciplines (such as chemistry and geography) can help to identify unexpected hazards such as ozone depletion.

The 'gender bender' controversy surrounding chemicals that appear to be damaging the reproductive health of animals, fish and possibly humans illustrates these issues of complexity and uncertainty. Sectors of the chemical industry seem to accept the view that:

> '. . . there are not necessarily safe doses of many of the chemicals we produce [and] with ordinary people being exposed to so many chemicals the problem of proving which is the most harmful to human health is almost insurmountable' (Institute of Materials PVC committee, 1996).

Yet, there are costs to economic interests when precautionary action is taken. What if 'early warnings' turn out to be false? In highly competitive global markets, what are the likely costs of being right or wrong with predictions of serious harm? And who will bear these costs? Who, in other words, should get the benefit of the doubt and why?

The answer to this depends upon what we think the costs of being wrong are likely to be, and how fairly they will be distributed. If the consequences of being wrong are likely to be serious, irreversible and unfairly distributed, then the benefit of the scientific doubt should be given to people and the planet, rather than to potentially damaging chemicals and human activities – but only if the costs of this 'precautionary principle' do not seriously outweigh the benefits of avoiding the hazard. For example, few people would think it was sensible to immediately close down all European coal and lignite mines today because of the early warnings of global warming that we now have, particularly if China and other countries expand their use of fossil fuels. However, most people today would like to see much greater investment and action on energy efficiency and renewable sources of energy in order to minimize the 'pipeline' problem of global warming in the future.

If we speed up the improvements in energy efficiency and the development of renewable energy sources in response to the threat of climate change, and it turns out not to be happening, then the cost of being wrong will have been some misallocation of society's resources. This will be offset by lower energy bills and the employment and technological progress from energy efficiency and renewable energy technologies. If we do not take action until after we get proof of climate change which is 'beyond reasonable doubt', then the costs of not accepting the early warning signs will be unstoppable sea-level rises, storms, floods, damage to agriculture, and increased diseases and other damage that will get worse over several decades before we have any hope of reversing the trends. The financial 'pipeline' costs of climate change will be very large (much greater, for example, than asbestos) and irreversible, at least for several decades.

This 'no regrets' approach to the uncertainty of climate change has been broadly accepted by the consensus scientific panel set up by the UN – the Intergovernmental Panel on Climate Change (IPCC), who have concluded that 'the balance of evidence . . . suggests a discernible human influence on global climate' (IPPC, 1995). It is now widely held that about a 50 to 70 per cent immediate reduction in carbon dioxide (CO_2) emissions would be needed to stabilize global CO_2 concentrations at the 1990 level by 2100 (EEA, 1999, p79). The level of proof required for decisions on long-term hazards with possibly serious and irreversible impacts is thus a key area of debate for science, policy and the media.

In environmental policy, choices must be made between 'precautionary' and 'profligacy' principles in the context of often high levels of uncertainty over environmental impacts.

Uncertainty and the Precautionary Principle

The one certainty in environmental science is that it will always be uncertain. The challenge is to manage it. If environmental hazards take a long time to appear, but the damage they do is serious and irreversible, how should the media report them? Should polluting processes such as acid rain, pesticides in groundwater, traffic fumes, ozone-damaging chemicals or 'greenhouse gases' such as CO_2 be given the benefit of scientific doubt ('innocent until proven guilty') until there is proof 'beyond all reasonable doubt' that they are hazardous? Or should people and the planet be given the benefit of the doubt and protected by the 'precautionary principle', which justifies preventative action on much less proof of damage?

The use of different levels of proof is common in law. For example, in UK law, a low level of proof ('balance of probabilities') is used in the civil courts, where injured parties are given the benefit of the doubt. However, in criminal courts a high level of proof ('beyond all reasonable doubt') is used, giving the accused the benefit of the doubt. In using these two levels of proof, society has accepted that the costs of being wrong in both types of courts are more acceptable than if different levels of proof were used.

Controversies over asbestos, acid rain, chlorofluorocarbons (CFCs), 'gender bender' chemicals, and, most recently, GM food illustrate the difficulties we have in handling scientific uncertainty. Such uncertainties will arise due to data deficiencies, ignorance of processes and pathways in both nature and humans, and to the 'surprises' that we can expect from nature. Non-linear responses and thresholds, in cases where both the critical dose (and how near we or nature are to that dose) are often unknown, are particularly difficult to deal with. More sophisticated risk assessment, with uncertainty-analysis guidelines being developed for each step in risk assessment will help (NRC, 1994). However, the unknowable complexity of dose/response models in the context of large-scale exposures of the public and nature to sources of seemingly irreversible damage calls for new ways of dealing with uncertainty. Questions about the underlying assumptions of risk-assessment methodologies also arise.

Wynne takes these issues a step further by exploring the issue of 'indeterminacies' which arise from the value and social systems within controversies over risk (Wynne, 1993). These help to explain why probabilistic risk assessments are inadequate at predicting actual risks, which are partly determined by unpredictable human behaviour. Examples include the cases of technicians at Three Mile Island who misread a dial that had gone round twice, and scientists in the 1970s dismissing the low satellite readings on ozone depletion because they did not match their expectations.

Scientists can make spectacular mistakes by adopting initial perceptions that turn out to be false. For example, the confident statement that radiocaesium from Chernobyl would be 'safe' some three weeks after its deposition on Welsh upland soils, on the assumption that human exposure would be direct rather than indirect via the food chain, turned out to be disastrously wrong, 'severely damaging the credibility of the scientists and institutions concerned' (Wynne, 1993).

In response to these uncertainties the precautionary principle is gaining ground, as it proves its efficacy in situations where societies have to deal with large-scale exposures and possibly irreversible effects (Santillo et al, 1998). The North Sea Conference in 1987 provides an early example of this approach being adopted. It agreed to reduce at source:

> '[p]olluting emissions of substances that are persistent, toxic and liable to bioaccumulate . . . especially when there is reason to believe that certain damage or harmful effects . . . are likely to be caused by such substances, even when there is no scientific evidence to prove a causal link between emissions and effects' (MINDEC, 1987).

This approach was extended from the sea to the whole environment by other conventions, and by the Rio declaration in 1992, which stated that: 'full scientific evidence shall not be used as an excuse for post-poning cost-effective measures to prevent environmental degradation' (UNCED, 1992).

The precautionary approach may appear to be costly for industry, but in reality it may not be so. If society, by adopting the lower level of proof required by the precautionary principle, takes a shorter time to decide that there is a hazard, then it may be possible in many cases for society to give industry a longer time to adjust through longer phase-out periods. Public trust in scientists increases, and costs to industry decrease, if society can negotiate a better time balance between the 'problem recognition' and 'problem control' phases of risk management. The history of 'late lessons from early warnings' (EEA, forthcoming) can show what the costs and benefits of heeding or ignoring scientific evidence of harm have been, who has gained and lost from these impacts, and what lessons we can learn that might assist in the practical application of the precautionary principle to current issues.

'HARD' PUBLIC VALUES AND 'SOFT' SCIENTIFIC FACTS: NEW CHALLENGES FOR POLICY MAKERS AND THE MEDIA

A range of authors and institutions have come to argue that public environmental values, deeply and widely held, are not sufficiently represented in decision making. Ravetz argues that 'a truly integrated assessment must take account of values, including those held by citizens' (1996). Similarly, Kasemir finds that 'results show that scientific uncertainty is not a hindrance to political action if it is communicated explicitly and discussed openly: talk with us, don't teach us, is the basic rule' (Kasemir, 1999).

Previous reliance on a combination of established expert bodies and public opinion polling have offered a distorted picture of public feelings about the environment. The inadequacies of this approach were demonstrated by the different approaches to the attempted introduction of irradiated food in the UK and Denmark. In the UK the Advisory Committee on Novel Foods and Processes decided that the process should be introduced. There was a hostile response from the public and industry was unable to use plant that it had installed. The Royal Commission on Environmental Pollution (RCEP) concluded that: 'The outcome might well have been avoided if there had been appropriate public debate before the decision was taken' (RCEP, 1998). The Danish parliament had available a very negative report by a lay panel and decided that irradiation of food should not be approved for general use. The resulting decision saved Danish industry considerable costs, and sustained existing levels of public trust in decision makers.

In this case the scientists' assessments of risks did not connect with the public's interrogation of the need for new products that carried uncertain and apparently unquantifiable risks. This is an increasingly prevalent issue in environmental debates over complex problems such as chemicals, radiation and GMOs, where increasingly 'hard' (ie strongly held) public or consumer values need to be reconciled with increasingly 'soft' (ie uncertain) scientific facts.

European governments and institutions are experimenting with new means of exploring uncertain and complex issues. Although there is limited experience and evaluation in this sphere, the use of focus-group research, lay panels, citizens' juries and consensus conferences may help to bridge the gulf of perception and understanding between publics and the policy and scientific communities.

However, these activities remain marginal and experimental. A failure to hold timely public debate about controversial issues can widen the gap between the public and governments, which can then lead to mistrust. Unfortunately, public authorities and industry are not considered by the European public to be very reliable sources of information, according to the 1999 Eurobarometer poll (EC, 1999).

Trust, and the perceived reliability of the information provided, are partly related to how information fits in with local experiences: information that cannot be related to local circumstances is often ignored (Macnaghten, 1995) This is a particular challenge for European institutions who need to produce pan-European information that reflects regional and local diversity.

CONCLUSION: CONTROVERSY AND CONSENSUS IN RAISING AND RESOLVING ISSUES

As other chapters in this book have shown, uncertainty, complexity and risk are not easy to represent within the existing formats of broadcast and print news. Yet there are signs of positive change. European institutions, such as the EEA, are increasingly recognizing the need to work directly with journalists. They need to be given access to well-researched, fully referenced and professionally edited materials that allow them to communicate the state of scientific and public debate. The range of transnational, national and local media can also respond to people's needs to have environmental debates set within contexts to which they can relate.

The media and a body such as the EEA serve to shape perceptions through the information they publish. However, the EEA's aim is to help reduce controversy by assisting people in agreeing on what is happening to the environment, whereas the media thrives on the creation of controversy. Both groups can improve the way they report on the environment by means of a better understanding of the science, the values and the interests at stake. However, it would be wrong to conclude that the media's interest in controversy prevents progress in dealing with environmental issues. Both controversy and consensus have their part to play in first raising then resolving environmental problems.

The EEA and the media, in their different ways, can help to identify and raise issues; other political institutions are needed to resolve them. The current environmental context of 'hard' values, 'soft' facts, uncertainties and media power calls more for innovation in the political machinery of democracy than for reforms in the media's handling of environmental issues.

REFERENCES

Burgess, J, Harrison, C and Filius, P (1996) 'Rationalizing environmental responsibilities', in *Global Environmental Change*, vol 6 no 3, pp215–234

Doble, J (1995) 'Public Opinion about issues characterized by technological complexity and scientific uncertainty', *Public Understanding of Science*, vol 4, pp95–188

European Environment Agency (1996) *Environmental Taxes: Implementation and Environmental Effectiveness*, EEA, Copenhagen

European Environment Agency (1998) *Making Sustainability Accountable: Eco-Efficiency, Resource, Productivity and Innovation*, EEA, Copenhagen

European Environment Agency (1999) 'Environmental information: Needs and Gaps', in *Environment in the European Union at the Turn of the Century*, Environmental Assessment Report No 2, EEA, Copenhagen

European Environment Agency website (1999) http://www.eea.eu.int

European Environment Agency (forthcoming) *The Precautionary Principle, 1898 to 1998: Late Lessons from Early Warnings*, EEA, Copenhagen

European Commission (1993) *Towards Sustainability: the European Communities Fifth Environmental Action Programme*, EC, Brussels

European Commission (1999) Eurobarometer, EC, Brussels

Factor 10 Club (1994) *Carnoules Statement to Government and Business Leaders*, updated in 1997, Factor 10 Institute, Carnoules

Fouquet, R (1997) *Environmental Information and the Demand for Super Unleaded Petrol*, Energy Economics Discussion Paper, No 90, University of Surrey, Guildford

Institute of Materials PVC committee (1996) *PVC 1996: Alarming Prospects*, April 1996 conference programme, Institute of Materials, London

IPPC (1995) *Climate Change: Second Assessment*, Cambridge University Press, Cambridge

Jamison, A (1998) Technology Policy Meets the Public, Pesto Papers No 2, Aalborg University Press, Aalborg

Kasemir, B (1999) *Focus groups: A new approach to stakeholder involvement in environmental policy*, Fifth Ulysses Workshop on Integrated Assessment, March

Keough, P G (1994) 'Changing Environmental Behaviour in the US through the use of Public Disclosure of Information', in *Proceedings of the 3rd International Conference on Environmental Enforcement*, Brussels

Macnaghten, P et al (1995) *Public Perceptions and Sustainability in Lancashire*, Lancaster County Council, Preston

Macnaghten, P and Urry, J (1998) *Contested Natures*, Sage Publications, London

MINDEC (1987) *Ministerial Declaration of the Second International Conference on the Protection of the North Sea*, 24–25 November 1987, London

NRC (1994) *Science and Judgement in Risk Assessment*, National Academy Press, Washington

OECD (1997) *Eco-labelling: Actual Effects of Selected Programmes*, Organization for Economic Cooperation and Development, Paris

Peto, J (1999) 'The European Mesothelioma Epidemic', *British Journal of Cancer*, vol 79, p314

Ravetz, J (1996) *Integrated environmental assessment: developing guidelines for good practice*, Research Methods Consultancy, London

RCEP (1998) *Setting Environmental Standards*, 21st Report, Royal Commission on Environmental Pollution, London

Santillo, D, Stringer, R L, Johnston, P A and Tickner, J (1998) 'The Precautionary Principle: Protecting against failures of scientific method and risk assessment', *Marine Pollution Bulletin*, vol 36, no 12, pp939–950

UNCED (1992) *The Rio Declaration*, United Nations Commission on Environment and Development, New York

UNESCO (1998) 'Environment and Society: Education and Public Awareness for Sustainability', in *Proceedings of the Thessalonika International Conference*, organized by UNESCO and the Government of Greece, M Scoulos (ed) 1997 UNESCO, Paris

Veenman, J C (1994) 'The Role of Communication for Implementing Enforcement Policy', Ministry of Spatial Planning and the Environment of The Netherlands, in *Proceedings of the 3rd International Conference on Environmental Enforcement*, Brussels

WBCSD/EPE (1999) *European eco-efficiency initiatives: a road map for business strategy and government action*, World Business Council for Sustainable Development, Geneva, and European Partners for the Environment, Brussels

Williams, W, Wilson, K and McConnell, M (1997) *Is there any knowledge out there? The impact of information on Practitioners*, the British Library Research and Innovation Report No 62, the British Library, London

Winward, J, Scheillerup, P and Boardman, B (1998) *Cool Labels: the first three years of the European Energy Label*, Energy and Environment Programme, Environmental Change Unit, Oxford University, Oxford

WWF (1999) *Chemical Trespass: A Toxic Legacy*, World Wide Fund For Nature, Godalming

Wynne (1993) 'Uncertainty and Environmental Learning', in T Jackson (ed) *Clean Production Strategies*, Stockholm Environment Institute, Stockholm

16 BRIDGING THE GAP BETWEEN SCIENCE AND THE MEDIA: THE CASE OF SEAWEB

Vikki Spruill

The devastating impacts of overfishing; a new generation of urban and agricultural pollution runoff; the demise of coral reefs worldwide; continuing impacts of commercial whaling; the maritime transport of a profusion of species to new marine habitats around the world; poor aquaculture practices; and the global increase in red tides and diseases in coastal environments – all these are evidence of a living ocean in trouble.

That the need for marine conservation has generated such little attention compared to terrestrial environmental issues is not altogether surprising. Though the oceans are expansive, they remain a mystery to most people. Even people who live near coasts relate to the marine environment from the safety of the beach or a recreational boat. Only fishers, divers and ocean researchers have developed some sort of intimate relationship with the ocean and its living creatures, and those relationships are limited in scope by how much area is covered and the shape of the 'window' used to view the life hidden within. Scuba gear and submersibles allow unrestricted views of macroscopic life over very small areas. Fishers' nets and scientists' over-the-side samplers may cover larger areas, but are highly selective in the types of life they capture and tell little about the habits and habitats of that life. There is so much we do not know about the biodiversity and ecology of marine environments and there is a general lack of interest among the media and politicians. It is clear, however, that this does not reflect a lack of interest on the part of the public, who visit aquariums by the millions each year and have an insatiable appetite for underwater films.

Protecting the broader marine environment means developing solutions to problems that are interconnected, perhaps even more so than on land. Yet, few conservation organizations and political leaders and institutions deal in an integrated way with the multiple causes of marine problems. Solutions must involve the land as well as the sea and must take into account the near and distant fates of discrete activities, as well as the global consequences of the synergy of numerous human activities around the world. Solutions will have to involve new approaches and large-scale initiatives by governments; but first, publics have to give governments the signal that they want this to happen.

Until the public comprehends the dramatic extent of destruction that has already occurred in the marine environment and its causes and implications for human populations around the world, policy makers will not take the steps needed to reverse the degradation of the ocean environment. Public interest in the ocean is growing in response to publicized evidence of the ocean's involvement in climatic events, such as El Niño, and the increasing awareness of the dire condition of some of the world's fisheries. Nevertheless, concern is not yet strong enough nor is understanding clear enough to spur the type of concerted action needed to protect the ocean and its living ecosystems.

While an informed public is the key, the process of informing the public involves some significant hurdles. Firstly, there is very little visual impact of what is happening to the ocean environment, since most of the effects are hidden from human sight by the opaqueness of the water. Only along the fringes of the ocean – in estuaries, tidal coastlines and wetlands – does the drama unfold before human eyes, so these habitats alone must stand as visual warnings of the much larger problem. Secondly, the scientific understanding of marine ecosystems is itself incomplete – so trying to paint a clear and complete picture for the public depends upon scientists being able to responsibly communicate what they do know without confusing the lay audience with the complexities of what they don't know or are unsure of. Scientists are reluctant to draw in black and white, but subtle tones of gray are not easily portrayed in most news media. Even when scientists are willing to communicate with the public, they often lose their credibility with that audience when they talk about uncertainties or when they disagree among themselves (which, of course, is the lifeblood of science). Finally, convincing people that there have been alarming changes in the ocean and its ecosystems and conveying the importance of these changes can be a daunting task. How to tie ocean happenings directly to the lives and experiences of humans in their daily lives is a challenge. 'What's the hook?', to use a common phrase in media relations.

With these problems in mind, it became clear that something was needed to link together scientists, government policy makers and the public towards developing a conservation ethic for the marine environment, and that a key element in this linkage was the media. But the media was disinterested and ill informed about the ocean, and it desperately needed that 'hook' to get it interested. As a result, SeaWeb was born. The Pew Charitable Trusts took it upon themselves to launch this organization in 1996 with the purpose of educating the media, and, by so doing, raising public awareness about the growing threat to ocean ecosystems and living marine resources. The long-term goal was to make ocean protection a high environmental priority in the US and around the world. Educating opinion leaders (journalists and others), who act as conduits of information to the public, was to be the strategy for attaining this goal.

How SeaWeb Designed Its Overall Strategy

SeaWeb was conceived with the belief that making credible, scientific information about the ocean environment accessible to the public is the most effective way to focus attention on marine issues and to instigate greater efforts to do something about the severe problems affecting coastal seas and the world ocean. The principle function of the organization is to educate. Even though the public is our ultimate audience, the various forms of media are the principle direct targets of SeaWeb's educational efforts. It is through these avenues that we believe the most effective and broadest education of the public will occur. SeaWeb's approach to accomplishing its goals has been science-based and objective – but not neutral. The organization has a clear bias to protect the ocean and its living ecosystems.

Prior to the final design and launch of its activities in 1996, SeaWeb undertook a comprehensive planning process, which included qualitative and quantitative research concerning public attitudes and the opinions of policy experts and conservationists. This process included more than 100 private interviews with NGO experts, opinion leaders, scientists, academicians and journalists in the US. Eight focus groups were held to seek insight and direction rather than quantitative or absolute measures, and a national telephone survey of 1300 adults was conducted for quantitative measures of public opinion.

Throughout this research, education was an underlying theme – what information is the public missing, what misconceptions are pervasive, what kinds of knowledge would the public respond to, who are the best and most trusted sources, and what would mobilize the public into effective action? Participants repeatedly expressed the view that the US public at large does not know that ocean ecosystems are threatened and does not understand the nature of the problems and that an educational effort would be effective.

Our findings that the public lacked solid scientific information about the ocean, but cared and wanted to learn more, led us to realize that 'the ocean is in trouble, and therefore so are we' was an issue waiting to be made. SeaWeb positioned itself to bridge the gap between the scientific community and the media. The idea was to ultimately establish a workable link between science and the public using the media's ability to inform the public about ocean issues. Our methodology had three basic components: to present articulate ocean scientists directly to the media; to alert the media to important ocean environment news and provide expert contacts for additional information; and to use media outlets to disperse our own parcels of ocean information formulated to be scientifically sound but also appealing to the general public.

Some findings of our early studies that were particularly helpful included the following:

- Although focus-group participants did not realize the ocean environment as a whole is in danger, they did recognize pollution, overfishing and endangered species as issues pertinent to the ocean.
- After some discussion, participants accepted that the ocean is not infinite, and that human action can and is having a negative impact.
- Respondents to the poll accepted that there is a connection between the condition of the ocean and our everyday lives; but it was not determined just which connections they were making.
- In developing a strategy for activism, focus-group participants agreed that efforts need to be personalized and localized: they would be willing to change personal behaviour and to work on behalf of a specific local issue, and they would feel a strong sense of personal satisfaction knowing they were doing their part to protect the ocean. They would be less interested in joining an environmental organization.

It became clear that our overall mission would be to convince the public that the ocean environment is in trouble; that the ocean's troubles impact our own lives; and that the causes are complex and interconnected but can be prevented by changes in human behaviour. We set out to accomplish that by marshalling the scientific community to educate the media so that the message could be effectively conveyed to the people.

SeaWeb's role has been, and continues to be, to create a favourable media climate for ocean conservation and, in general, to enhance the policy debate. Within the ocean conservation community, SeaWeb seeks to represent a neutral voice and is perceived among journalists to be an 'honest broker' of ocean conservation news. Other opinion leaders, especially scientists, also appreciate SeaWeb as a credible source of ocean conservation information and a reliable conduit for their information to reach the media. By using a diverse group of credible voices in our many media outreach activities, SeaWeb has helped to bridge the gaps between science, media and the public.

Polling the Public

Early in the process, SeaWeb commissioned a public opinion poll (by the Mellman Group in Washington DC) to gauge public attitudes towards the ocean. The purpose was to help guide our packaging of information about the ocean environment and to provide one of several tools for assessing the importance of SeaWeb's communications programme. The research provided a sense of what will work best to get the attention of the media and the public and be useful starting points for framing and discussing more significant issues.

The survey, conducted by telephone in May 1996, interviewed a nationwide sample of 900 adults, with a separate oversample of 400 residents of coastal communities, for a total of 1300 individuals. The statistical margin of error for the base sample as a whole is ±3.3 per cent; for the coastal oversample it is ±4.9 per cent. The results portray the perception of the public and do not necessarily correspond to SeaWeb's knowledge about the ocean and its environmental troubles.

In general, the survey found:

- The ocean does not rank high on people's list of everyday anxieties, or even as a top environmental issue, but there is recognition of the ocean's importance, concern about its health, and a sense of responsibility to protect the ocean for present and future generations (Spruill, 1997, p149). This conclusion suggests that there is a strong latent concern for the fate of the ocean – so efforts to increase people's awareness and knowledge about marine environments can be effective.
- While interest and concern about the ocean are high, information is deficient. The issues that Americans identify as the most serious threats to the ocean are not necessarily those that would be chosen by experts – for example, oil pollution and oil companies consistently

ranked at the top of the list of offenders, even though other environmental maladies pose more imminent threats to the life of the ocean (Spruill, 1997, p150–151). It was also significant that, although people recognize there are differences of opinion between citizens and scientists, a majority feel that the citizens' concerns should be given more attention than those of the scientists (Spruill, 1997, p150).

- Government action and personal action are popular. A majority believe that the government should do more to protect the ocean, including devoting more resources to ocean exploration. However, although people profess themselves likely to take personal action, they are not inclined to join environmental groups, lobby governments or participate in organized activity (Spruill, 1997, p151).

Polls such as this are useful in guiding how informational messages to the media are shaped to attract the most public attention. They also provide a baseline for subsequent polls to assess changes in public attitude with the passage of time and increased exposure to information about the ocean.

OBJECTIVES

SeaWeb's primary objective is to create a favourable media climate for ocean conservation to enhance the policy debate. Within this broader framework, SeaWeb has worked hard to establish itself as a broker of ocean news that is trusted by the media and academics alike. As such, when SeaWeb has specific issues and information to present to the media, it is well received.

SeaWeb's primary audience is the media (national and local print and electronic outlets including journalists, radio programmers and station managers, publishers, film producers and the Internet) as the primary gatekeeper to reaching and influencing the public. Indirect audiences include opinion leaders, the scientific, academic and conservation communities, NGOs, policy makers, and government representatives. We seek to influence their opinions only through the dispersal of sound information and through public opinion generated by such information. We do not lobby.

In maintaining our credibility with the media and the scientific community, however, SeaWeb has not always been able to maintain trusting relationships with government agencies and with business when they have agendas that are not supported by the information we are sending to the public. Nevertheless, we have been able to influence them via the media and the public.

SeaWeb's principal impact has been to influence coverage of, and attention to, ocean issues through the use of multiple communications techniques and thereby to raise awareness of the threats facing the world ocean and its biodiversity. By reaching out with reliable and useful information to opinion leaders, namely key decision makers and journalists as conduits to the public, SeaWeb helps to create a more favourable atmosphere to impact policies in support of ocean conservation.

TACTICS AND ACTIVITIES

SeaWeb has significantly contributed to an increased awareness of ocean issues in the US. A recent editorial in the nation's principal fishing industry magazine said, 'SeaWeb has captured the media's – and thus the public's – attention about ocean issues' (Smith, 1998, p3). Our success has be greatly enhanced by synergism with other environmental organizations. At times, the media is ready to receive our information related to an ocean problem because it has already been alerted to the issue by NGOs working for relevant policy changes. Conversely, NGOs pushing for changes have been able to capitalize on our preconditioning and education of the media to make it aware of, and prepared to report on, particular ocean issues.

SeaWeb's mission to increase public awareness of the ocean is executed with a sophisticated mix of communications activities. A brief description of SeaWeb's activities and a profile of the results they have produced over the past two years are provided below.

Bringing Ocean Science to the Media

SeaWeb's inhouse team of professionals is poised to feed ideas to the media and respond to queries based on a wide range of sources. Many journalists who are looking for story ideas or access to resources often contact SeaWeb first. Hundreds of substantive stories have appeared in the media – including major pieces in *Time International* (Earle, 1996, p54), *The New York Times* (*The New York Times*, 1998, p20), *The International Herald Tribune* (Reichert, 1997), and virtually every major newspaper – as a result of a combination of SeaWeb activities. Much of this impact has been the result of dozens of briefings to news outlets that have been conducted in every major US media market by SeaWeb over the past two years. A team of scientists was recruited, and was media-trained and taken by SeaWeb for indepth meetings with editorial boards and science and environment writers. Journalists have been openly grateful for the breadth of information conveyed by the scientists, and the scientists have in turn been appreciative of the opportunity to convey complete ideas (as opposed to sound bites) to a receptive media audience.

Reaching Out to the Scientific Community

Over the past several years, SeaWeb has gained the respect of the scientific community. Through presentations of SeaWeb-generated polling data, new life has been breathed into an ongoing dialogue about the appropriate role of science and scientists in the public debate and policy-making process. Members of the international scientific community are increasingly seeking to have their work and perspectives included in the SeaWeb newsletter, and SeaWeb staff receive frequent calls from reputable scientists who want to be involved in the organization's outreach activities to journalists. Conversely, SeaWeb has recruited scientists who are doing important marine research and are willing to talk to the media.

Producing Information for the Media and Public

SeaWeb has its own research capability to provide the resource material for the production of a daily radio show, *The Ocean Report*, that is presently aired on over 100 public radio stations and is heard by more than one million listeners. SeaWeb maintains a database of more than 1700 journalists, NGOs and opinion leaders who regularly rely upon SeaWeb materials such as the monthly newsletter *Ocean Update* and the *SeaWeb Ocean Briefing Book*, a loose-leaf collection of factsheets. These have all proven to be effective ways of reaching both the media and the public with packaged tidbits and newsworthy research regarding the ocean environment and marine conservation.

Maintaining an Active Website

The SeaWeb website (www.seaweb.org) has been critically acclaimed and receives over 80,000 visits per month. It is the only US site that serves to link together a wide network of groups and organizations working on marine conservation issues nationwide. It provides a breadth of information, such as abstracts of important ocean research papers, our news letter and briefing papers, and information about the staff. Keeping it updated with new information is essential, since our visitors include journalists, students, teachers and other professionals who use the information in their work, as well as the general public.

Maintaining an Ocean Information Database

SeaWeb stays abreast of current scientific knowledge on the ocean environment (eg biodiversity, atmosphere–ocean interactions, fisheries) and on human health and seafood safety (eg biotoxins, pathogens and xenobiotics), and is able to delineate key researchers and programmes involved in specific issue areas. SeaWeb regularly monitors approximately 135 peer-reviewed science journals (eg *Nature*, *Deep Sea Research*, *Global Change Biology*) and some 15 technical Internet listservers (eg *Seabird-L*, *MarMam*, *ProMed*) in addition to government press release services (eg USFWS, USDA). Information from these sources, including articles, abstracts and information sources, are disseminated by SeaWeb and provide up-to-date information for use in media briefings, factsheets and other SeaWeb publications. All abstracts, documents, published papers and books are incorporated into the 'SeaWeb Ocean Information Database' and are filed inhouse. More than 6000 documents, books, reports and abstracts have been entered to date. The SeaWeb database and library provide readily accessible information on virtually all aspects of the marine environment for SeaWeb reports and programmes and information requests from the media and public.

SeaWeb's Writers

In addition to opinion editorials in major newspapers, SeaWeb staff members have published various reviews and issue stories. These include articles on seafood safety, whaling and bycatch in the International Labor Organization's *Encyclopaedia of Occupational Health and Safety*; algal blooms, coral reefs and aquaculture in issues of *BBC Wildlife*; ballast water introductions in *The New Scientist*; the Year of the Ocean in *E Magazine*; ocean pollution in *Nature and Environment*; marine reserves in *Science*; a report on global ocean issues published by the Independent World Commission on the Ocean; and a book on marine biodiversity, *The Living Ocean*.

A Fisheries-specific Campaign

SeaWeb launched a successful swordfish consumer campaign designed to draw consumer attention to the plight of North Atlantic swordfish and the broader issue of overfishing. The campaign, called 'Give Swordfish a Break', involved mobilizing chefs along the East Coast of the US who had been convinced by information provided by SeaWeb that the North Atlantic swordfish was being severely depleted by overfishing. The chefs agreed to remove swordfish from their menus in order to educate their customers and to protest against ineffective government regulation of the fishery. Press coverage was significant, and the responsible government agency is reviewing current regulations with the intent of making them more effective.

The swordfish campaign was an outgrowth of SeaWeb's initial public opinion research, which indicated that one of the most compelling ways to reach the public about ocean issues is through the food on their plates. The groundwork had already been laid with journalists during the first nine months of SeaWeb's media outreach. Our reputation as a scientifically reliable source of information was crucial. We carried that standard into the swordfish campaign by selecting a fishery for which there is irrefutable scientific evidence that overfishing is leading to serious depletion of fish populations. The 'preconditioning' of the media allowed SeaWeb to more aggressively make its own news about overfishing issues.

The swordfish campaign has already had an important impact upon the regulation of that fishery, but the future will tell us whether it has been effective in raising awareness of the broader overfishing and bycatch problems. Unrealistic management policies coupled with overcapitalized, oversized and overmechanized, and subsidized fisheries have led to the depletion of numerous fish populations. The incidental catch of marine mammals, seabirds, sea turtles and non-target species of fish, along with the destruction of habitat by bottom-dragging gear, now threaten entire ecosystems. Overfishing poses significant, and possibly the most imminent, threat to biodiversity in the ocean, especially in coastal waters. The effectiveness of our 'poster fish' in drawing attention and inspiring action on the whole host of overfishing problems has yet to be measured.

OBSTACLES

The obstacles SeaWeb has encountered are many and include political, economic, philosophical and structural challenges. A summary of the principal obstacles follows:

- People do not see the degradation in ocean environments because it is hidden by the water. When the damage becomes so bad that it is no longer concealed, it is too late to prevent it and often too late to correct it. As long as the problems are out of sight, it is difficult to attract attention to the threats and the need to prevent further harm.
- It is very difficult to articulate, in a way that is relevant to the general public, the importance of the ocean and how various threats to that environment will impact individuals' lives. It is a challenge to personalize specific issues (such as overfishing and ocean pollution), let alone to convey an intimacy between the whole ocean ecosystem and human affairs.
- The vastness of the oceans makes it difficult for people to comprehend the problems, much less the solutions. People are reluctant to accept that this ocean and its fish are finite.
- Ocean environmental issues are generally treated on a case-by-case level – eg hunting too many whales, overfishing the cod, killing dolphins when fishing for tuna. It has proven difficult to integrate issues so that the public understands how one problem is related to another and how the solutions must be holistic.
- In a political climate dominated by the economic value of virtually everything, the ocean conservation community is woefully unprepared and lacks the relevant data to engage in the economic debate on the current and future value of the ocean and its resources.
- Living ocean resources (fish and shellfish) are seen as commodities with far more value dead than living. The need to conserve live fish for the sake of the ecosystem thus becomes a more difficult argument than conserving the ecosystem for the sake of the fishery; and, once the fishery is depleted, the ecosystem appears to lose its value.
- The marine conservation (NGO), scientific and foundation (funding) communities are fragmented and often work in isolation from one another. This makes the development of cohesive messages that support ongoing conservation efforts particularly challenging for large issues such as fishing and coastal development.

- We should not overestimate how much the media audience understands about the ocean and its environmental issues. Our messages have to begin at a fundamental level that explains the issue as well as offers possible solutions. It is important to understand that a great deal of misinformation has already been circulated – some of it by industry and others with particular agendas.
- Solutions to problems such as overfishing are not simple and concise. Therefore, it is challenging to present the options without confusing the audience to the point of disinterest.
- When focusing on a specific issue and a specific solution, it is difficult to frame the media message in the context of the whole. For example, a campaign to dissuade people from buying severely overfished North Atlantic swordfish can lead people to think that by taking that one fish off their menus, they have helped to solve the overfishing problem for the ocean. Follow-up is essential to make the media and public understand the one issue in the context of the larger issue.
- There is a fine line between providing neutral and scientifically solid information about an ecosystem and shaping a media message to support a particular action that will help that ecosystem. When the line is crossed, the 'honest broker' of information reputation may be endangered. If an action campaign is undertaken, it is essential that it has the strong backing of scientific knowledge and preferably of the scientists themselves.

TRANSFERRING SEAWEB TO OTHER PLACES

There are compelling reasons to believe that the general SeaWeb model would be successful in raising awareness of the importance of particular environmental issues in other parts of the world as well. However, if this model is to be transferred to other geopolitical regions, it is essential that the first step – the ground survey – should not be skipped. It cannot be assumed that the US survey results, around which the SeaWeb model was designed, will apply everywhere – in fact, it is safe to assume that they will not. Public attitudes and knowledge about the environment, economic and political climates, and the relationships among governments, the media and NGOs will dictate the most effective design for a media outreach programme such as SeaWeb's. One of the fundamental decisions will be to decide if such an organization should be pointedly independent, as SeaWeb is, or if, in some regions of the world, it would be more effective to work in close association with other organizations – environmental NGOs, the media itself or other opinion leaders. It is essential that the planning and implementation be done from within the designated region and not be imposed from outside.

In Latin America, for instance, SeaWeb has done preliminary research in several countries (Mexico, Chile, Argentina, Venezuela, Ecuador and Peru) that indicates that the elements of an effective message must stress economic concerns first and wildlife/habitat concerns second. Furthermore, countries in this part of the world vary considerably with respect to the freedom and influence of their press, the prominence and popular appeal of their NGOs, and the influence which scientists and the public have upon governmental decisions. It is important to assess these dynamics before designing a workable media strategy for the ocean or any other environmental issues.

In developing a SeaWeb-type model for a specific region of the world, the following phases and steps, which were followed in the US, are recommended.

(1) Commitment Phase: funding and leadership

- Secure a committed source of funding for a minimum of three years.
- Secure a minimum three-year commitment of qualified and motivated leaders to implement the programme.

(2) Design Phase: assessing attitudes towards ocean conservation (or other environmental focus) and finding ways to use communications and media techniques to initiate policy and regulatory changes

- Conduct an issues assessment among NGOs, government, media and scientific communities, and a public attitudes survey.
- Assess obstacles to achieving the basic goal of educating the media, other opinion leaders, the public and policy makers.
- Profile the NGO and scientific communities to determine how a strong SeaWeb might be best able to support their efforts to educate the public about the issues.
- Construct a detailed operational blueprint (programme structure, essential staff, organizational hierarchy and location) and a budget.

(3) Implementation Phase: implementing the designed programme to achieve the overall goal of educating the media, opinion leaders and the public about the ocean ecosystem (or other environment) and the human activities that threaten it

- Hire director and staff and establish a local presence (independent or associated with another organization identified in the design).
- Identify and begin executing specific communications tactics to implement the programme and achieve its goals.
- Establish working relationships with important communities and individuals (scientists, NGOs, media representatives, other opinion leaders).
- Evaluate and modify the programme in accordance with successes and failures and as new opportunities arise.
- Make sure that there is follow-up on initiatives so that long-term goals as well as short-term goals are achieved.

CONCLUSION

To establish SeaWeb as an effective national media outreach programme, the initial financial commitment was critical. It would not have worked to start it on a small scale. Nor would it have been effective to establish it as part of an existing NGO – at least, that is true in the US. Whether they deserve it or not (in many cases they do not), NGOs are viewed by this country's media as being biased sources of information. A new model was needed, and SeaWeb has provided that and is building momentum with the continuing support of the media, the scientific community and the broader foundation community. That is not to say that SeaWeb works alone in its media outreach. Synergism, and at times deliberate coordination, with the NGO community is essential. We lay the groundwork for each other as we work from different angles to raise the media's awareness of ocean environmental issues.

SeaWeb, so far, is the success story of a concentrated effort to use media outreach to build a bridge from the scientific community – the keepers of the knowledge – to the public and policy makers in order to enable greatly needed changes in US ocean environmental policies. The transfer of knowledge has been overwhelmingly successful, as evidenced by a marked increase in accurate, often indepth, portrayals of ocean environmental issues in the media. The public response is encouraging, and the level of interest and participation in the restaurant-based swordfish campaign is a good indication of the willingness of people to mobilize around ocean conservation issues. The transfer of this increased interest and knowledge into marked changes in government policies and regulations will be slower; but there are signs that changes are forthcoming and that regulators are becoming much more uncomfortable sitting on their hands. The regulation of ocean fisheries, in particular, is finally beginning to change, in large part due to the public attention it has received in recent years; but it remains to be seen whether new initiatives will be effective in stemming the decline of so many fish species. Certainly, the height to which fisheries issues have risen in the media over the past two years provides an open door for SeaWeb and others to continue the public education process and to keep the pressure on the policy makers.

REFERENCES

Earle, S (1996) 'Oceans the well of life', *Time Magazine International*, vol 148, no 18, pp54–57

The New York Times (1998) 'Saving Swordfish', editorial, *The New York Times*, New York, 21 January, p20

Reichert, J (1997) 'Stop Wasteful Fishing and Save Marine Life', *International Herald Tribune*, 15 August

Smith, S (1998) 'Fit to Print', *National Fisherman*, vol 78, no 12, p3

Spruill, V N (1997) 'US public attitudes toward marine environmental issues', *Oceanography*, vol 10, pp149–152

APPENDIX 1
CLIMATE CHANGE: A NOTE BY THE UK CHIEF SCIENTIFIC ADVISER, SIR ROBERT M MAY, SEPTEMBER 1997

This note sets out my personal view of a subject in which there remain significant uncertainties. The main source for assessing the science is the UN Intergovernmental Panel on Climate Change (IPCC). This is supported by 150 nations, and the UK chairs its science working group. Its last scientific assessment drew on the work of some 3000 of the world's leading scientists.

THE GREENHOUSE EFFECT AND CONCERNS ABOUT IT

The physical principle of the greenhouse effect is well established. Put simply, the Earth's surface temperature depends upon the balance between incoming short-wave energy from the sun and outgoing long-wave energy emitted from the Earth's surface and atmosphere. Some gases ('greenhouses gases') in the atmosphere allow short-wave solar radiation to pass through and warm the Earth's surface; but at the same time these gases trap some of the long-wave infrared radiation emitted by the ground, and keep the Earth warmer than it would otherwise be. Were it not for these natural 'greenhouse gases', the most important of which is water vapour, the earth would be roughly 30° Celsius colder, and we would not be here.

Concern arises because human activities are increasing the concentration of greenhouse gases, particularly carbon dioxide CO_2 and methane. While these facts are certain, the implications for changes in average temperatures, both global and local, are less certain. The ultimate effects of such temperature change on rainfall and storm patterns – floods and droughts – and on other aspects of our environment are hard to predict in detail, although the broad outlines seem clear. In what follows, I expand on these themes, sketch some likely consequences for different parts of Britain and other places and outline some policy choices.

FACTS ABOUT GREENHOUSE GASES

Concentration of CO_2 in the atmosphere has increased by about 25 per cent over the past 100 years (see Figure A1.1). If current trends in fossil-fuel burning continue, CO_2 will be present in the atmosphere at twice pre-industrial levels by around the middle of the 21st century. Once atmospheric concentrations have been increased they take a long time, characteristically around 100 years, to decrease even if no more CO_2 is added. As with turning a large ship, there are long lags between actions aimed at levelling-off CO_2 levels, and the levels actually stabilizing. This is a strong argument for early action.

Other gases, including methane, nitrous oxide and chlorofluoro-carbons (CFCs), also contribute to the greenhouse effect. They too have been increasing in the atmosphere. Methane levels have doubled over the last 100 years. Nitrous oxide levels are currently rising at around 0.25 per cent each year. As for CO_2, all these increases are clearly caused by human activities, largely connected with energy generation, transport and agriculture.

Carbon dioxide contributes most to human-caused global warming, accounting for around 70 per cent of the total. The other gases contribute the remaining 30 per cent, with methane accounting for about 20 per cent.

GREENHOUSE GASES AND GLOBAL TEMPERATURE

Over the past 130 years, global average temperature has risen about 0.6° Celsius (see Figure A1.1). This may sound trivial. But the temperature difference between today and the extreme of the last ice age, 20,000 years ago, is only about 5° Celsius (although this was a decrease, rather than an increase, in temperature). The estimated range of variability in global temperature over the past 1000 years is around 1° Celsius.

Direct attribution of these temperature changes to human activities is complicated by the fact that climate varies naturally from year to year, and from decade to decade. Long-term human-induced warming has to be distinguished against this natural background. Although we do not have data reaching back many hundreds of years, by comparing observations of global mean temperatures with natural variability estimated from climate models, we find the warming has, over the past couple of decades, extended beyond the bounds of our estimates of natural variability. This is why the IPCC considered it valid to conclude that the balance of evidence suggests a discernible human influence on global atmosphere.

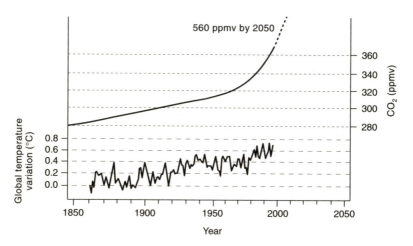

Note: ppmv = parts per million by volume

Figure A1.1 *Global temperature variation – CO_2 ppmv*

In order to predict how increases in atmospheric concentrations of CO_2 and other greenhouse gases will affect global temperature and other climate variables in the future, complex mathematical models of the Earth's climate system have been developed. There is no dispute that, all other things being equal, a doubling of atmospheric CO_2 concentration would, by itself, lead to an increase in average global temperature of around 1.2° Celsius.

The difficulty is that other things are not equal. A serious problem is that the models are highly non-linear. A doubled input does not necessarily lead to a doubled output; two and two do not always add up to four. These mathematical arcana are often manifested in feedback effects, which can amplify or ameliorate global warming. Importantly such feedbacks in global climate models arise from water vapour, cloud cover, ocean circulation, reflection from icecaps and other things.

With a warmer atmosphere, more evaporation occurs from the oceans and from wetland surfaces. On average, a warmer atmosphere will possess a higher water vapour content. Water vapour is a powerful greenhouse gas, so a positive feedback results, amplifying the warming effects.

The effect of cloud cover seems to be very variable, depending upon local conditions and on the kind of cloud. Clouds reflect some solar radiation back to space, thereby reducing the global warming effect. However, they counter this by acting as a blanket for thermal radiation from the Earth's surface, thus increasing average temperatures. Which of the two effects dominates depends upon cloud temperature, height and optical properties (whether it is ice or water, thick or thin). In general, low clouds cool global climate, whereas high clouds tend to increase temperature. Feedback can therefore be positive or negative, making the modelling difficult, with the effects varying from place to place.

Ocean circulation is particularly important because the ocean acts as a big heat reservoir, redistributing heat globally via its circulation. The time scales involved in ocean circulation are much longer (typically decades) than those in the atmosphere, and so couplings between oceans and atmosphere, and possible changes in ocean circulation, must be taken into account in predictions of climate change. Quite small changes in regional transportation by oceans can have a large, but difficult-to-predict, influence on local climate change. Conversely, it is possible that small changes in regional climate could result in large, and possibly abrupt, changes in ocean circulation patterns. All this introduces major uncertainties, particularly at the regional level.

Another feature of non-linear systems is that, under certain circumstances, quite small changes in a 'forcing' variable (for example, atmospheric CO_2) can lead to abrupt and large changes in a dependent variable (for example, ocean circulation). A possible example of this is the disruption we have seen to the El Niño system. This is a region of unusually warm water which appears every three to five years in the Equatorial Pacific and which strongly influences weather patterns, especially in tropical and subtropical areas. In recent years, intense El Niño phenomena have been recorded, which are thought to have led to extreme weather events in the Americas, Australia and Africa. If global warming continues, perturbation to weather systems like this are likely to become more common.

The IPCC predicts that when all these feedback effects are taken into account, a doubling of atmospheric CO_2 would lead to an average global temperature increase of between 1.5 and 4.5° Celsius, most probably 2.5° Celsius.

Any prediction will depend, of course, upon the assumptions we make about future emissions of CO_2 and other greenhouse gases. These, in turn, depend upon assumptions about future populations, economics and energy generation. The IPCC approaches these uncertainties by spelling out a range of possible scenarios, and then predicting the climate change for each.

Figure A1.2 offers a summary – and a dramatic summary at that – of the IPCC findings. The left-hand side of the figure shows the outcome of the IPCC's various scenarios for atmospheric CO_2 concentrations for the next two centuries. Each of these scenarios describes atmospheric CO_2 levels eventually stabilizing at some steady level; in the case, for example, of S450 this happens around the year 2075, but in most of the scenarios it takes longer. The right-hand side of the figure shows the predicted rise in average global temperature associated with each scenario, once CO_2 levels have reached their steady state; the horizontal line shows the range of predicted temperatures, and the dot the best guess (for example, for S450, the temperature increase is predicted to lie between 0.8 and 2.1° Celsius, with a best guess around 1.3° Celsius). The figure on the right also displays three vertical lines. The first (labelled 'a') represents the estimated range of variability in global temperature over the past 1000 years (around 1° Celsius), and the second (labelled 'b', at 2° Celsius) represents double this millennial variability and could be taken as a level at which man-made warming would be self-evident, beyond all dispute. The third (labelled 'c') shows the difference between the last ice age and the warmest time since (around 5° Celsius).

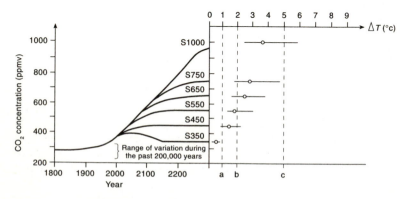

Figure A1.2 *IPCC scenarios of CO_2 concentrations*

These IPCC scenarios represent the levels at which atmospheric CO_2 will stabilize. To achieve any of these, CO_2 emissions (from transport, power generation, agriculture, etc) will not just have to stop growing, but will have to be reduced below the present level. For example, S450 assumes that global CO_2 emissions will fall below current levels by about 2035, and will reduce below 40 per cent of current levels after 2100. Presented this way, the assessments make stark viewing. If the 'best guess' estimate for global warming associated with any of the IPCC scenarios is accepted, only scenarios below S550 – which I rate as rather optimistic, given current trends in emissions – keep temperature increases below the 2° Celsius threshold.

CONSEQUENCES OF GLOBAL WARMING: GENERAL

So far, this chapter has focused on average global changes in temperature. Of great practical interest is how climate change will affect individual regions. Broadly, temperature increases will be greatest at high northern latitudes, in part because the melting of sea ice will allow more solar radiation to be absorbed, thus amplifying warming in this region. Warming is also likely to be greater over land areas than over the oceans, due to the slow thermal response of the latter. The models predict extensive areas where rainfall will become greater, and others where the opposite is predicted. In general, places which already get heavy rainfall are likely to see it get heavier; conversely, where rainfall is now light it is likely to get lighter. But the geographical details of these findings remain, at present, uncertain.

I note a few general conclusions, before turning in more detail to the UK. One class of consequences of climate change relates to sea-level change. As the ocean warms, it will expand and sea level will rise. Some land ice will melt, and so changes to the large ice masses over Greenland and Antarctica will have additional effects. A rise of some 50 centimetres in average sea levels may be expected over the next century, but there will be larger local effects. As heat diffuses slowly to the deeper ocean, it will cause further expansion; hence, at any given time, the observed sea-level rise will only be a fraction of that which will inevitably follow. Even if there were to be no further change in climate (which would require, for example, a 60 per cent decrease in CO_2 emissions), sea-level rise will continue for hundreds of years.

Temperature change also has effects upon the hydrological cycle, which effectively translates into changes where rain falls and where water ends up. As global warming increases, the world will see more and worse droughts and floods.

By the year 2020, climate change in Britain is likely to correspond roughly to a northward shift in climate characteristics of some 100 to 200 kilometres. This and other changes will have major effects upon the habitats and ranges of many species of plants, animals and microorganisms. Many of the species, and indeed ecosystems, thus affected will not be able to respond fast enough to 'move with the temperature change'. The overall effects are extremely complicated, and vary from region to region, in all cases surrounded by a good deal of uncertainty. Rather than make any attempt to survey these questions, I observe that a major recent study has attempted to assess the economic value of the 'ecosystem services' delivered by natural ecological processes: soil formation, water supplies, nutrient cycling, waste processing, pollination, and much else. The assessment, necessarily very rough, is around UK£10 to £34 trillion per year, with a best guess of around UK£21 trillion, most of it outside the market. This is roughly twice the conventional global GNP, at around UK£11 trillion per year. Large swathes of this UK£10 to £34 trillion are at risk from the possible environmental and ecological changes sketched by the IPCC.

CONSEQUENCES OF GLOBAL WARMING: BRITAIN

Climate models are not sufficiently accurate at present to give reliable predictions of local climate changes. In the UK, however, climate change may already be having an appreciable effect. Of the five warmest years in central England's 337-year-old temperature records, three (1989, 1990, 1995) have occurred in the past ten years. The summer of 1976 was the warmest ever, and that of 1995 the second warmest; in summer 1995, temperatures in central England were 3° Celsius warmer than the average between 1961–1990. 1997 is challenging these records.

In the summer of 1995, rainfall in central England was about two-thirds of the normal amount. Overall, the most obvious impact was in the energy sector, with net savings to the consumer for the period November 1994 to October 1995 of about UK£335 million. There were negative impacts on agriculture (about UK£180 million), water supply (UK£96 million) and the building insurance sector.

With global warming, we can generally expect the weather to become more extreme and more variable: more heat waves, more floods, more droughts. The deep depression, or 'hurricane', which wrought such havoc in southern Britain in late 1987 resulted in damage estimated at UK£1.9 billion. The indications from climate models are that the number of deep Atlantic depressions is expected to increase; by the middle of the next century, the incidence of gales across the country is predicted to increase on average by 30 per cent if no major global actions are taken to reduce emissions of greenhouse gases. There may already be some evidence for this. Since the 'hurricane' in 1987, there have been 'billion dollar' storms around the world, each year. 1990 as well as 1987 was a particularly bad year for storms in Europe.

Climate change scenarios suggest that, as well as becoming more windy, the south of the UK is likely to become hotter and drier, with very warm days becoming much more frequent and the demand for water increasing. In contrast, the north-west is likely to become wetter. Drought in the south-east and flooding in the north-west are both likely to become more common. Storm damage will be more frequent, with effects on flooding and erosion of coastal areas and on the cost of flood defence. As temperature increases and precipitation patterns change, natural habitats, wildlife species and farming zones will steadily migrate northwards (insofar as they are able to) by around 50 to 80 kilometres per decade.

In the longer term, and more uncertain, are possible effects on ocean currents and productivity around the UK. As mentioned earlier, there is an important link between deep ocean circulation and the hydrological cycle. Increased precipitation in the North Atlantic region, and increased freshwater runoff, will reduce the salinity of surface water. Water will therefore be less dense and will not sink so readily. Such changes in marine salt balance could modify the fluid dynamics which ultimately drive the Gulf Stream. I emphasize that the Gulf Stream, in effect, transports towards the British Isles 'free' heat which amounts to 27,000 times the total power generation capacity of the UK! The possibility that this might be significantly reduced, much less turned off, is an awesome prospect.

More generally, the world may also be affected by migration of populations from areas severely affected by changes in sea level. For example, over six million individuals in Bangladesh will be displaced, and seven million in Egypt severely affected, by a one-metre rise in sea level (assuming these populations do not increase, which is unrealistic).

WHAT TO DO

I believe the world must aim to reduce the emission of greenhouse gases, especially CO_2. The prime minister's personal appearance at the special session at the UN General Assembly in June, where he affirmed the UK's target of a 20 per cent reduction in CO_2, was a valuable demonstration that the UK takes these issues very seriously. Kyoto in December will present another opportunity for the deputy prime minister to work with our partners, moving further towards concrete international actions to combat global warming.

The UK has already taken exemplary steps to reduce CO_2 emissions, mainly as a result of the moves from coal to gas power generation in the late 1980s and early 1990s (which will result in our CO_2 emissions in 2000 being 4 to 8 per cent below 1990 levels). Although painful to the coal industry in the UK, these changes entailed relatively little cost in overall measures of environmental protection or changes in national lifestyle. The next steps in the UK will be a lot harder.

The UK's atmospheric input of CO_2 can be broken down, by end user, into road transport (around 22 per cent), domestic uses (about 27 per cent), and industry (about 28 per cent); a miscellany of other categories (including other transport, and heating and other energy use in shops and offices) makes up the remaining 23 per cent. Thus, the task of reducing such inputs potentially falls very broadly.

And we need to think long. Whatever target for 2010 is agreed at Kyoto can only be a first step for the international community. A long-term view of policy options is necessary; effective decisions in the short term must not hinder our options for taking measures to meet future reductions targets.

In the short term, significant reductions in greenhouse gas emissions are technically possible, and can be economically feasible. Policy measures to accelerate technology development, and to encourage diffusion and transfer of new technologies to all centres, will help. An integrated transport policy, plus strict air quality standards, should help to reduce vehicle emissions, but will not of itself be sufficient without development of cleaner fuels, more efficient engines and alternative energy sources. The same is true for energy supply for industrial and domestic uses. New technologies will need to include reductions in emissions of greenhouse gases in the 'harvesting' and subsequent use of fossil fuels, switching to non-fossil-fuel sources of energy and a better efficiency of energy use where possible. Better management of the natural environment can also help. Improvements in how we develop and sustainably use forests, agricultural lands and soils in general could play an important part in reducing emissions and in enhancing the rate at which carbon is biologically fixed.

UK industry should see climate change as opportunity not as threat. Industry should be constructively addressing climate change in its forward planning. Mitigation of climate change will require big changes in the energy, transport and construction industries, in terms of much greater efficiency in production and use (which, in turn, will bring greater industrial efficiency and competitiveness) and the development of appropriate, known, technologies. Many aspects of the UK government's Foresight initiative are addressing these questions.

Most of these actions will be impossible unless the public in general is persuaded of the need for them. For example, if we are to cut transport emissions not just per vehicle but in aggregate, then some tough choices may have to be made about private car usage. I believe that there is a crucial role for ministers collectively to play, leading the British people to appreciate the need to take firm and early action.

The quality of the UK's contribution to research on climate change, in the broadest sense, is strong out of all proportion to our relative size or research spending. We should aim to maintain this strength, in order to have international policy underpinned by fundamental understanding, to continue our position of international policy and scientific leadership in this arena, and to help persuade the world's sceptics that climate change is a real and serious problem.

Ultimately, the problem of climate change demands international cooperation and coordination. No matter how good a job we do in the UK, its global effects will be marginal compared with what happens over the next few decades in, say, China. Developed countries, with the highest level of emissions, need to take the lead. We need to promote among developed countries an understanding that serious and urgent action to limit emissions is needed, and to press for a solid result in Kyoto. I also believe that the government should use the moral authority conferred by the UK's conscientious efforts to meet its own targets – combined with our disproportionate contributions to basic understanding of the underpinning science – to help developing countries reconcile sustainable development with amelioration of atmospheric greenhouse gas emissions as far as possible. By this, of course, I do not mean patronizing moral exhortations nor throwing money at problems, but rather partnerships in which we explore appropriate forms of help. The Global Environment Facility and, on a small scale (around UK£3 million per annum), the post-Rio Darwin Initiative for helping developing countries record and conserve their biological diversity, are models.

APPENDIX 2
THE PRESENT STATUS AND THE FUTURE PROSPECTS FOR BIOLOGICAL DIVERSITY

Sir Robert M May

How well do we know the world of plants, animals and micro-organisms with which we share this planet? The answer, by any one of a variety of objective measures, must be: not very well. Firstly, estimates of the number of species that have been named and recorded (a simple, factual question, like how many books in the library catalogue) range from 1.4 million to 1.8 million. Secondly, estimates of the total number of species present on Earth today range over more than an order of magnitude, from a low of around three million, to a high of 30 million or possibly much more. And thirdly, we have even less idea of the rates at which species may currently be becoming extinct, as a result of habitat destruction and other consequences of human population growth.

THE PAST

The history of life on Earth, written in the fossil record over the past 600 million years since the Cambrian explosion in the diversity of multicellular organisms, is one of broadly increasing diversity, albeit with many fluctuations and punctuated by episodes of mass extinction. As reviewed in more detail elsewhere (Sepkoski, 1992; May et al, 1995), the average lifespan of a species in the fossil record, from origination to extinction, is around five to ten million years. There is, however, much variation within and among groups, and some groups have lifetimes significantly longer or shorter than this. Comparing the five-to-ten-million-year average lifespan with the 600-million-year fossil record span, we might estimate that 1 to 2 per cent of all species ever to have lived are with us today. However, allowing for the fluctuating but steady average growth in species diversity since the Cambrian, a better estimate might be 2 to 4 per cent. And if we recognize that most of today's species are terrestrial invertebrates (mainly insects), whose patterns of diversification began around 450 million years ago and whose average lifespan may be characteristically longer than 10 million years, it could be that today's species represent more like 5 to 10 per cent of those ever to have graced our planet.

NUMBERS OF SPECIES TODAY

The systematic naming and recording of species began relatively recently, with Linneaus's canonical work, which in 1758 recognized some 9000 species. Today the total number of living species named and recorded is around 1.7 to 1.8 million. Amazingly, no centralized catalogue exists. But there is a problem with synonymy (the same species unwittingly recorded under different names by different researchers). Known rates of synonymy run around 20 per cent, and could be higher, so that a better estimate may be 1.4 million recorded species (May et al, 1995).

Some groups are much better known than others, reflecting patterns in the taxonomic workforce which derive from intellectual fashions rather than analytic assessments of priorities. Bird and mammal species are comparatively well documented; even though three to five new bird species and around ten new mammal species are found each year, such numbers are small fractions of the totals recorded in these classes (approximately 9000 species of birds and 4000 of mammals). The roughly 270,000 recorded species of vascular plants probably represent 90 per cent or so of the true total. But comprehensive explorations of invertebrate groups in previously unstudied places – tropical canopy insects; deep-sea benthic macrofauna; fungi – typically find that 20 to 50 per cent, or even more, of the species are new to science. Taxonomists are distributed roughly evenly between vertebrates, plants and invertebrates. But there are roughly ten plant species for each vertebrate animal species, and conservative estimates suggest around 100 insect species for each vertebrate one. Thus current patterns of knowledge reflect the fact that the average vertebrate species receives ten times more taxonomic effort than the average plant species, and 100 times more than the average invertebrate (Gaston and May, 1992). This is a bad way to run a business.

The true total number of living species is very uncertain. My guestimate is around three to eight million (May, 1994). Dramatically higher numbers have been proposed: 30 million insects on the basis of studies of beetles in tropical canopies; tens of millions of benthic invertebrates on the basis of a deep-shelf transect off the north-eastern US; 1.5 million fungi on the basis of scaling up the species ratio of fungi to vascular plants in Britain; and others. I am sceptical of all these estimates, but they could be correct. The fact that reasonable estimates vary so widely says a lot about how little we know.

Understanding Diversity

The lack of systematic compilations of information about recorded species, much less about the true species totals, greatly impedes our understanding of the causes of biological diversity and of the likely consequences of its impending reduction. Various patterns – some more general than others – have been tentatively documented. None are fully understood (May, 1990; Wilson, 1992; Lawton, 1995).

For most groups of organisms, there is a marked 'latitudinal species diversity gradient'. This is particularly notable for tree species, where the enormous diversity of tropical forests gives way to the almost monospecific conifer forests of northerly latitudes.

Other things being equal, there is a relation between a region's area and the number of species found in it. A tenfold reduction in area (as when a reserve is established, and its surroundings modified) roughly halves the number of species; more generally, $S=cA^z$, where the constant c varies from group to group, and the exponent z is usually in the range of 0.2 to 0.3.

There are broad trends in the relative abundances of species within a community or ecosystem. In old established communities, these patterns of species-relative abundance tend to be more even (often described by a subset of lognormal distributions) than those for early successional or highly disturbed situations. These 'canonical' lognormal patterns can be interpreted as a rising from the multiplicative interplay of many ecological and evolutionary factors, and the observed species-area relations can be derived from them (under the additional assumption that total numbers of individuals scale roughly linearly with area).

The numbers of species in different categories of physical size vary systematically: for terrestrial animals, a decrease by a factor of ten in characteristic linear dimensions (or 10^3 in mass) roughly results in 100 times more species. This rough rule holds down to size categories around a few species numbers fall away below this.

Patterns in the relations between the body sizes and the geographical ranges of species are only just beginning to receive systematic attention. It is possible that geographical ranges are typically more extensive for relatively large organisms and for microorganisms (protozoa and below) than for mid-size organisms (insects). If true, such patterns (which are entwined with the species-size effects) are relevant, amongst other things, to possible range modifications associated with climate change.

EXTINCTION RATES

Over the past century, rigorously documented extinctions in well-studied groups – primarily birds and mammals – have run around one species per year. Because tropical species typically receive less attention, true extinction rates of birds and mammals are undoubtedly higher. But even one per year among the roughly 13,000 species of birds and mammals translates to expected species' lifetimes, based on documented recent extinction rates, of around 10^4 years. Although seemingly long, this is shorter by a factor of order 10^{-3} than the background average lifespan of five to ten million years seen in the fossil record. That is, recent extinction rates in well-documented groups have run 10^3 faster than the average background rates.

Looking toward the immediate future, three different approaches to estimating impending rates of extinction suggest species' life expectancies of around 200 to 400 years. One of these approaches is based on species-area relations coupled with assessments of current rates of habitat loss. The other two are based in different ways on the International Union for the Conservation of Nature's current catalogue of 'endangered' or 'vulnerable' species, for better-known groups such as birds, mammals or palm trees (May et al, 1995). Such figures correspond to likely extinction rates of a factor of 10^4 or more above background, over the next century or so. This represents a sixth great wave of extinction – fully comparable with the Big Five mass extinctions of the geological past – but different in that it results from the activities of a single other species rather than from external environmental changes.

As we face this future, we must ask: does it matter more if we lose 25 per cent of all mammal species than if we lose 25 per cent of the vastly more numerous insect species? Or does it matter equally? Or less? There is need not only for more taxonomic information, but also for a 'calculus of biodiversity' based on this information. Such a calculus should, ideally, quantify the taxonomic uniqueness, or amount of independent evolutionary history, inherent in individual species. Increasingly, such quantification should replace emotion (although embracing emotional elements, perhaps, as part of such quantification) in assigning conservation priorities and places on the 'Ark'. For a review and further introduction to this topic, see May et al (1995).

WHY VALUE BIOLOGICAL DIVERSITY?

One argument for the preservation of biological diversity is narrowly utilitarian. It correctly emphasizes the benefits already derived from natural products, such as foods, medicines, and so on. Currently, 25 per cent of the drugs on the shelves in the pharmacy derive from a mere 120 species of plants. But, throughout the world, the traditional medicines of native peoples make use of around 25,000 species of plants (about 10 per cent of the total number of plant species); we have much to learn. More generally, as our understanding of the natural world advances, both at the level of new species and at the level of the molecular machinery from which all organisms are self-assembled, the planet's genetic diversity is increasingly the raw stuff from which our future can be constructed. It seems a pity to be burning the books before we can read them, and before we can create wealth from the recipes on their pages.

Another class of arguments is more diffusely utilitarian. The interactions between biological and physical processes created and maintain the Earth's biosphere as a place where life can flourish. With impending changes in climate caused by the increasing scale of human activity, we should be worried about reductions in biological diversity – at least until we understand its role in maintaining the planet's life-support systems. The first rule of intelligent tinkering is to keep all the pieces.

For me, however, a third class of argument is the most compelling. It is clearly set out in the UK government's *White Paper: This Common Inheritance* (HMSO, 1990, Chapter 1.14): 'the starting point for this government is the ethical imperative of stewardship ... we have a moral duty to look after our planet and hand it on in good order to future generations'.

REFERENCES

Gaston, K J and May, R M (1992) 'The Taxonomy of taxonomists', *Nature*, vol 356, pp281–281

HMSO (1992) *This Common Inheritance: Britain's Environment Strategy*, HMSO, London

Lawton, J H (1995) 'Population dynamics principles', in J H Lawton and R M May (eds), *Extinction Rates*, pp147–163, Oxford University Press, Oxford

May, R M (1990) 'How many species?', Philosophical Transactions of the Royal Society of London, vol B330, pp292–304

May, R M (1994) 'Conceptual aspects of the quantification of the extent of biological diversity', *Phil Trans Roy Soc*, vol B345, pp13–20

May, R M, Lawton, J H and Stork, N E (1995) 'Assessing extinction rates', in J H Lawton and R M May (eds), *Extinction Rates*, pp1–24, Oxford University Press, Oxford

Sepkoski, J J (1992) 'Phylogenetic and ecologic patterns in the Phanerozoic history of marine biodiversity', in N Eldredge (ed), *Systematics, Ecology and the Biodiversity Crisis*, pp77–100, Columbia University Press, New York

Wilson, E O (1992) *The Diversity of Life*, Harvard University Press, Cambridge, Massachusetts

INDEX